D0598557

The
Cookie Party
Cookbook

The
Cookie Party
Cookbook

The Ultimate Guide to Hosting
a Cookie Exchange

Robin L. Olson

St. Martin's Griffin

New York

Northern Plains Public Library
Ault Colorado

THE COOKIE PARTY COOKBOOK. Copyright © 2010 by Robin L. Olson. All rights reserved. Printed in the United States of America. For information, address St. Martin's Press, 175 Fifth Avenue, New York, N.Y. 10010.

www.stmartins.com

Book design by Phil Mazzone

Illustrations by Sally Mara Sturman

Library of Congress Cataloging-in-Publication Data

Olson, Robin L.
    The cookie party cookbook : the ultimate guide to hosting a cookie exchange / Robin L. Olson.—1st ed.
        p. cm.
    ISBN 978-0-312-60727-2
    1. Cookies.   2. Entertaining.   I. Title.
    TX772.O47 2010
    641.8'654—dc22

                                                                                                2010030354

First Edition: October 2010

10   9   8   7   6   5   4   3   2   1

In memory of the woman who taught me how to bake,
my mother-in-law, Sylvia Olson.
Even though you're not here anymore, you're always near,
especially when I'm in the kitchen baking your cookie recipes.

Contents

Creating Your Cookie Exchange Party

Introduction

In 1980, I became engaged to Kim Olson. That first innocuous invitation to bake Christmas cookies with my fiancé and his family was the beginning of what would become a treasured lifetime activity. The Olson family baking tradition started with my husband's grandmother Anna West Olson, born 1886, and continues to this day, with the chain unbroken. Our daughter, Stephanie, is an avid cookie baker as well.

I began baking under the tutelage of my future mother-in-law, Sylvia. Little did I know what I was in for, as I was twenty-one and she was fifty-nine, and of strong personality. It was no match, and I was immediately conscripted into baking boot camp before I even knew it. Syl's daughters, Beth and Jackie, were married with families of their own and lived elsewhere.

Christmas was Syl's favorite holiday and much work and detail went into the making of an Olson Family Christmas. On a scale of one to ten, Syl was a ten. The kickoff of the holiday season was the annual cookie "bake-a-thon" right after Thanksgiving. The majority of the thousands of cookies baked were destined to be shipped to relatives across the country.

That first year and in the ensuing years, we would bake double to triple batches of ten to twelve types of cookies the first week in December, eight hours a day, for three days. There were stacks and stacks of cookies everywhere, around two thousand cookies. There were no excuses, and it was expected that I would show up and assist, and I did for the next twelve years, until we moved back East.

Syl was an excellent baker who made *the best*-tasting cookies. Syl always hand-stirred all her dough. I don't think she even owned an electric hand mixer. She was very particular about her measurements and also of not leaving *a smidgen* of dough in the bowl, which I credited to her growing up during the Great Depression. "Waste not, *want not!*"

The cookie stance: Syl would stand in the middle of the kitchen, place a large mixing bowl in the crook of her left arm, and, wielding a large wooden paddle in her right hand, she would then proceed to beat the butter and sugar into submission, using *a lot* of elbow grease. Syl always proclaimed, "This is what makes my cookies taste better than all the others." She was old-fashioned about many things, and her cookie-baking technique was one of them. However, I, being young and impatient, used an electric hand mixer at home when out of her sight, but Syl never knew that!

Syl's mother, whom we called Gram Parker, was not a baker. Syl was taught how to bake by her mother-in-law, in the early 1940s, when Syl was a newlywed. Anna, a lifelong avid baker, did not just bake cookies, she baked everything: breads, rolls, cakes, and pastries. After Anna was widowed, she went to live with my in-laws; that was very common back then. Anna then went with the family when they moved from Indiana to California in 1960. The Olsons had three children, Beth, seventeen; Jackie, eleven; and Kim, who was four.

Kim has fond childhood memories from the mid-1960s of sitting in the kitchen listening to baseball games on the radio with Anna, who was a huge baseball fan. The Olsons were originally from the South Side of Chicago and Anna never missed a "Ladies Day" at Old Comiskey Park.

While they'd listen to the baseball games, Anna would knead bread dough or roll and cut cookies. Even after she went blind in her old age, Kim remembers that his grandmother would measure and handle everything she needed as if she could see.

My favorite cookie is the Crisscross Peanut Butter Cookie (page 92) that came from Anna. Year after year, Syl pieced together the three yellowed scraps of paper with the original handwritten recipe on it. She'd bend over the kitchen countertop with her nose practically touching the recipe as she tried to read the crumbling, faded, stained pieces of paper.

Every single year I'd ask Syl if she would let me take the recipes and photocopy them. But alas, she'd never let me take any of her crumbling, handwritten recipes out of her house. To her, these handed-down recipes were her family jewels. Syl passed away in 2005 at the age of eighty-five, so I now have all of the crumbling, handwritten recipes, ancient cookbooks, and clippings, thanks to my sister-in-law Jackie Thomas, of San Diego. I'd like to think that Syl would be pleased to know that not only did I not lose her beloved recipes (apparently her greatest fear), but I'm publishing them, so they will never be lost or forgotten.

Parchment Paper!

In his later years, my father-in-law, Melvin Olson, had a retirement job as General Manager at the Jesuit Novitiate in Montecito, California, from the mid-1970s until he died in 1988, at age sixty-eight. Mel was also a World War II hero, a tailgunner in the United States Army Air Corps. He sat in the back of the B-17 bombers, in subzero temperatures, shooting at the enemy. It was a dangerous job and many did not survive it. Mel was in Jimmy Stewart's squadron and he flew twenty-seven missions, the most allowed. He was the typical strong, silent type of the 1940s and he *never* bragged about himself. (That was Syl's job.) As a couple, opposites attract: where he was quiet, Syl was outgoing. They moved in unison, always got along, and were happily married for forty-eight years.

The Novitiate had a huge commercial kitchen to feed all of the Brothers, Superiors, and Novices. Mel would bring home industrial-size sheets of parchment paper that his friend, Chef Veane, had given him. Veane told Mel that lining the baking sheets with parchment paper was the "professional baker's secret." Well, if it was good enough for professional bakers, it was good enough for the Olsons. Mel's job for the home bake-a-thon was to cut the parchment sheets with scissors to fit a home-size baking pan. His other job was to chop all the nuts in a little old-fashioned nut grinder before he retired to his workshop.

Syl started her own business, a hobby and miniatures store called Sylvia's Memories in Miniature, when Kim was in high school. Because Syl didn't get home from work until 5:30 P.M., we didn't start baking until after dinner. For at least eight hours, three nights in a row, we would have a production line of cracking eggs, measuring ingredients, mixing and rolling the dough, slicing, nut chopping, sprinkling, timer setting, baking, transferring the cookies to the cooling racks, and then doing the icings and toppings.

That first year, 1980, Kim and I were engaged, not married. Both fiancé and future father-in-law helped with everything for that first baking experience for the entire evening, which probably lasted until midnight with the four of us working hard. I was impressed, and thought it was so sweet that the whole Olson family baked together. When the next year's baking session rolled around, we were married. Things started out well, but after an hour and a half, the men quietly slipped out of the room, one at a time . . . and disappeared . . . *forever*. For the next eleven years that I baked with Syl, it was just the two of us, until two-thirty in the morning.

How I Discovered Cookie Exchanges

In 1989, I was telling my good friend Holly Murphy how many cookies I'd baked the previous three days with Syl. Holly became very excited by the thought of a bake-a-thon and having thousands of cookies to give away, so she suggested that we bake cookies together. Well, I was on baking burnout, but figured that I'd recover by the following week. A few days later, I went to a bookstore in search of cookie recipe books for our little baking venture. After nine years of baking with Syl, I was only familiar with her cookie recipes and wanted to try some new ones. There on the bookshelf in the cookie recipes section was a book entitled *The Wellesley Cookie Exchange Cookbook,* and I bought each of us a copy. I'd never heard of a cookie exchange before, and the concept *really* appealed to me!

The next day I handed the book to Holly and said: "Why don't we do a cookie exchange like they do in this book? This way we can sample dozens of cookies that we don't have to bake!" We both had young children and not a lot of extra time. Holly loved the idea, and now it's been two decades and many thousands of cookies later. At the time, we both lived in Santa Barbara, California, and Holly and I co-hosted the early cookie exchanges together.

When we moved to Maryland in 1994, I knew I had to keep the tradition going. Holly has kept the original cookie party that we started together going strong. She has sixty-five to eighty-five attend, and instead of limiting guests due to space, she moved the party to a country club ballroom. Holly's party (girls only) has become a much anticipated annual event in Santa Barbara. In 2009, I flew out there to attend "our twentieth." I helped Holly bake her cookies. They were holly-shaped sugar cookies—ten dozen!

I enjoy continuing the Olson family tradition of baking. Our daughter, Stephanie, is an avid cookie baker, and my sisters-in-law, Jackie and Beth, and their daughters, Heather and Debbie, all bake the same cookie recipes as well, so the tradition continues within all of our families. Our boys, David and Sean, are more interested in eating cookies than in baking them, continuing their Dad's tradition.

Thank you, Syl and Mel, for teaching me how to bake, and for your only son, and for passing down the love of your favorite holiday, Christmas.

The Cookie Exchange

What Is a Cookie Exchange?

Many hands make light work," as the old saying goes. That is the essence of an old-fashioned cookie exchange.

To host a cookie exchange, you invite a group of friends, relatives, and neighbors over to your house to exchange homemade cookies. Every person brings about six dozen of one type of cookie. The cookies are laid out on the dining room table and exchanged. The result is that everyone goes home with an assortment of six dozen different types of cookies. The recipes are also swapped, so that if you take home a new cookie that you really like, you will be able to make it yourself. The cookie party can be given at any time during the year; however, most cookie exchange parties occur in December.

There are as many ways and reasons to host a cookie exchange party as there are people who give them. The party could be hosted as a one-time-only event, every couple of years, or annually. The majority who host a party for the first time are looking forward to making it an annual tradition for their friends and family. We all lead such busy lives, and a cookie exchange is a great time to reconnect with people you may not see on a regular basis.

Even though most cookie exchanges are given during the holidays, which is by far busiest season of year, it's still the best time of year to do this party. On top of "normal life," you then have the added workload of making "Christmas magic" by rushing around, trying to find parking spaces at busy malls, waiting in lines, buying and wrapping presents. You're tired, stressed, your feet hurt, and you're wondering where the meaning is in all of this hustle-bustle.

> ## A Moment in Time
>
> *The Marion Daily Star,* Marion, Ohio—September 13, 1895
>
> ---
>
> ### TOMORROW.
>
> At the ladies' exchange at the Free Will Baptist church there will be found home-made bread, brown bread, cakes, pies, fried cakes, cookies, ginger bread, veal loaf, fresh eggs, dressed chickens, etc. A liberal patronage is earnestly desired.

I might even feel guilty asking you to add one more thing to your long to-do list. However, the cookie party gives back. It rejuvenates, and gives meaning and inspiration to the holidays, embodying the qualities that we all love best—friendship, food, and festivity. There is something about baking that forces you to slow down, and sharing cookies, which is edible proof of time spent for the benefit of others, is healing and giving at the same time. While you are baking, you also know that soon, very soon, you'll be coming over to my house for a party and we are going to have a lot of fun!

The bonus for the guests, especially for those who describe themselves as non-bakers, is that after they leave the party they'll go home with a yummy assortment of six dozen homemade cookies. Store-bought cookies just don't compare. Your non-baking friends will now have home-baked cookies for their families, or they can give out little plates of home-baked love as gifts to their friends, relatives, and associates. Once you've started the tradition of hosting cookie exchanges, the holidays won't seem the same without them!

Each person who goes to a cookie exchange party has her own reasons for attending. For my group of girls, who mostly identify themselves as non-bakers, coming to my cookie party is an opportunity to get a selection of different types of homemade cookies.

> ## A Moment in Time
>
> *Portsmouth Herald,* Portsmouth, New Hampshire—December 30, 1916
>
> ---
>
> The Willing Workers connected with the Government Street M.E. church are making plans for a cookie party in the near future.

Some people who attend don't care as much about the cookies, but wouldn't want to miss the party for anything! However, they know their ticket to get in the front door is a tray of home-baked cookies, so they dutifully bake.

Story time is always fun, *especially* when you have a group of non-baking friends "who killed themselves" to bake cookies to the best of their abilities and get to the party. Do you have a group of "non-bakers"? Here's a party tip: Print out my baking tips and include them with the basic invitation and the Rules of the Cookie Exchange (see www.cookie-exchange .com/baking_tips.html).

While cookies are the focal point of the party, the guests are the real reason to host a party. A cookie exchange enables you to bring together people of various backgrounds, ages, and interests; they all have something in common on that one day. Everyone involved has had to spend the same amount of time, energy, money, and thought to participate. They all brought home-baked cookies, and all have stories to share of the baking adventures (or misadventures!) that they had before they got to my door.

> ## A Moment in Time
>
> *Sheboygan Press*, Sheboygan, Wisconsin—January 5, 1925
>
> ---
>
> ### ST. MARK'S LADIES AID SOCIETY MEETS
>
> The Ladies Aid Society of St. Mark's church will meet Wednesday afternoon in the church parlors. The officers will be the hostesses and it will be a cookie party. All members and friends are invited to attend.

At weddings, birthdays, anniversaries, and graduations, the focus of the party is on the one or two people being honored. At a cookie exchange, every single person is highlighted and the focus is on each guest for a few minutes as they talk about their cookies. Everyone is a star! New friendships are forged, and after time they, too, become old friends who enjoy seeing each other, year after year, at the annual cookie exchange.

The History of the Cookie Exchange

In the earliest days of documentation, over one hundred years ago, they were referred to as "cookie parties." By the 1930s, they began to be called "cookie exchanges." The term "cookie swap" wasn't popularized until the 1950s.

Historically, cookie exchange parties have been a ladies-only event. Exchanges were hosted by friends, relatives, neighbors, social groups, clubs, office co-workers, teams, schools, and churches. That's currently changing, as other types of cookie exchange parties are emerging and becoming commonplace now: families with children included, men only, men and women, and cookie exchange parties used as a fund-raising tool. I'm often asked, "How old is the cookie exchange?" and "Who invented it?"

Throughout the millennia, sharing food has been the most elemental form of communication. If one were to encounter a group of semi-hostile strangers who spoke a different

A Moment in Time

Syracuse, New York—January 20, 1936

HOME BUREAU UNITS HOLD 11 MEETINGS

COOKIE EXCHANGE WILL BE FEATURE OF ERWIN GROUP

Eleven meetings of Syracuse Home Bureau units are to be conducted this week and will deal with methods of remodeling hats and setting the luncheon table. The schedule follows:

Monday—Lincoln Unit meets at the home of Mrs. H. K. Seeley, 300 Hickok Avenue, at 2 o'clock to study planning and setting the luncheon table. Erwin Unit meets at the home of Mrs. I. B. Stafford, 242 Kensington Place, at 2 o'clock for a cookie exchange meeting. South Side Unit meets at the South Side Library at 1:30 for a lesson on remodeling hats given by Miss Maude Loftus.

language, nothing says "I come in peace" more than outstretched arms containing platters of food. If you're going to nourish someone, it's likely that your intentions are peaceful.

The humble roots of the American Thanksgiving come to mind. The Pilgrims felt indebted to the Native Americans for teaching them how to live off the land. To show their appreciation, the Pilgrims invited the Indians over for a three-day celebration, and foods were shared from the harvest. Many parties are celebrated and forgotten. But this feast wasn't; it launched a tradition celebrated by millions annually. What does that have to do with a cookie exchange? It's completely natural to ask strangers to your feast: PEOPLE + FOOD = SHARING.

We'll never know who first thought of the cookie-only exchange. However, the tradition of sharing foods has been going on for thousands of years, and will continue, for survival and celebration, for thousands more.

How to Host a Cookie Exchange

There are no absolutes on how to host a cookie exchange. You can throw the party any way that you choose, and customize it so that it fits your needs. Once you learn the basics of organizing a cookie exchange, you can then go up and down the sliding scale from simple to elaborate.

A lot of planning goes into creating a cookie exchange party. As the event date gets closer, sometimes the details become overwhelming. The more you take care of in advance, the better off and more relaxed you'll be on party day.

Things to Consider Before Hosting a Cookie Exchange

Before you host your first cookie exchange:

- How many people do you want to invite? Take into consideration how many guests can comfortably fit into your home.
- Invite anywhere from one-third to twice as many guests as you actually want to attend, as calendars fill up quickly during the holidays. Not everyone will be able to attend.
- By September and no later than October 15, decide the date for your party and send out a Save the Date notification by e-mail, postcard, or magnet. A Save the Date will improve

A Moment in Time

Nevada State Journal, Reno,
Nevada—January 26, 1944

ELKO HOMEMAKERS
HEAR BOOK REVIEW

"Chicken Every Sunday" by Rosemary Taylor was reviewed by Mrs. George Ogilvie at the Elko Homemakers' club meet, January 18, at the home of Mrs. Daniel Glaser. A teatime cookie exchange with recipes, continued a club project to collect recipes for a mimeographed leaflet, to be issued through the office of Mrs. Helen S. Tremewan, home demonstration agent for Elko County. This is the third recipe exchange of the current club year. Vocal solos by Mrs. M. W. Means completed the program, which was arranged by Mrs. Oscar Upwall. Mrs. J. A. Sharp conducted the business meeting.

your attendance. If you don't send a Save the Date, 50 percent will come. If you do send a Save the Date, 70 percent will come.

- Send the actual invitation four weeks before the party.
- How many platters of cookies can fit on your dining room table? Do you have room to set up extra folding tables, if needed? Is there enough room to accommodate guests walking around the table to gather cookies?
- Decide what kind of refreshments and foods to serve at your party.
- Think about whether you want to arrange a craft activity, play games, or hold contests.
- Are you going to give prizes and/or parting gifts?
- Decide how many cookies to ask for from each guest. How many cookies do you want to end up with? Be realistic about your group's baking capabilities.
- Decide if you want open cookie platters or prepackaged. There are pros and cons to both methods.
- Decide if you're going to have a cookie theme for the party. Cookie theme examples for first-timers are: Family Favorites, Heritage Cookies, must have (or not have) chocolate in the recipe, and Christmas Classics. Use your imagination!
- For hostesses who have given several cookie exchanges, contemplate implementing a party theme. (This is different from a cookie theme.)
- Decide what rules or guidelines to apply. This is highly recommended for best quality so that *everyone* goes home happy.
- The last consideration you need to decide upon is: What time to host your party? Based on a poll of nearly 500 votes on my Web site, cookie-exchange.com, 57 percent prefer afternoons, 33 percent prefer evenings, and 10 percent prefer a morning party. Do what is most comfortable for your lifestyle and that of your friends.

I'll share what I do, because on the sliding scale from simple to elaborate and easy to complicated, the way I give my cookie party falls right in the middle, and the majority of hostesses give their parties in a very similar way.

My favorite range of guests for a cookie party is fifteen to twenty-five, so I'll invite thirty-five to forty. This number of guests allows time to chat with everyone and catch up with those I may not have seen for a while. If you have the space, larger parties (thirty plus) are fun in their own boisterous way. Just be aware that it will be more work to get everyone organized for the swap and that you probably won't have time to chat with every single person at the party.

When you get a group of women in one room who haven't seen each other for a year, it can be quite a gab fest! For larger parties (eighteen plus), when I have to gather everyone into different rooms for the actual cookie swapping or to initiate games, I'll ring a gold Christmas bell to get everyone's attention before making announcements. It's a lot more elegant—and effective—than attempting to yell above the crowd.

After everyone has chatted, mingled, and eaten, which is about an hour into the party, I'll gather everyone into the den to play a couple of party games and hand out prizes to the winners. After that, I'll call the cookie swap to order. (This begins the last hour of my three-hour party.) I'll ring my little gold bell and guide the guests into the dining room, where the cookies are laid out on the table.

A Moment in Time

The Daily Herald, Chicago, Illinois—December 22, 1950

FAVORITES FOR FLAVOR

Christmas is only three days away, and there is still much to do—one more batch of cookies to bake, one more gift to finish up, last-minute wrapping, so many little details. This is certainly no time to try out new recipes.

Thinking of cookies, it is nice to have a plate of them ready to serve whenever friends drop in during the holidays. Rich little Christmas cookies, gaily decorated, that melt in your mouth. There are so many good recipes, it is hard to choose which ones to make. Even four or five varieties takes more time than many a busy Mother can spare. Here is an idea that has caught on in Mt. Prospect. You might like to file it away for next year.

It is a cookie exchange. It was originated last year and has spread until this season there are a number of groups following the plan.

The number of participants vary. Six to eight is a large enough group. Each one makes a large batch—twelve times the number in the group—of one kind of cookies. Almost every cook has some extra special kind: trilbys, almond crescents, spritz, filled cookies, frosted cookies, pinwheels. Then one afternoon the group gathers, and over a cup of coffee the cookies are exchanged. Net result, each one has as many dozen cookies as there are members of the group. Six members, six kinds of cookies, a dozen each.

Well, now we've rested up a bit while reading the paper. Back to all the happy hubbub that makes Christmas so exciting.

A Moment in Time

Ames Daily Tribune, Ames, Iowa—
December 4, 1954

ACADEMY OF FRIENDSHIP

. . . will meet at the Moose hall Tuesday at 8 p.m. Dues for the Academy are due. Margaret Elding and Maxine Miller are hostesses. There will be a gift exchange.

❧

ONTARIO FRIENDLY 24

. . . will meet Wednesday at 2 p.m. at the home of Mrs. J. Clarence Iden. Co-hostess will be Mrs. R. Earl Houck. There will be a gift exchange and cookie swap.

A Moment in Time

The Daily Herald, Chicago, Illinois—
December 12, 1957

Ruth Vogeler, 3505 Kingfisher Lane, acted as hostess for the cookie exhange she and 9 other gals from the block had planned. Each of the gals participating in the cookie exchange were to bake a specific kind of cookie, pack them in a shoe box and decorate the box. Prizes were awarded for the 3 best decorated boxes. First prize went to Lavern Grafton; second to Barbara Marsh; and third was won by Carol Colberg. Others present were Marie Mueler, Pat Baker, June Carl, Giles Talik and Ann Enderle. Refreshments were served and when the gals returned home that evening, their boxes contained a variety of cookies.

After everyone has gathered around the table in front of their cookies, I start by thanking everyone for attending my annual cookie exchange and give an overview of how we're going to do the actual cookie swap. I'll announce that everyone will have a chance to talk about their cookies and the story behind them.

Then I'll say, "Whoever is new here, please raise your hands!" We all cheer and clap and welcome the newest "cookie swap virgins" to the party. Some women get nervous when they realize they'll be expected to speak aloud, so this first-timers' welcome really helps break the ice for them.

Since I'm the hostess and want to set the example, I'll introduce my cookie first and tell the story behind it, plus share any problems I had in baking it. Then, I'll turn to my left, and say, "Okay, Joyce, your turn!" Have everyone state their name, the name of their cookie, and their baking story. Examples: "My grandmother passed down this recipe" or "I burned the first two batches, and then switched recipes" or "I sent my husband to the store at midnight because I ran out of ingredients." This part is fun, because there's always a story behind a baking experience, the stories are always different, and there's always a lot of laughter.

After the last person has spoken, everyone steps forward to the table, elbow to elbow, with empty containers in hand, and we slowly walk around the table clockwise, everyone taking three to five cookies from each platter. You can provide the containers or ask guests to bring their own. By the time we've rotated around the table three times, the cookies are gone and everyone goes home with the same number of cookies they came with. After the exchange, everyone sets their containers down on the dining room table. I provide the plastic wrap and advise everyone to take off their name tag and stick it on top of their cookies to avoid confusion.

Keep your camera handy, and take pictures of the cookie table before the exchange starts, and remember to take group photos as well. A common regret from others is that they get so busy during the party, they forget to take pictures. A solution is to enlist the help of a few friends to bring their cameras. Another option is to purchase several disposable cameras, leave them around the party area, and invite guests to snap away.

The party will start to wind down after the swap, and soon it will be over. My family will come home and attack the leftover appetizers and cookies, which they always look forward to. I'll make some tea and nibble on my cookies, while reflecting on the things that I liked best about the party, and also what I may want to do differently the next year.

> ### A Moment in Time
>
> Elk Grove Village, Illinois—
> January 12, 1961
>
> ---
>
> Mrs. Dolby gave a reading from the Bible, and members participated in the singing of Christmas carols and hymns. A Christmas cookie exchange was also held, in which each woman brought two dozen cookies which were exchanged for a comparable number of cookies someone else had baked.

Planning Timeline

Two to Three Months Before the Party

1. Pick the date for your party by September and no later than October. Send out a Save the Date notification by e-mail, postcard, or refrigerator magnet. Not everyone does a Save the Date, but I do recommend it for best attendance. Sending a Save the Date allows your guests to mark their calendars early so they don't schedule over your party. If you decide to send magnets by mail, use a holiday-themed note card and sturdy envelopes. Hand-write or make a sticker that says "Hand Cancel" so the postal machines don't ruin them.

2. If this is your first party, you might consider making phone calls to friends in October to explain the concept, as they might not know what a cookie exchange is.

A Moment in Time

Star News, Pasadena, California—
December 14, 1973

COOKIE SWAP

The female residents of New Milford, Conn., found an answer to the Christmastime problem of quantity cookie baking—a cookie swap. The plan is simple. Gather neighbors and friends, each bringing three dozen or more of her favorite cookies to sample and exchange with the others in attendance. The guests return home with a delicious assortment that would have taken many hours for one person to produce.

3. Buy or make the invitations. Some hostesses are using online invitation services alone or along with paper invitations. The online method (such as Evite.com or MyPunchbowl .com) can be a great way to track RSVP's and everyone can see what cookies other guests will be bringing.

One Month Before the Party

4. Send invitations out the first or second week in November, at least one month before your party. Send the online invitation shortly after the mailed invitation.

5. Use technology to your advantage. Stay in touch with your group by sending friendly e-mails with baking tips, recipe links, and ideas. Share some of the fun things you're planning!

6. Create a holiday music mix on your iPod, or arrange your Christmas CD collection.

7. A small percentage of hostesses only serve drinks such as hot chocolate, coffee, tea, and soda, and then sample the cookies at the party. This is a very good way to have a low-cost cookie exchange. However, it is very common to serve appetizers and/or main courses at the party and only swap the cookies, not eat them. If you plan to serve food, research your recipes and make a menu and a list so by the time you go shopping, which should be two to three days before the party, you'll have a well thought-out plan. Planning saves time as well as money by eliminating frantic last-minute purchases. Whatever can be done days ahead, like casseroles and dips, should be.

8. Do some research and decide which activities or games to play. Set aside a box with all the materials you'll need for games: pencils, pens, clipboards or magazines to write on, and props. Some hostesses opt to do craft projects. These could easily be set up in October or November and stored in a box until needed.

9. Make a contest box, wrap all prizes, and store until needed. Hold contests for Best-tasting Cookie, Best-looking Cookie, Best Theme Outfit, Best Cookie Platter Presentation, or Most Creative Packaging.

10. Purchase or hand-make parting gifts as a thank-you for participating. Parting gifts are an old-fashioned ritual that goes back to the beginnings of the cookie exchange. It's optional, but it is very common to do so. Wrap and store gifts in a box in a handy place until needed. Pull them out the day before the party and set up a table display near the front door.

11. As soon as holiday paper goods like paper plates, napkins, cups, plasticware, and tablecloths become available, buy them for the best selection. Alternatively, you could buy them for 50 percent off at the after-holiday sales to use the following year. If you're going to store them in an attic, a garage, or a basement, store in airtight plastic containers to keep the items clean and pest free.

A Moment in Time

Piqua Daily Call, Piqua, Ohio—
December 10, 1976

COOKIE SWAP SHOP PLANNED AT YWCA

YWCA members will have the opportunity to fill their cookie jars with a variety of cookies Thursday at 1:30 p.m. at the YWCA tea and cookie exchange.

Each person attending should bring five dozen Christmas cookies packaged in bags of one dozen each with a copy of the recipe attached to each bag.

You may then swap your five dozen for five dozen cookies from other kitchens. This exchange is open to all YWCA members.

Two Weeks Before the Party

12. Name tags and cookie platter place cards: You could purchase ready-made name tags, or you could follow an easy and inexpensive method at home. Take thirty-to-a-sheet Avery mailing labels and add holiday themes by using rubber stamps, clip art, or placing stickers on the labels after they're printed out. Make labels for the whole invitation list and then on the day of the party, remove the names of guests who won't attend. Another method is to have a check-in table near the front door, and have the labels ready, with pens in a little basket or other cute holiday container, for guests to fill in their own names.

For easy cookie place cards, cut heavy white paper stock to size, and fold in half like a tent, then use rubber stamps to decorate. If you're crafty, get out the glue and glitter, too. Have these handy on the cookie table for guests to fill in their name and the name of their cookie.

A Moment in Time

The Capital, Annapolis, Maryland—
November 8, 1987

WOODLORE HOMEOWNERS

The Woodlore Homeowners Association will hold its annual neighborhood cookie exchange from 2 to 4 p.m. Sunday at 1724 Woodlore Road.

Santa Claus will arrive in a West Annapolis Fire Department truck to present a gift to each child.

One Week Before the Party

13. Create a party staging area in your home so that you can remain organized. Take inventory! Keep lists to stay organized.

14. Stock up on beverage, bar, and soda needs.

15. Get out table linens and clean them if necessary. Take stock, survey, and organize serving pieces, silverware, wineglasses, and paper goods. Just know where everything is.

Three Days Before the Party

16. Bake your cookies. Keep baked cookies in airtight containers in a cool, dry place.

17. Make your cold dips; they refrigerate and hold well. Make any other foods that keep well.

18. Gather folding tables and chairs from the basement, garage, or attic and set up the party room, if possible.

Two Days Before the Party

19. Go grocery shopping for all the perishables to be served. Take the groceries home, and put them away. Now, go get your nails done! You deserve it!

20. Miscellaneous: Get the candles out, and place matches nearby. Do your fresh floral displays and theme decorations. Find your camera and make sure the batteries are fresh or charged and ready to go.

One Day Before the Party

21. If you can afford to do so, have your house professionally cleaned.

22. Make the appetizers and store them in the fridge.

23. Set up your cookie swap table. Make sure there's enough room for each attendee's platter. If you have fifteen guests, make sure fifteen platters fit on the table.

24. Pull out the serving trays and silverware for the foods you are serving. Set up the buffet table without food. Make sure you have Sterno ready for chafing dishes.

The Night Before the Party

25. Send hubby or your significant other to the store for last-minute items.
26. Get the family involved in the process. My daughter, now an adult, helps make the party food and bake cookies. I must say, the extra set of hands really improves my party. If you can find someone to help you, by all means accept the help!

On the Morning of the Party

27. My husband's job is to set up the bar and make a fire in the fireplace right before he leaves the house. My sons move the furniture around, and set up extra tables and chairs.
28. Double-check your lists to make sure everything is out, ready, and in place. The only thing left on party day should be preparing the foods that could not be made in advance.
29. One hour before the party, take a deep breath, relax, and get dressed. Promise yourself to have more fun than anyone!

How to Do the Actual Cookie Exchanging

There are several methods of exchanging cookies. Plus, there are two different kinds of cookie presentations: prepackaged and open platters. Seventy-five percent of hostesses prefer open platters of cookies, 25 percent prefer prepackaged cookies. Decide which method you prefer and inform your guests accordingly.

How Many Cookies to Ask For?

The two most common choices are:

- One dozen per person attending.
- Six dozen per person attending. (Alternatively, any amount you care to specify ranging from two to ten dozen.)

The One-Dozen-Per-Person Method

First and foremost, you must know your group's baking capabilities. For avid bakers, if you have twelve people attending, then twelve dozen cookies (144 cookies, two to four batches) is doable. If you invite a non-baker, expect to hear a "No, thank you." As the hostess, you'll have to keep on top of RSVP's because you have to notify your guests of how many cookies to bake a few days before the party. I would only recommend this type of party for eight people or less, unless you have über bakers. A slight problem would be if you think that twelve people are coming and everyone baked twelve dozen cookies each, but only nine actually show up. You'll have to split twelve dozen cookies among nine bakers. Since these one-dozen-per-person parties usually require prepackaged cookies, you may have to do some last-minute repackaging to fix the odd numbers at the party.

A Specified Amount

Ask for a specified amount, like six dozen cookies, because that's only one large batch of cookies or two smaller batches. It's completely doable, even for non-bakers, and seventy-two cookies fills up a nice-size platter. Ask for whatever amount you're comfortable with.

If everybody brings six dozen cookies, they go home with six dozen cookies. It doesn't matter if you have ten, fifteen, or thirty cookie swappers. Everyone will go home with the same amount of cookies they came with, which is six dozen.

What does change is the quantity of cookies each participant gets. If there are ten guests, each person gets seven cookies of a kind. If there are fifteen guests, everyone gets four to five cookies of each kind. If there are twenty people, everyone gets three to four cookies. It still ends up to be six dozen, just with more cookie varieties the more guests there are.

Here's the formula: Divide the number of cookies by the number of guests. For instance, 72 cookies divided by 15 guests is 4.80 cookies. Tell each person to take four to five cookies of each type. It all works out in the end and everyone should leave with similarly sized, proportioned cookie platters, containers, or baskets.

I'm all about fairness for participants. Don't worry about having the group count their cookies after the swap. If all the trays look the same, it's all good. If you're concerned about exact even numbers, then you should consider doing the prepackaged cookie swap.

. . . And then there are the wild cards. You instruct, "Please bring six dozen cookies," but one guest will bring six and one-half to seven dozen cookies and another will bring five and one-half dozen cookies. Someone else may have split their six dozen cookies in half, bringing three dozen of two types of cookies. There are usually some odd numbers of cookies to deal with. *What to do?* We need even, perfect numbers, right?

I always make this announcement right after the group has shared their stories, and right before we do the actual swap: "If you see a platter and it looks like it has six dozen cookies (like most of the platters will have), take three to four cookies. If you see a cookie platter that has an obviously higher yield, take five to six cookies. If you see a platter with a low amount, for instance those two smaller platters over there with three dozen cookies each, only take two cookies from those platters." From my experience, everyone "gets it" right away and any problem is solved before it happens.

Ways to Swap

Circle the Cookie Table

The cookies are on open platters. Everyone circles around the cookie table at the same time, elbow to elbow, taking a few cookies per tray until all the cookies are gone. The group usually circles the table up to three times. Everyone has an even selection of the cookies offered. This is the most common style of cookie swapping and it's my favorite method. For a party of about fifteen, it will take approximately ten minutes, start to finish.

Pros: A sensory experience that is the highlight of the cookie party.

Cons: When the swap is finished, the cookies are all in one tray and will have to be separated by the guests when they get home. You could also provide baggies in case anyone wishes to separate cookies at the party.

The Prepackaged Cookie Table

The hostess instructs guests on how many packages of cookies to take. This can be done in a similar style as open-platter swapping, by circling a table and taking the cookie packages. The table can also be against the wall.

Pros: All the cookies are prepackaged and the swapping is done quickly. Some hostesses like this method of swapping because they think it's more sanitary. (No extra touching of the cookies, other than by the baker.) The hostess often holds a "best presentation" contest for the most creative packaging.

Cons: They miss the aforementioned sensory experience of elbow-to-elbow cookie grabbing!

The Hostess Method

The hostess exchanges the cookies for everyone, usually prepackaged. She leaves the party briefly and goes into a separate room. She swaps the cookies and then emerges and distributes the already-divided cookies and hands guests a bag or box with their name on it.

Pros: Hostess control.

Cons: Not as much fun as a live exchange.

The Group Circle

The group sits in a circle, either at a table or in a den, and hands around prepackaged cookies in groupings of three to six cookies per package, or whatever your hostess specifies.

Pros: The feel would be similar to a baby or bridal shower. It may be a good method for an older crowd.

Cons: It limits freely moving around and chatting.

The Reverse Swap

Line your dining room table with bakery boxes, trays, baskets, or other types of containers, preferably symmetrical. Have guests walk around the table, carrying the containers of cookies they brought with them to the party, and distribute their cookies into the prepared containers on the table. Instead of picking up cookies, you're putting down cookies.

Pros: Good if you're short on table space because the hostess controls symmetrical container size.

Cons: It's unusual.

The Free-for-All

The cookies are on a table at the party and people are free to wander around and take whatever they want, whenever they want, of any cookie they choose.

Pros: None that I can think of.

Cons: I've heard complaints from attendees about this method, so I wouldn't recommend it. If it's open platters, all the best cookies will be taken first; sounds disorganized and chaotic.

Take a Number

The hostess assigns each person a number and when your number is called, you go to the cookie table and select whatever cookies you want. Hostess may specify how many cookies to take.

Pros: The first numbers called get to pick and choose the best cookies.

Cons: The last numbers called get . . . well . . . you can figure it out. This is the most complained-about method. Someone's feelings are bound to be hurt if their cookie tray is full and untouched by the end of the party. I don't advise it, unless the cookies are prepackaged to eliminate cherry-picking.

The Rules of the Cookie Exchange

The goal should be the equitable distribution of high-quality, home-baked cookies, so that everyone goes home happy. All hostesses should implement some sort of ground rules for their parties. The purpose is to ensure quality and fairness for the majority who attend your party. You should honor the people who spent significant time and energy baking for your party. You want everyone to go home happy, right?

The most common complaints are from people who went to a no-rules cookie exchange in which they brought good-quality, home-baked cookies that were time-consuming to make, and went home with burnt, low-quality, no-bakes, or store-bought cookies. I am not necessarily blaming the attendees. Some people just aren't bakers, and they'll often admit it. It is the hostess's responsibility to guide her guests in the right direction.

Hostesses, please think about this. You have one baker who works full time, comes home, makes dinner for her family, and then spends three evenings in a row making cookies for your party. The first evening, she makes double batches of dough, investing an hour to make it plus cleanup. The second evening she spends three hours rolling, cutting out shapes, and baking the cookies. The third evening she spends two to three hours icing and decorating each cookie. That is a minimum of *seven hours* of work. If there are no rules at your party, this person may end up going home with pretzel rods dipped in chocolate that took five minutes to make, meringue cookies that took ten minutes if left in the oven overnight, a bar cookie that takes one hour from start to finish, or worse yet, store-bought cookies. Is this equal distribution of time, money, and talent? What do you think she's thinking when she gets home? What is her husband going to say when he saw her bake his favorite cookies and walk out the door with them, only to return with no-bakes, low-quality, burnt, or store-bought cookies? Rules for your party will keep this from happening.

If you want to make your party an annual event that your friends look forward to, be known for your high-quality cookie exchanges and create a lasting tradition.

And a final note: If someone brings cookies that look less than desirable, or not according to your rules, never say a word. The rules exist simply to ensure that the *overall* majority of cookies will be good. That's all one can ask for in an imperfect world. Lastly, I have never not invited someone due to their baking capabilities, and I've seen much improvement from my friends over the years. I've been able to create a long-standing cookie exchange out of a group of women in which 80 percent call themselves non-bakers. If I can do it, you can do it.

Modify the Rules to Your Specifications

1. All cookies should be homemade, baked, and the main ingredient must be flour.
2. No plain chocolate chip cookies, no-bakes, meringues, or bars. (Alter to your needs.)
3. Please bring six dozen total cookies. (Alter to your needs.)
4. The theme is "Christmas Cookies." (Insert your theme, if you have one.)
5. Creatively arrange cookies in a basket or platter and bring a large container to carry home your cookies. (Or you can provide guests with a take-home container.)
6. E-mail a copy of your recipe before the party. (Or bring a copy of the recipe to the party.)
7. Christmas attire is encouraged! (Or whatever theme you're implementing.)
8. RSVP as soon as possible and let me know what type of cookies you're planning on baking—no duplicate recipes are allowed.
9. There will be a prize for the best Christmas outfit. (Or whatever contest you'd like.)
10. If you don't have time to bake, or have burnt your cookies, but still want to attend, you must go to a real bakery and buy six dozen high-quality cookies.

A Word About the Toughness of the Rules

The example above is about as tight as you should get on the rules. If you add an item to #2, take something else off. I get letters from people asking me to review their customized rules before they send them to their guests. Some of the rules I've seen are so tough that I can't even think of what cookie their guests would be allowed to bring.

Here is the rationale behind *my* exclusions:

- CHOCOLATE CHIP COOKIES: too common, everyone bakes them anyway, so no one needs the recipe. How boring would the stories be if six out of twelve bakers brought them?
- NO-BAKES: not cookies, more like candy or a treat. They usually take five minutes to make, not enough effort. (Again, where's the story?)
- MERINGUES: made with whipped egg whites and sugar, and left on a pan in the oven overnight. Too easy, not enough effort. Pros: A good cookie for dieters as they contain no flour or butter. Enjoy these on your own, but not for a cookie party.
- BARS: not as transportable as cookies. Most bars have a crumb base, fall apart easily, and are often gooey. They're made with similar ingredients as cookies but with less effort. However, many hostesses allow them, which is fine with me. That rule is just my personal preference. Let's be honest, it's a lot easier and less time consuming to make pan bars than individual cookies, isn't it?

Although the above items are banned from my cookie exchange, I like to *eat* everything listed above. I will assume that you can make all of the above on your own, too. I always give away plates of cookies to people in my life during the holidays. I'll make cookies, bars, tartlets, and no-bakes and then use the cookie party cookies to round out the offering, so that each little plate has a wide variety of different cookies and treats.

A newer problem that's spawned complaints are dry cookie mixes. Some hostesses also object to cake mixes as a base, so think about whether you mind those items or not, and adjust your rules accordingly.

Another thing I've seen done is incorporating baking tips inside the rules, so it looks bossy, as if you're telling people how they must bake. Send some simple baking tips on a separate sheet of paper with the invitation if your group is primarily a non-baker group. Copy my easy baking tips at cookie-exchange.com/baking_tips.html.

When Should You *Not* Use Rules?

- A children's cookie party
- A one-time event
- When most of the bakers are older than sixty

- An office cookie exchange
- When you have a group of advanced bakers

Just use common sense. If you're a hostess who has maintained a long-standing cookie exchange and haven't used any rules thus far, then you obviously don't need them. However, if you're a seasoned hostess who has noticed a continual drop in attendance, then you may want to consider implementing some rules to jump-start your party. There are reasons that cookie parties die out and I firmly believe it's the quality issue. Believe it or not, most of your guests will actually appreciate the quality control. Many of your cookie bakers are already following the rules. If you get a complaint about the rules from your guests, it won't be from the cookie bakers who made a good effort, it will be from the ones who tend to bring the same old cookies, no-bakes, candy, or meringues every year.

I've received thousands of letters of thanks since I posted the "Rules of the Cookie Exchange" on my Web site back in 1997, and they've helped hostesses launch successful cookie exchange parties all over the world.

The Recipes

Cookie Recipes from All Over the World

This recipe collection contains something for everyone. There's a variety of recipes for every skill level. The recipes are from all over the world because I like seeking out unusual, old-fashioned, forgotten, regional, foreign, historic, and ancient recipes. For simplicity, they've been divided into four categories: Classic Cookies; International Cookies; Bars, Tartlets, and Turtles; and Easy Treats.

The ultimate purpose of the cookie exchange party is to share favorite or beloved recipes, as well as the cookies themselves. I just love the surprise and discovery factor! Once you find a keeper, you'll take that recipe and incorporate it into your own life, outside of the cookie exchange.

I've also added hints for the types of use for each cookie—Holiday 🎄, Anytime ☺, Good for Kids 🐘—and the ability level for each recipe—Easy ⁄, Intermediate ⁄⁄, For Advanced Bakers ⁄⁄⁄. The designation "For Advanced Bakers" doesn't necessarily mean difficult or impossible, it simply means it's a time-consuming recipe and may also require skills that a novice or non-baker doesn't have, such as experience, patience, and confidence in one's baking abilities. There's only one way to gain experience, and eventually confidence: Start baking!

If you're going to host or attend a cookie exchange party, I recommend baking cookies from the Classic and International chapters. I love to eat bars, but it's my preference not to include them at my cookie party, because they're often crumbly, sticky or gooey, and are generally not as transportable. They're also not as time-consuming to make as cookies. However, I do consider bars to be a legitimate part of a cookie exchange party, therefore the choice is left up to each hostess to decide whether to include bars or not.

Use the Bars and Easy Treats sections for your family all year long, or to complement the cookie tins that you'll be giving away to family and friends. These recipes are generally easy, therefore, they're also great for kids to make! (If you allow Easy Treats at your party, promise me that your invitation will reflect that by stating: "You're invited to a Cookie and Treat Exchange Party" or "Cookie and Candy Exchange Party.")

This recipe collection isn't just for your cookie party, because that's only one day a year. Nor should the pleasure of eating home-baked cookies be reserved just for the holidays. Keep this cookbook handy in your kitchen and you'll discover new favorites to share with your family and friends all year long.

Happy baking!

Baking Tips

These are my best cookie baking tips plus cookie storage and mailing information.

1. **Always use fresh ingredients.** Buy new baking soda and baking powder every six months or at least every year. Age tends to weaken these ingredients and render them ineffective.
2. **Butter is better.** Butter adds incomparable flavor and texture to baked goods. For centuries, butter was considered a luxury. Take that, margarine! When baking, use unsalted, or sweet, butter, so you can control the salt content in your recipes.
3. **Be prepared before you bake.** Have all the ingredients out on the countertop before you start, so that you don't spend time looking for ingredients and then forget which step you were on. (Did I already add salt?) For beginning bakers, I recommend premeasuring all small spices and baking powders into little cups, so when it's time to add it, the cup will be empty and you'll easily be able to keep track of your steps. This is how chefs bake professionally and on TV, and it makes perfect sense.
4. **Measure ingredients accurately.** A level measurement means flat at the top of the measuring spoon or cup; use a metal spatula to level off dry ingredients. An extra pinch of salt can make cookies too salty. Not enough sugar, too bland.
5. **Sticky ingredients.** Use a nonstick cooking spray, or a fine coat of oil or butter, to coat measuring cups for gooey ingredients like honey and molasses—they'll slide out easier, and you'll have less waste and easier cleanup.
6. **Follow directions.** Beginning bakers should follow the recipe directions as closely as possible. It's hard to troubleshoot when you wander away from the original rec-

How to Make Brown Sugar in a Pinch

Making your own brown sugar costs about half the price of store-bought, processed brown sugar and tastes much fresher.

1 cup white granulated sugar
1–2 tablespoons molasses (1 tablespoon for light, 2 tablespoons for dark)

Give a quick spin in your food processor, or use your electric mixer to combine.

Store in an airtight container.

ipe. Advanced bakers can make changes, because they have an idea of the outcome. If you do change ingredients, methods, or baking times, make notations. That way if you like the new version that you came up with better, you'll be able to replicate it.

7. **Drop cookies.** Use a good-quality ice cream scoop for drop cookies. It makes the process faster and gives professional results. All the cookies will be the same size and proportion. Most cookies are spaced 2 inches apart, unless the recipe specifies differently. See Resources, page 330.

8. **Sinking nuts and fruits.** To keep dried fruits like raisins, and chopped nuts, from sinking to the bottom, toss them in a bit of flour, using part of the flour from the recipe.

9. **Tough cookies.** Once the flour has been added, overmixing the dough can create too much gluten and the result could be tough-textured cookies. When it's time to add the flour, mix or stir *until just combined* on a low speed or do the final mixing by hand with a wooden paddle.

10. **Rolling dough.** Use a pastry rolling mat (ideally, with baking guidelines printed on it) or parchment paper to roll your dough onto when using cookie cutters.

11. **Baking surface.** Use parchment baking paper to line cookie sheets, as parchment prevents the cookies from sticking and overbrowning. It's easy to see how cookies are doing while baking on parchment versus on an aluminum or dark baking sheet.

12. **Set the timer for one minute early.** If you detect a slightly dark ring around the base of cookies, chances are, the cookies are done. Remember that cookies still cook

for a few moments after they are removed from the oven. Reuse each parchment sheet until they are slightly browned, then toss.

13. **Perfect bars.** Line bar cookie baking pans with parchment paper overlapping the sides. When slightly cool, lift the entire bar out of the pan. Let cool completely before cutting and you will have perfectly sized bars and no sticking or breakage.

14. **Transferring cookies after baking.** Allow cookies to cool and set on the baking sheet for one minute before transferring to cooling racks to keep them from cracking or breaking. The cookies will continue baking before you transfer them to the cooling rack. The underside of a perfectly baked cookie should be the same color as the top.

15. **Don't overbake!** Some bakers tend to overbake their cookies, thinking that they don't "look" done when they are done. Follow the recipe time, you can't always tell by looking at them, and some cookies puff up and then settle down. Set the timer one minute early and check. It's easy to bake cookies an extra minute, but impossible to undo overbaking. The oven will be hotter toward the end of your batch; either lower the temperature or pull them out that crucial minute early. A cookie that is crunchy soon after baking is overdone. A cookie that's supposed to be crunchy should be moist and chewy soon after baking and then firm up after cooling.

16. **Release the moisture.** Stack your cookies in groups of six to eight, cool on racks overnight. Lay a sheet of wax paper loosely over them. Do not seal the cookies for at least eight hours to let all the moisture out. Freshly baked cookies, sealed too soon, may crumble. Allowing excess moisture to be released keeps cookies fresh for about three weeks under the right conditions.

17. **Short-term cookie storage.** For the holiday season, store cookies in tins, one type of cookie to a tin to prevent flavors from mixing, layered with wax paper. Keep tins in a cool, dry place. The keyword is "cool." In the winter, I store my cookie tins in the garage, but if you have a second refrigerator, that would work well, too, and the temperature is regulated. In my opinion, cookie tins that are stored at room temperature (70°F/21°C) last no more than two weeks. Using my method, the cookies will stay fresh for four to five weeks; however, this depends on how cold it is in the winter where you live. If you live in a warm climate, store them in a fridge or freezer. If you want cookies to retain moisture, or if they've hardened a bit, place a clean, slightly damp paper towel in the tin and seal. Make sure the tin is airtight by placing a piece of wax paper larger than the lid on the top and press the lid down.

18. **Longer-term cookie storage.** Most cookies freeze well for longer storage and will last up to at least three to four months, if packaged well. Cookies only take about 10 to 15 minutes to thaw on the countertop.

19. **If making cookie dough ahead of time.** Most cookie doughs such as for drop or rolled cookies can be made ahead of time. They'll keep well in the refrigerator for up to a week, if wrapped and stored properly. Cookie dough easily absorbs other aromas (like garlic and onions!), so wrap tightly. I like to wrap logs or disks in wax paper and then tightly in plastic wrap, but you can use all plastic wrap, too. I find wax paper releases frozen dough easier than plastic, if caught in the crevices. Using the same type dough, separately wrapped logs or disks can be wrapped together en masse. Be sure to label and date the package. Cookie dough lasts in the freezer for two to three months. It really depends on if your freezer smells funny or not. See Resources, page 330, for that fix.

20. **Shipping cookies.** If you intend to ship cookies through the mail as gifts, send them in sturdy, airtight tins. Be sure to heed the advice in #16, as it's very important, so the recipient doesn't get a box of crumbs. Cut out several rounds of wax paper and top each layer of cookies, with the same type cookie on each level to prevent flavors from mixing. Fill the can to the top so the cookies don't move around. If there is still space, crumble wax paper to make sure the cookies are tight and don't move around when you shake the can lightly. Even delicate cookies can be shipped successfully, if they're packaged properly. Cookies will absorb other flavors, so for fragrant and/or spicy cookies that have strong aromas like chocolate, ginger, allspice, and cardamom, pack in separate tins before shipping.

21. **No freshly baked cookies on cookie exchange day.** Bake your cookies 2 to 4 days before the cookie exchange for all the reasons listed above. I find that people obsess on the freshness factor. Not only is it unnecessary *and* stressful to bake on cookie party day, the cookies are more delicate and less transportable. How long can some cookies last? Well, some German bakers store their cookies for six months to a year! Some cookies are baked with the express purpose of aging (Nürnberger Lebkuchen and English Parkin), just as fine wines and cheeses are, and continue to get more flavorful with age. Syl taught me the concept of releasing the moisture thirty years ago, and after thirty years of practice, I can assure you this method works well. In a nutshell: Release excess moisture, and store in airtight tins, in a cool, dark place.

Cookie Baking Troubleshooter Tips

The most common question is "How do I fix flat cookies?"

1. Use fresh baking soda and baking powder. Both ingredients are leavening agents, which become less effective with the passage of time. The purpose of baking powder is to do most of the leavening, while the baking soda neutralizes the acids in the recipe and helps with texture. You could try reducing the amount of baking soda if your cookies continue to flatten.

2. Never use melted butter in a cookie recipe unless the recipe specifies it. Use chilled or softened butter, according to the recipe directions.

3. If you *prefer* flatter and chewier cookies, then use melted butter, and add a higher-protein flour like unbleached flour or bread flour (the highest protein flour) and use more brown sugar than white sugar.

4. For cake-like cookies, use shortening instead of butter and use a soft, lower-protein flour like cake flour.

5. If your impression is that the butter is causing the flatness, try using a 50/50 mix of shortening and butter. Of note: Shortening is 100 percent fat, while butter is 80 percent fat, plus water and milk solids. I generally use unsalted, or sweet butter for baking. However, if your cookies are consistently going flat, use salted butter, as the extra salt toughens the glutens in the flour, making a stiffer cookie.

6. Overmixing can cause problems like flattening because it whips too much air into the ingredients. What goes up must come down.

7. Buy a good-quality oven thermometer for accuracy. Hire a repair person to calibrate your oven, if necessary.

8. Check humidity levels in your house. High humidity can cause flatness.

9. If you're intent on salvaging dough that you've already made, use chilled cookie dough and place on cool baking sheets. Keep dough in the fridge until ready to use. If dough is too warm or sticky after placing it on a baking sheet, put the whole sheet in the refrigerator for 10 minutes, or in the freezer for 5 minutes, then take it out and put it straight into the oven. Bake the cookies at a higher temperature for a shorter amount of time.

10. If these flat cookie rescue tips don't work for you, *throw the whole mess away* and skedaddle over to your favorite bakery as quickly as possible. As long as you arrive at

the cookie exchange with delicious cookies that anyone would want to eat, *you and your cookies will be welcome!*

Recipe Conversions

Europeans have always measured ingredients by weight, rather than volume. Most of the early American settlers from the 1600s were of European descent. So why *didn't* we carry on the tradition of our ancestors? The reason why Americans don't weigh ingredients when they cook and bake is simple, according to baking expert and author of *The Cake Bible* and *The Pie and Pastry Bible* Rose Levy Beranbaum. When the pioneers had to cross the great divide, they were forced by circumstance to discard all unnecessary items from the covered wagons. This included pianos and other valuable items, including scales. But they still had to have cups to drink from, so they converted from weighing ingredients to measuring by volume using those ubiquitous cups!

If you were to ask the average baker this question: "One cup of flour = how many ounces?" they'd most likely answer "8 ounces," but they'd be weigh (sic) off base! Please view the chart below for the right answer. (Note that if you stir up the flour before measuring you will get slightly less.) The dip-and-sweep method is done by stirring up the flour, then dipping the measuring cup into it, and using a knife to sweep away the excess at the top of the cup.

1 cup all-purpose flour, bleached		Ounces	Grams
	sifted	4 ounces	114 grams
	lightly spooned	4.2 ounces	121 grams
	dip and sweep	5 ounces	145 grams
1 cup all-purpose flour, unbleached			
	lightly spooned	4.6 ounces	130 grams
	dip and sweep	5.2 ounces	148 grams

(Courtesy of Rose Levy Beranbaum, author of nine cookbooks on baking.)

Many American cookbooks, like this one, simply use volume as the common measure.

However, other countries, European ones especially, use weight as opposed to volume to measure ingredients. To follow a recipe by weighing the ingredients on a scale means that you will be able to replicate the original recipe almost *exactly*. Our volume measuring system is more imprecise and, when baking, often causes problems. Sometimes we don't know why a recipe didn't work out, but there is a good chance that there was too much or not enough of an ingredient. Some recipe books do list ounces and grams, but most of us have trained ourselves to simply ignore those directions.

So why do you need this information? In this multicultural, no-borders world that we all live in now, if you simply own a digital kitchen scale, you can cook or bake any recipe that you find on the Internet, as long as the ingredient weight is provided. Press a little button and it goes from grams to milliliters to ounces. In writing this book and culling recipes from all over the world, I had a heck of a time trying to convert recipes from other countries using math, which is just not my subject. I bought a scale and all of a sudden conversion went from difficult to easy. If you bake a lot, I advise you to buy a digital scale. Once you use a scale, you'll wonder why you didn't buy one sooner.

One last tip in favor of scales that Rose told me: If you forget to add an ingredient, instead of playing a guessing game with yourself, add up all the weights of your ingredients from the recipe. Then weigh your bowl with the ingredients in it. Subtract the bowl weight by the original ingredients' combined weight. Voilà! Whatever number you're off by should be the exact amount of the missing ingredient. How brilliant is that? Of course, this only works easily if your recipe was listed by weight, not volume. However, you could attempt to use the charts on pages 37 and 327 to translate your recipe from volume to weight, if you wish.

Cookie Decorating 101

Piping with Icing!

Susan J. Sias, Chocolatier, Wilton Method Instructor, Lafayette, Colorado

To frost and then decorate cookies using piping with icing, you should be relaxed and unhurried. Follow the recipe and these easy instructions to create hair, fur, leaves, petals, snow, and monograms as well as many other textures, and soon you'll be cookie decorating like a pro!

Royal Icing Using Meringue Powder

4 cups confectioners' sugar

3 tablespoons meringue powder

½ teaspoon extract (vanilla, lemon, or almond)

5 to 6 tablespoons warm water, plus more to thin down icing later

Food coloring (I use Wilton's Icing Colors, which can be found online or in cake decorating and party stores)

Using an electric mixer, beat the confectioners' sugar and meringue powder until combined. Add extract and water and beat on medium speed until very glossy and stiff peaks form (5 to 7 minutes). Tint with food coloring. The icing needs to be used immediately or transferred to an airtight container as royal icing hardens when exposed to air. Cover with plastic wrap when not in use.

Fill your bag with the prepared royal icing to outline the cookies. To thin royal icing for filling in outlines, add a few drops of water at a time to the full-strength royal icing you have remaining in the mixing bowl. To cover or "flood" the entire surface of the cookie with icing, the proper consistency is when you lift the beater, the ribbon of icing that falls back into the bowl remains on the surface for a few seconds before disappearing, or a count of 7. When finished, fold over or seal up those bags for later use.

Makes about 3 cups

Tools Needed

    Offset spatula
    Wilton's 12-inch Disposable Decorating Bags or
        Ziploc Freezer Bags (1 quart and 1 pint sizes)
    Sharp scissors
    Scotch tape
    Tweezers
    Decorative paint brush (small tip)
    Wilton's Decorating Couplers (for royal icing)
    Wilton's Decorating Tips (for royal icing)
    Wilton's Icing Bag Ties (for royal icing)

To fill the Wilton Disposable Decorating Bag or the Ziploc Freezer Bag, hold the bottom of the bag in one hand and fold the upper half of the bag inside out over the top of your hand, so that only one-third of the bag is open in the palm of your hand. (If using Wilton Couplers, insert the lower half of the coupler at this time.)

Using an offset spatula, fill the bag inside of your hand with the icing of your choice. Lift the edges of the bag up and around the icing, press out any extra air, and seal the bag. (If using a Wilton Tip, snip off the end of the bag, insert the tip [Wilton tip 1, 2, 3, or 4], insert the coupler top, and apply the Icing Bag Tie.) Reinforce the corner of the bag with the icing in it with six overlapping layers wound with Scotch tape. Squeeze or pinch the taped corner flat. For a small plain tip, use your scissors to cut a very small ($\frac{1}{16}$-inch) corner off of the bottom. Vary the size. For a larger-size plain tip, use your scissors to cut a small ($\frac{1}{8}$-inch) corner off the bottom (Wilton tip 5, 6, 7, 8, 9, 10, 11, or 12).

To create flower petals and leaves, you will do the same for both, just with different icing colors and tips if using Wilton tips. Hold the bag(s) open and with your offset spatula push the icing down into one corner of the bag. (If using a Wilton Coupler, insert coupler at this time before inserting icing.) Reinforce the corner of the bag with the icing in it with six overlapping layers wound with Scotch tape. Squeeze or pinch the taped corner flat. Use your scissors to cut a small V-shape from the corner. (If using the Wilton Tip, snip off the end of the bag, insert the tip [Wilton Tip 103, 104, 352, 67, 68, 69, 2D], insert the coupler top, and apply the Icing Bag Tie.) Beginning on the perimeter of your cookie, place the tip flat on the surface of the exterior edge of the cookie. Squeeze the bag, pulling away from the center and using small wiggling motions or side-to-side motions to give the petal or leaf its shape. You want to work toward the center of your cookie in concentric circles, overlapping the layers of icing just slightly.

To create fur or any holiday decoration, you may need two to three colors of icing. Hold the bag open and with your offset spatula, spread two of the colors down opposite sides of the bag. Fill the bag with your third color, if using. Lift the edges of the bag up and around the icing and press out any extra air, then seal the bag. Reinforce the corner of the bag with the icing in it with six overlapping layers wound with Scotch tape. Squeeze or pinch the taped corner flat. Use your scissors to cut a small (⅛-inch) M-shape in the corner by cutting two small V's side by side. (If using a Wilton Tip, insert the inner coupler before adding icing, add the icing as directed above, snip off the end of the bag, insert the tip, insert the coupler top, and apply the Icing Bag Tie.) Beginning on the perimeter of your cookie, put the tip of the bag on the surface of the cookie and squeeze, until you have the length of icing you wish. Release the pressure and pull away. Piping in concentric circles and just slightly overlapping the pattern will achieve the wonderful fur-like icing or wreath-like icing we all desire. Try multicolored hues of red, green, and white, or blue and white; they are truly lovely. Enjoy presenting your beautifully decorated cookies at your next cookie exchange party!

Cookie Key

Everyday 🍪   Holiday 🍪   Good for Kids 🐘

Easy ▭   Intermediate ▭   Advanced ▭

Classic Cookies

Best Ever Sugar Cookies

Robin Olson

This is my favorite sugar cookie recipe, and the cutouts hold their shapes very well, along with tasting great!

Dough

    4 cups sifted all-purpose flour

    3 teaspoons baking powder

    ½ teaspoon salt

    1⅓ cups (2 sticks plus 2⅔ tablespoons) butter

    1½ cups sugar

    1 teaspoon grated orange zest

    1 teaspoon vanilla extract

    2 large eggs

    2½ tablespoons milk

Icing

    1 (1-pound) box confectioners' sugar

    Pinch of cream of tartar

Milk or cream to thin
Red and green food coloring
Multicolored sprinkles

In a medium bowl, sift or whisk together the flour, baking powder, and salt; set aside. In another bowl, cream together the butter, sugar, orange zest, and vanilla. Add the eggs and beat until light and fluffy, then add the milk. Gradually add the sifted dry ingredients and mix into the creamed mixture until well blended. Divide the dough in half, shape into disks, and wrap in wax paper. Chill for 1 hour.

Preheat the oven to 375°F/190°C. Line the baking sheets with parchment paper.

Roll out the dough on a lightly floured surface or pastry rolling mat, to a thickness of ¼ inch. Cut out the dough with cookie cutters of your choice. Transfer to the lined baking sheets.

Bake 8 to 10 minutes. Transfer the cookies to wire racks to cool.

Meanwhile, make the icing. In a medium bowl, sift together the confectioners' sugar and cream of tartar. Stir in milk or cream a little at a time, to thin to the desired consistency. Put some of the icing in two other separate bowls and tint with red and green food coloring, leaving some white, too. When the cookies have cooled, spread with the icing. Use multicolored sprinkles to decorate the iced cookies. Place the decorated cookies on wire racks to allow the icing to dry for a few hours before storing in an airtight container.

Makes 6 dozen cookies, using 3-inch cutters

Robin's Favorite Gingerbread

Recipe courtesy of Rose Levy Beranbaum, New York, New York

Rose Levy Beranbaum is an award-winning cookbook author and baking expert. This is my favorite gingerbread recipe and I've made it for several of my cookie exchanges. Rose graciously agreed to let me share it with you. (Thank you, Rose!) This recipe is for true gingerbread lovers; it's dark, spicy, and holds its shape very well. In the "Food Network Holiday Cookie Swap Special" that I was featured in, my friend Debby Griffith exclaimed "I love your gingerbread!" What Debby was really saying was that she loves Rose's gingerbread!

Dough

3 cups bleached all-purpose flour
¼ teaspoon salt
1 teaspoon baking soda
2 teaspoons ground ginger
1 teaspoon ground cinnamon
½ teaspoon grated nutmeg
¼ teaspoon ground cloves
¾ cup firmly packed dark brown sugar
¾ cup (1½ sticks) unsalted butter, softened
½ cup light molasses, preferably Grandma's brand (use a greased
   liquid measuring cup to measure)
1 large egg

Royal Icing

3 large egg whites
4 cups confectioners' sugar

Measure the flour using the dip-and-sweep method (see page 37). In a medium bowl, sift together the flour, salt, baking soda, and spices, then whisk together to mix evenly. In a separate bowl, using an electric mixer, cream together the brown sugar and butter until fluffy. Add the molasses and egg to the creamed mixture and beat until blended. On low speed, gradually beat in the flour mixture until incorporated.

Scrape the dough onto a sheet of plastic wrap and use the wrap, not your fingers, to press the dough together to form a thick flat disk. Wrap it well and refrigerate for 2 hours.

Preheat the oven to 350°F/180°C. Lightly grease the baking sheets.

On a floured surface or pastry rolling mat, roll out the dough to about a thickness of ⅛ inch. Use gingerbread cutters to cut out the dough. With a metal spatula, transfer the cut dough onto the prepared baking sheets, placing them about 1 inch apart. If desired, make holes in the cookies for hanging as ornaments.

Bake for 8 to 10 minutes for small cookies and up to 10 to 12 minutes for the larger ones, or until firm to the touch. Cool the cookies on the baking sheets for about 1 minute, then transfer to wire racks to cool completely. When completely cool, decorate with royal icing.

To make the icing: In a bowl, using an electric mixer, beat the ingredients on high for 5 to 7 minutes.

Variation: While the cookies are still hot, press raisins, currants, cinnamon red-hots, or other decorative candies as eyes and buttons. Decorations can also be attached, using dots of royal icing as glue, after the cookies have cooled. Store in an airtight container.

Makes 19 dozen (2 × ¼-inch) small cookies or 40 (5 × 3 × ¼-inch) large cookies

Basic Butter Cookies

Suzie Troia, Hilton Head, South Carolina

I win the award for longest travel to Robin's cookie exchange . . . 605 miles!

Suzie was my neighbor, two doors down, until she moved away.—Robin

1 cup (2 sticks) butter, softened
1½ cups sifted confectioners' sugar
1 large egg
1 teaspoon vanilla extract
2½ cups all-purpose flour
1 teaspoon baking soda
1 teaspoon cream of tartar
¼ teaspoon salt

In a medium bowl, cream the butter, then gradually add the confectioners' sugar and beat until light and fluffy. Beat in the egg and vanilla. In a separate bowl, sift the dry ingredients and gradually add to the creamed mixture, mixing until well blended. Shape the dough into a ball and wrap in wax paper. Chill for 1 hour.

Preheat the oven to 350°F/180°C. Line the baking sheets with parchment paper.

Roll out the dough in sections and cut out the cookies with cookie cutters of your choice. For easier cookie cutting, dip the cutter into confectioners' sugar prior to cutting the dough. Transfer the cutouts to the lined baking sheets.

Bake the cookies for 8 to 10 minutes, or until the edges begin to turn golden brown.

Variations: Sprinkle the dough with colored decorator's sugars before baking. Or, after baking, while the cookies are still warm, lightly brush with melted butter and then sprinkle with colored sugars. Another option is to frost or ice the cookies after they are completely cool. Store in airtight containers once the icing has set.

Makes 3 to 4 dozen cookies, depending on the size of the cutters

Apricot-Almond Thumbprint Cookies

Donna Dlubac, Gaithersburg, Maryland

These are so simple, yet everyone loves them.

1 cup (2 sticks) butter, softened
¼ cup sugar
1 teaspoon almond extract
2 cups all-purpose flour
1 cup ground almonds
1 cup apricot jam, or jam of choice

Preheat the oven to 350°F/180°C. Line the baking sheets with parchment paper, or use ungreased sheets.

In a medium bowl, cream together the butter, sugar, and almond extract. Add the flour and incorporate. Shape the dough into teaspoon-size balls and roll in the ground almonds. Place the cookies on baking sheets 2 inches apart. Indent the centers with your thumb and fill with jam.

Bake for 10 to 12 minutes. Transfer the cookies to racks to cool.

Makes 4 dozen cookies

White Chocolate–Macadamia Nut Cookies

Joyce Buttrey, Gaithersburg, Maryland

1¼ cups all-purpose flour
½ teaspoon baking soda
½ teaspoon salt
½ cup (1 stick) butter, softened
¾ cup sugar
1 large egg
1 teaspoon vanilla extract
1 cup white chocolate chips
1 cup coarsely chopped macadamia nuts

Preheat the oven to 375°F/190°C. Line the baking sheets with parchment paper.

In a small bowl, whisk together the flour, baking soda, and salt; set aside. In a medium bowl, cream together the butter and sugar. Beat in the egg and vanilla. Gradually add the flour mixture to the creamed mixture and mix until well blended. Stir in the white chocolate and nuts. Drop the cookies by heaping teaspoonfuls, about 2 inches apart, onto the lined baking sheets.

Bake for 8 to 10 minutes, or until lightly browned. Transfer to wire racks to cool.

Makes about 2½ dozen cookies

Butter Pecan Cookies

Leslie Jackson Kelly, Laurel, Maryland

¾ cup chopped pecans
½ cup (1 stick) unsalted butter, softened
⅓ cup sugar, plus more for coating
1 teaspoon vanilla extract
⅛ teaspoon salt
1 cup all-purpose flour

Preheat the oven to 350°F/180°C.

Toast the pecans on a baking sheet in the oven, until fragrant, about 6 minutes. Let cool completely, then finely chop.

In a medium bowl, using an electric mixer, cream the butter for about 1 minute. Add the sugar and cream until light, about 1 minute more. Beat in the vanilla, salt, and flour, and continue beating, scraping down the sides of the bowl, just until the dough comes together. Fold in the pecans.

Separate the dough into 15 pieces. Shape each piece of dough into a ball. Roll each ball in sugar. Place the balls, 3 inches apart, on ungreased baking sheets. Gently flatten each ball with the bottom of a glass, reshaping the sides if necessary. Sprinkle with additional sugar.

Bake the cookies about 15 minutes, or until golden brown, rotating the baking sheets halfway through the baking time. Sprinkle with more sugar. Transfer the cookies to wire racks to cool.

Makes 15 cookies

Oatmeal Toffee Cookies

Mary Jean Anderjaska McCarthy, Towson, Maryland

1½ cups (3 sticks) butter, softened
1 cup firmly packed light brown sugar
2 large eggs
2 teaspoons vanilla extract
2 cups all-purpose flour
½ teaspoon salt
1 teaspoon baking soda
3 cups old-fashioned rolled oats
1 cup chopped pecans
4 cups Heath Bits o' Brickle Toffee Bits

Preheat the oven to 300°F/180°C. Line the baking sheets with parchment paper.

In a medium bowl, cream together the butter and brown sugar. Stir in the eggs and vanilla and beat until smooth. In a separate bowl, whisk together the flour, salt, and baking soda, stir into the creamed mixture, then stir in the rolled oats. Finally, stir in the chopped pecans and the Bits O' Brickle. Drop the dough by rounded tablespoonfuls 2 inches apart onto the lined baking sheets, and flatten slightly.

Bake the cookies for 10 to 18 minutes. Transfer to wire racks to cool.

Makes 6 dozen cookies

Cocoa Peppermint Pretzels

Angela Sammarco, Gaithersburg, Maryland

Chocolate pretzels with crushed peppermint candy "glued" on. Kids love them!

2½ cups all-purpose flour
½ teaspoon salt
½ cup unsweetened cocoa powder
1 cup confectioners' sugar
1 cup (2 sticks) butter, softened
1 large egg
1½ teaspoons vanilla extract
½ cup vanilla baking chips (or white chocolate chips)
1 teaspoon shortening
⅓ cup crushed peppermint candy

In a medium bowl, whisk together the flour, salt, and cocoa powder; set aside. In a large bowl, using an electric mixer, combine the confectioners' sugar, butter, egg, and vanilla, and beat until light and fluffy. Gradually add the flour mixture to the creamed mixture and beat on low speed until a soft dough forms. Cover the dough in the bowl with plastic wrap. Chill for 2 to 3 hours, or until firm.

Preheat the oven to 375°F/190°C. Line the baking sheets with parchment paper, or use ungreased baking sheets.

Roll the dough into 9-inch-long ropes about ½ inch in diameter. Shape each rope into an upside-down U. Bring the ends together and twist in the middle. Take the ends to the top of the pretzel and press the dough to secure. Place the pretzels 2 inches apart on the lined or ungreased baking sheets. Bake for 8 to 9 minutes, or until set. Cool completely on the baking sheets.

Put the baking chips and shortening in a small microwave-safe bowl and microwave on high for 2 to 4 minutes, stirring often until melted. Dip one side of each pretzel into the melted chips, then roll the dipped side into the crushed candy. Place the pretzels on wax paper–lined baking sheets and let dry completely before storing.

Makes 4 dozen pretzels

Colorful Cream Cheese Pinwheels

Iris Grundler, Gaithersburg, Maryland

¾ cup (1½ sticks) butter, softened
1 (8-ounce) package cream cheese, softened
1 egg, separated
½ cup granulated sugar
1 teaspoon vanilla extract
2 cups all-purpose flour
1 tablespoon baking powder
¼ cup pink colored sugar
¼ cup yellow colored sugar
¼ cup blue colored sugar
¼ cup green colored sugar
30 M&Ms

Beat the butter, cream cheese, egg yolk, sugar, and vanilla in a medium bowl until smooth. Add the flour and baking powder and combine. Cover the dough with plastic wrap and refrigerate for 1 hour.

Preheat the oven to 350°F/180°C. Line baking sheets with parchment paper.

Roll out the dough to ¼-inch thickness, one-half at a time, between two sheets of wax paper. Using a knife, cut the dough into 3-inch squares and place, 3 inches apart, on ungreased baking sheets. Lightly beat the egg white and brush the squares with it. Using a knife, cut the dough in, diagonally, from each corner, about ½ inch. Sprinkle about 1 teaspoon of colored sugar over each square. Fold alternate corners of the square to the center to form a pinwheel, overlapping the dough at the center and pushing down gently to seal. Press one M&M in the center of each pinwheel.

Bake the cookies for 12 to 15 minutes. Cool for 1 minute on the baking sheets, then transfer to wire racks to cool completely.

Makes 2½ dozen pinwheels

Strawberry-filled Tea Cookies

Leslie Jackson Kelly, Laurel, Maryland

These tea cookies are tender little pillows filled with strawberry preserves.

1½ cups (3 sticks) butter, softened
1½ cups (12 ounces) cream cheese, softened
4½ cups all-purpose flour
2 cups strawberry preserves (or substitute red raspberry preserves or seedless blackberry jam)

Place the butter and cream cheese in a medium bowl and beat with an electric mixer until softened and thoroughly blended. Slowly mix in the flour, beating until blended. Roll the dough into 1-inch balls, cover with wax paper, and refrigerate for at least 8 hours.

Preheat the oven to 350°F/180°C. Line the baking sheets with parchment paper, or use ungreased baking sheets.

Roll or press the balls flat. Place ½ teaspoon strawberry preserves in the center of each cookie. Fold the outer edge upward and pinch closed. Place, pinched side up, on ungreased or lined baking sheets.

Bake the cookies for 20 to 25 minutes, or until golden brown. Cool on the baking sheets for 5 minutes, then transfer to wire racks to cool completely.

Makes 26 to 30 cookies

Sweeties

Donna Dorsch, Gaithersburg, Maryland

Almond-flavored and chewy, this is a pretty cookie with pink swirls.

Dough

2 cups sugar

1 cup (2 sticks) butter, softened

3 large eggs

2 teaspoons almond extract

4 cups all-purpose flour

1 tablespoon baking powder

½ teaspoon cream of tartar

2 to 3 drops red food coloring

Glaze

1 cup confectioners' sugar

1 to 3 teaspoons milk

1 teaspoon almond extract

Preheat the oven to 375°F/190°C. Grease baking sheets.

In a medium bowl, cream together the sugar and butter. Beat in the eggs and almond extract. In a separate bowl, mix together the flour, baking powder, and cream of tartar. Add the dry ingredients to the creamed mixture and mix well. Swirl red food coloring, by hand, into the dough to create a ribbon-like appearance. Using a 2-inch ice cream scoop, scoop the dough onto the baking sheets, placing the cookies 2 inches apart.

Bake for 10 to 12 minutes; the cookies should have a chewy consistency. Transfer to racks to cool.

Meanwhile, make the glaze. Mix the confectioners' sugar with 1 teaspoon milk, adding more milk as needed until you reach the desired consistency.

Glaze the cooled cookies on nonstick cooling racks so that icing drips down the side.

Makes 2 to 3 dozen cookies

Lemon Melting Moments

Robin Olson

The name perfectly describes this lovely, lemony, crumbly cookie with a sweet frosting.

Dough
1 cup all-purpose flour
²⁄₃ cup cornstarch
¹⁄₈ teaspoon salt
1 cup (2 sticks) butter, softened
¹⁄₂ cup confectioners' sugar
1 tablespoon freshly squeezed lemon juice

Frosting
4 teaspoons butter, softened
2 cups confectioners' sugar
2 to 3 tablespoons freshly squeezed lemon juice

1 tablespoon grated lemon zest
Sprinkles (optional)

Preheat the oven to 350°F/180°C. Line the baking sheets with parchment paper.

In a medium bowl, whisk or sift together the flour, cornstarch, and salt; set aside. In a separate bowl, using an electric mixer, cream together the butter and sugar. Slowly add the flour mixture to the creamed mixture and mix until combined. Add 1 tablespoon lemon juice. Using a teaspoon or a small scoop, form the dough into 1-inch balls and place 2 inches apart on the lined baking sheets.

Bake for 12 to 15 minutes, or until lightly browned around the edges. Transfer to wire racks to cool. When completely cool, ice the cookies.

To make the frosting, in a medium bowl, combine the butter, confectioners' sugar, lemon juice, and lemon zest. Gently beat with a whisk until combined. Decorate with sprinkles, if desired, while the icing is still wet.

Makes 2 to 3 dozen cookies

Christmas Spice Cookies

Julie Buschek Jones, Holly Springs, North Carolina

¾ cup sugar
⅔ cup (1 stick, plus 2⅔ tablespoons) butter, softened
¼ cup freshly squeezed orange juice
½ cup dark corn syrup
½ cup dark molasses
4½ cups all-purpose flour
¾ cup whole wheat flour
1 teaspoon baking soda

1 teaspoon salt
½ teaspoon ground cloves
½ teaspoon ground nutmeg
½ teaspoon ground allspice
2 teaspoons ground ginger

In a medium bowl, cream together the sugar and butter; blend in the orange juice, corn syrup, and molasses. In a separate bowl, combine the flours, baking soda, salt, and spices. Add the dry ingredients to the creamed mixture. Chill the dough in the bowl for 3 to 4 hours.

Preheat the oven to 350°F/180°C. Lightly grease the baking sheets.

Roll out a portion of dough on a lightly floured surface to a thickness of ¼ inch. Cut into desired shapes. Place 2 inches apart on the prepared baking sheets.

Bake the cookies for 12 to 14 minutes. Transfer the cookies to wire racks to cool.

Makes 6 to 7 dozen cookies

Snickerdoodles

Julie Buschek Jones, Holly Springs, North Carolina

This is the best Snickerdoodle recipe, all puffy and cinnamony! Enjoy these with a tall glass of milk.

My cousin Julie brought this to one of my early exchanges and it's become a family favorite must-bake every year. My kids love it.—Robin

Dough
3¾ cups all-purpose flour
½ teaspoon cream of tartar

½ teaspoon baking soda
½ teaspoon salt
1 cup (2 sticks) butter, softened
2 cups sugar
2 large eggs
¼ cup milk
1 teaspoon vanilla extract

Cinnamon Sugar

3 teaspoons sugar
1 teaspoon ground cinnamon

Preheat the oven to 375°F/190°C.

In a medium bowl, stir together the flour, cream of tartar, baking soda, and salt. In a separate bowl, cream the butter for 30 seconds, then add the sugar and beat until light and fluffy. Add the eggs, milk, and vanilla and beat well. Add the dry ingredients to the creamed mixture and beat until well blended.

Form the dough into 1-inch balls. Roll the balls in the cinnamon sugar made by mixing sugar with cinnamon. Place the balls 2 inches apart on baking sheets.

Bake for 8 minutes. Transfer to wire racks to cool.

Makes about 5 dozen cookies

Jumbles with Browned Butter Glaze

Julie Buschek Jones, Holly Springs, North Carolina

I moved to North Carolina so I can't attend my cousin Robin's cookie exchange party anymore, but if I could come, this is what I would bring!

Dough

2¾ cups all-purpose flour
1 teaspoon salt
½ teaspoon baking soda
1 teaspoon ground cinnamon
¼ teaspoon ground cloves
½ cup shortening
1½ cups firmly packed dark brown sugar
2 large eggs
¾ cup applesauce
1 teaspoon vanilla extract
1 cup raisins
½ cup chopped walnuts or pecans

Browned Butter Glaze

¼ cup (½ stick) butter
2 cups confectioners' sugar
1 teaspoon vanilla extract
1 to 2 tablespoons milk

Preheat the oven to 375°F/190°C. Lightly grease the baking sheets.

In a medium bowl, whisk together the flour, salt, baking soda, cinnamon, and cloves; set aside.

In a large bowl, using an electric mixer, beat the shortening and sugar until blended. Beat in the eggs until the mixture is light and fluffy, about 2 minutes. Add the applesauce and vanilla. Gradually add the flour mixture to the creamed mixture and beat until well blended. Stir in the raisins and nuts. Drop the dough by tablespoonfuls, about 2 inches apart, onto the prepared baking sheets.

Bake the cookies for 10 to 12 minutes, or until the edges are golden brown. Transfer to wire racks to cool.

Meanwhile, make the glaze. In a small saucepan, heat the butter over low heat until golden brown. Remove from the heat, and blend in the confectioners' sugar and vanilla. Stir in the milk a little at a time until you reach spreading consistency. Spread the cooled cookies with the Browned Butter Glaze.

Makes about 3 dozen cookies

Cherry Bonbons

Patrice Datovech, Gaithersburg, Maryland

Dough
1 cup (2 sticks) butter, softened
½ cup sugar
1 teaspoon vanilla extract
2¼ cups all-purpose flour
⅛ teaspoon salt
15 maraschino cherries, cut in half
15 pecans, cut in half

Icing
1 cup confectioners' sugar
2 tablespoons maraschino cherry juice
2 tablespoons butter, melted

Preheat the oven to 325°F/160°C.

In a medium bowl, cream together the butter and sugar until well blended. Add the remaining ingredients except for the cherries and pecans. Mix the dough with your hands to blend. Using a small cookie scoop to measure the dough, scoop out a small piece of dough and form a ball. Flatten the ball and place a cherry half and a piece of pecan in the center. Wrap the dough around cherry and nut to form a firm ball. Repeat with the remaining dough, cherries, and nuts.

Place the balls 2 inches apart on ungreased baking sheets.

Bake for 15 to 20 minutes; the bottoms of the cookies should be light golden brown. Let cool for a few minutes on the baking sheets, then transfer to wire racks to cool.

Meanwhile, make the icing: Combine the ingredients together until the mixture is smooth. When the cookies are completely cool, ice the tops.

Makes 2½ dozen cookies

Old-fashioned Cracked Peppermint Sugar Cookies

Lisa Cullen, Gaithersburg, Maryland

⅓ cup peppermint candy
1¼ cups granulated sugar
2 cups all-purpose flour
2 teaspoons baking soda
½ teaspoon salt
2 teaspoons cream of tartar

1 cup shortening

½ cup firmly packed light brown sugar

1 large egg

1 teaspoon vanilla extract

Preheat the oven to 350°F/180°C. Line the baking sheets with parchment paper.

Between sheets of wax paper, gently pound the peppermint candy with a mallet; you will need ⅓ cup. Transfer to a bowl and combine with ¼ cup of the sugar; set aside. In a medium bowl, combine the flour, baking soda, salt, and cream of tartar, whisk together; set aside. In a large bowl, cream together the shortening and sugars. Add the egg and the vanilla and beat until light and fluffy. Gradually add the flour mixture and mix until combined.

Shape the dough into balls the size of a walnut, and roll in the crushed peppermint-sugar mixture. Place the balls 2 inches apart on the lined baking sheets. Bake for 10 to 12 minutes. Transfer to wire racks to cool.

Makes about 4 dozen cookies

Cream Wafers

Robin Olson

A delicate butter cookie with a creamy filling. Great for special occasions like weddings or baby showers.

Dough

1 cup (2 sticks) butter, softened

2 cups all-purpose flour

⅓ cup heavy cream

⅓ cup sugar for dipping cut-out dough

Cream Filling

¾ cup confectioners' sugar

1 teaspoon vanilla extract

¼ cup (½ stick) butter, softened

Milk or water for thinning

A few drops food coloring of your choice

Using an electric mixer, cream the butter and then mix in the flour until well combined. Add the cream and mix well to combine. Divide the dough in half and form into 2 disks. Wrap in wax paper and chill for 1 hour.

Preheat the oven to 375°F/190°C. Line the baking sheets with parchment paper.

Roll out one disk of the chilled dough on a lightly floured pastry rolling mat to a thickness of ⅛ inch. Cut out the dough into 1½-inch rounds. Put the ⅓ cup sugar in a shallow bowl and dip both sides of the cut-out cookie in the sugar. Place 2 inches apart on the lined baking sheets. Poke each cookie with the lines of a fork four times.

Bake the cookies for 7 to 9 minutes. Meanwhile, mix all the filling ingredients until smooth, adding a few drops of milk or water if needed, and the food coloring. When the cookies are done, transfer to wire racks to cool. When cool, fill with the cream filling and sandwich together.

Makes 5 dozen sandwich cookies

Chocolate Mocha Crescents

Leslie Jackson Kelly, Laurel, Maryland

2 cups sugar

½ cup vegetable oil

4 (1-ounce) squares unsweetened chocolate, melted

2 teaspoons instant coffee crystals

2 teaspoons hot water

1 teaspoon vanilla extract

4 large eggs

3 cups all-purpose flour

2 teaspoons baking powder

¼ teaspoon salt

½ cup semisweet chocolate chips and ½ cup vanilla chips (or white chocolate chips)

4 teaspoons shortening

In a large bowl, combine the sugar, oil, melted unsweetened chocolate, coffee crystals, water, and vanilla. Using an electric mixer, beat at medium speed until well blended. Beat in the eggs. Gradually add the flour, baking powder, and salt. Beat on low speed until a soft dough forms. Cover the dough with wax paper and chill for several hours until firm.

Preheat the oven to 350°F/180°C. Line the baking sheets with parchment paper.

Shape rounded tablespoonfuls of the dough into crescent shapes. Place the crescents 2 inches apart on the lined baking sheets.

Bake the crescents for 12 to 15 minutes, or until set.

Cool several minutes on the baking sheets, then transfer to wire racks to cool completely.

Melt the semisweet chocolate and vanilla chips separately in the microwave or a double boiler, each with 2 teaspoons of shortening. Drizzle the melted vanilla chips over the cookies and repeat with the melted semisweet chocolate. Let dry completely before sealing in tins or airtight containers.

Makes 5 dozen crescents

Dipped Vanilla Almond Crescents

Anne Goldman, Montgomery Village, Maryland

½ cup (1 stick) butter, softened
½ cup ground almonds
¼ cup sugar
1 teaspoon vanilla extract
1 cup all-purpose flour
2 tablespoons cornstarch
2 (1-ounce) squares semisweet chocolate
½ teaspoon shortening

Preheat the oven to 375°F/190°C. Lightly grease the baking sheets.

In a medium bowl, cream together the butter, almonds, sugar, and vanilla. Add the flour and cornstarch and mix to form a dough. Roll the dough into 1-inch balls, shape into crescents, and place on the prepared baking sheets.

Bake the crescents for 8 to 10 minutes, or until lightly browned. Cool completely on wire racks.

Melt the chocolate and shortening in the microwave or a double boiler; stir until smooth. Dip one end of each crescent into the melted chocolate and cool on wax paper–lined baking sheets. Refrigerate for about 30 minutes to firm the chocolate.

Makes about 2½ dozen crescents

Chocolate Reindeer Cookies

Robin Olson

Chocolate Reindeer rank very high on the cuteness meter. Kids will love helping make these cookies, and they're very festive-looking. This is a modified version of my favorite cutout sugar cookie. You'll need a bell-shaped cookie cutter for this recipe.

Dough

2 cups sifted all-purpose flour

1½ teaspoons baking powder

¼ cup unsweetened cocoa powder

¼ teaspoon salt

⅔ cup (1 stick, plus 2⅔ tablespoons) butter, softened

1 cup sugar

½ teaspoon vanilla extract

1 large egg

1½ tablespoons milk

Decorations

1 large bag mini braided pretzel twists

Chocolate chips

Small red gumdrops

Royal icing (page 39, pages 44–45)

In a medium bowl, sift together the flour, baking powder, cocoa powder, and salt; set aside. In a separate bowl, using an electric mixer, cream together the butter, sugar, and vanilla. Add the egg and beat until light and fluffy, then beat in the milk. Gradually add the sifted dry ingredients to the creamed mixture and beat until well blended. Divide the dough in half, shape into disks, and wrap in wax paper. Chill for 1 hour.

Preheat the oven to 375°F/190°C. Line the baking sheets with parchment paper.

Roll out the dough on a lightly floured surface or pastry rolling mat to a thickness of ¼ inch. Cut out the rolled dough with bell-shaped cutters. Transfer the cookies to the lined baking sheets.

Bake the cookies for 8 to 10 minutes. Decorate while still warm and on the baking sheets.

Make the reindeer: The bottom of the bell is the top of the reindeer's head and the top of the bell is where the mouth should be. Using 2 pretzels, place antlers on the top of head. To make the eyes, use chocolate chips or, to create "silly eyes," use royal icing for the white part of the eye and black dots or chocolate chips at the bottom of the eye. Use a red gumdrop for the nose. Transfer the cookies to wire racks to cool.

Makes about 2½ dozen cookies using a 3-inch bell-shaped cutter

Caramel Apple Cookies

Cheryl Berger, Gaithersburg, Maryland

These little Caramel Apple Cookies are irresistibly cute!

Filling
⅓ cup chopped peeled apple
⅓ cup evaporated milk
⅓ cup granulated sugar
⅓ cup chopped pecans (or peanuts)

Dough
½ cup (1 stick) butter, softened
¼ cup firmly packed light brown sugar
¼ cup confectioners' sugar
1 large egg

1 teaspoon vanilla extract

¼ teaspoon salt

2 cups all-purpose flour

Coating

1 (14-ounce) package caramels

⅔ cup evaporated milk

Popsicle sticks cut in half, or colored toothpicks

1 cup finely chopped pecans

Preheat the oven to 350°F/180°C. Lightly grease the baking sheets.

In a small saucepan, combine the filling ingredients. Cook and stir over medium heat until thickened; set aside to cool. In a bowl, cream together the butter and sugars. Add the egg, vanilla, and salt and beat well. Add the flour and mix until well blended. Shape the dough into 1-inch balls. Flatten each ball, and place ¼ teaspoon of the filling in the center of each. Fold the dough over the filling and reshape into a ball. Place the balls, 1 inch apart, on the prepared baking sheets.

Bake the cookies for 12 to 15 minutes, or until lightly browned. Transfer to wire racks to cool.

In a saucepan over low heat, cook the caramels with the evaporated milk, stirring occasionally, until the caramels have melted. Insert a popsicle stick or toothpick into each cooled cookie and dip into the caramel until completely coated (the popsicle stick or toothpick becomes the stick). Dip the cookie bottoms into the chopped nuts. Place on wire racks to set.

Makes about 3 dozen cookies

Apricot-Cream Cheese Thumbprints

Donna Dlubac, Gaithersburg, Maryland

1½ cups (3 sticks) butter, softened
1½ cups granulated sugar
1 (8-ounce) package cream cheese, softened
2 large eggs
2 tablespoons freshly squeezed lemon juice
1½ teaspoons grated lemon zest
4½ cups all-purpose flour
1½ teaspoons baking powder
1 cup apricot preserves
⅓ cup confectioners' sugar for decoration

In a large bowl, cream together the butter, granulated sugar, and cream cheese until smooth. Beat in the eggs one at a time, then stir in the lemon juice and lemon zest. In a separate bowl, combine the flour and baking powder and stir into the cream cheese mixture until just combined. Cover and chill the dough until firm, about 1 hour.

Preheat the oven to 350°F/180°C. Line the baking sheets with parchment paper.

Roll tablespoonfuls of the dough into balls, and place them, 2 inches apart, on the lined baking sheets. Using your finger, make an indention in the center of each ball, and fill with ½ teaspoon of apricot preserves.

Bake the cookies for 15 minutes, or until the edges are golden. Allow the cookies to cool on the baking sheets for 2 minutes, then transfer to wire racks to cool completely. When cool, sprinkle with confectioners' sugar.

Makes 7 dozen cookies

Eggnog Logs

Debby Griffith, Gaithersburg, Maryland

Delicate, eggnog-flavored cookies, dipped on each end in delicious creamy vanilla frosting, and then rolled in chopped pecans.

Debby first brought these to my 1994 cookie exchange. Every time she says "I don't know what to make for this year's cookie exchange," I say, "Bring Eggnog Logs!"—Robin

Dough

1 cup (2 sticks) butter, softened

¾ cup sugar

1 large egg

2 teaspoons vanilla extract

1 teaspoon rum flavoring

3 cups all-purpose flour

1 teaspoon grated nutmeg

Vanilla Frosting

¼ cup (½ stick) butter, softened

2 cups confectioners' sugar

2 tablespoons milk

1 teaspoon vanilla extract

¾ cup chopped pecans for dipping

Preheat the oven to 350°F/180°C.

In a medium bowl, using an electric mixer, cream together the butter and sugar. Add the egg, vanilla, and rum flavoring and beat until light and fluffy. Combine the flour and nutmeg, and gradually add to the creamed mixture until incorporated. Divide the dough into

10 portions, and roll each portion into a rope 15 inches long. Cut each rope into 5 logs. Place the logs on ungreased baking sheets.

Bake the logs for 10 to 12 minutes. Transfer to wire racks to cool.

Make the frosting: Beat the butter, confectioners' sugar, milk, and vanilla together until smooth. Dip the ends of the cooled logs into the frosting and roll in the chopped nuts.

Makes 6 dozen logs

Pecan Lace Sandwich Cookies with Orange Buttercream

Peggy Ols, Gaithersburg, Maryland

Everybody loves these cookies!

Dough

¼ cup (½ stick) unsalted butter
⅓ cup sugar
2 tablespoons light corn syrup
⅓ cup all-purpose flour
1 cup coarsely ground pecans
1 teaspoon vanilla extract

Filling

1 cup confectioners' sugar
¼ cup (½ stick) unsalted butter, softened
1 tablespoon freshly squeezed orange juice
¾ teaspoon grated orange zest

Preheat the oven to 350°F/180°C. Line the baking sheets with parchment paper.

Stir together the butter, sugar, and corn syrup in a heavy-bottomed saucepan over low heat until melted and smooth. Increase the heat to medium-high, and bring to a boil, stirring constantly. Remove from heat. Stir in the flour. Add the nuts and vanilla and stir to combine. Drop the dough by teaspoonfuls onto the lined baking sheets, spacing them 2 inches apart.

Bake the cookies, one sheet at a time, until bubbly and lightly browned, about 11 minutes. Cool on the baking sheets for 10 minutes, then transfer to wire racks to cool completely.

Make the filling. In a medium bowl, whisk all the ingredients until smooth. Spread 1 teaspoon of the filling onto the bottom of one cookie. Top with a second cookie, bottom side down, pressing lightly to adhere. Repeat with the remaining cookies.

Variations: Use different extracts to flavor the filling: for example, almond, coconut, or raspberry.

Makes 18 to 20 cookies

Banana Bread Cookies

Zina Merritt, Gaithersburg, Maryland

Dough

    1 cup butter-flavored shortening
    1 cup sugar
    2 large eggs
    ½ teaspoon vanilla extract
    ½ teaspoon banana extract
    1 banana, peeled and mashed
    2 cups all-purpose flour
    1 teaspoon baking soda
    ½ teaspoon salt

Glaze

   3 tablespoons butter
   ⅓ cup confectioners' sugar
   1 to 2 tablespoons cream or milk
   1 teaspoon banana extract (or use rum extract)

Preheat the oven to 350°F/180°C. Line the baking sheets with parchment paper.

In a medium bowl, cream together the shortening and sugar until smooth. Beat in the eggs, vanilla and banana extracts, and the mashed banana. In another bowl, combine the flour, baking soda, and salt and blend thoroughly into the creamed mixture to make a sticky dough. Drop the dough by rounded tablespoons onto the lined baking sheets.

Bake the cookies for 10 to 15 minutes, or until lightly browned.

Meanwhile, make the glaze. In a bowl, blend together the butter, confectioners' sugar, cream or milk, and banana extract.

Remove the cookies from the oven and transfer to wire racks. Drizzle the glaze over the warm cookies.

Makes about 4 dozen cookies

Chocolate Pinwheel Cookies

Ann Hallock, Gaithersburg, Maryland

   1 cup (2 sticks) butter, softened
   1 cup sugar
   2 large egg yolks, beaten
   3 cups all-purpose flour

1 tablespoon baking powder
Pinch of salt
6 tablespoons milk
1 teaspoon vanilla extract
2 (1-ounce) squares unsweetened chocolate, melted

Preheat the oven to 350°F/180°C. Lightly grease the baking sheets.

In a medium bowl, cream the butter and add sugar gradually. Add the egg yolks and beat well. Sift together the flour, baking powder, and pinch of salt. Add to the creamed mixture with the milk and vanilla, mixing well. Divide the dough in half. Add the cooled, melted chocolate to one-half of the dough. Roll or pat each half of the dough into an oblong, thin sheet of the same size on wax paper. Place in the refrigerator to firm.

Place the chilled chocolate dough over the chilled white dough, and roll up tightly as for a jelly roll. Wrap the roll in wax paper or plastic wrap and return to the refrigerator until firm.

When firm, slice the rolls ¼ inch thick and lay, cut side down, on the prepared greased baking sheets. Bake for 8 minutes. Transfer to wire racks to cool.

Makes about 4 dozen cookies

Hidden Kisses

Tracy Thomas, Adamstown, Maryland

1 cup (2 sticks) butter, softened
⅔ cup granulated sugar
½ teaspoon vanilla extract
½ teaspoon almond extract
1¾ cups all-purpose flour

¾ cup finely chopped pecans

1 (9-ounce) package Hershey's Kisses

1½ cups confectioners' sugar

In a large bowl, cream together the butter, sugar, and vanilla and almond extracts. Stir in the flour and blend well. Add the pecans and blend well. Cover the bowl and refrigerate the dough for 1 hour.

Preheat the oven to 375°F/190°C.

Unwrap the candy kisses. Press a scant tablespoon of dough around each kiss, covering it completely. Shape into a ball. Repeat with the remaining dough and kisses. Place the cookies 2 inches apart on ungreased baking sheets.

Bake the cookies for 10 minutes. Cool slightly on the baking sheets, then transfer to wire racks to cool completely. Roll the cooled cookies in the confectioners' sugar.

Makes 4 dozen cookies

Chocolate Snowballs with Snowy Glaze

Debby Griffith, Gaithersburg, Maryland

Dough

1½ cups all-purpose flour

½ teaspoon baking powder

¼ teaspoon salt

¼ cup (½ stick) butter, softened

½ cup sugar

1 large egg

1 (1-ounce) square unsweetened chocolate, melted and cooled

1 teaspoon vanilla extract

Snowy Glaze

1 cup confectioners' sugar

1 tablespoon plus 2 teaspoons milk

$\frac{1}{2}$ teaspoon vanilla extract

White or clear decorator's sugar, for sprinkling

In a medium bowl, whisk together the flour, baking powder, and salt until combined; set aside. In a separate bowl, cream the butter, add the sugar, and beat until light and fluffy. Add the egg, melted chocolate, and vanilla extract and beat well. Slowly add the flour mixture to the creamed mixture and mix until combined. On wax paper, form the dough into a large ball, wrap, and chill for 2 hours.

Preheat the oven to 350°F/180°C. Line the baking sheets with parchment paper.

Shape the chilled dough into 2-inch balls. Place the balls 2 inches apart on the lined baking sheets. Bake for 10 to 12 minutes. Cool on wire racks.

Meanwhile, make the glaze. Combine the confectioners' sugar, milk, and vanilla and beat until smooth.

When the cookies are completely cool, apply the glaze. After applying the glaze, sprinkle with white or clear decorator's sugar for a sparkly, eye-catching affect. If your grocery doesn't carry decorator's sugar, make a trip to your local craft store or baking supply store for clear or white pearlized sugar, also called decorator's sugar, sanding sugar, or pearl sugar.

Makes about 2 dozen cookies

Surprise Cookies with Caramel Nest

Iris Grundler, Gaithersburg, Maryland

The caramel nest helped me win the presentation prize at Robin's cookie party!

Dough

¾ cup (1½ sticks) butter, softened
½ cup firmly packed light brown sugar
1½ teaspoon vanilla extract
⅛ teaspoon ground cinnamon
1½ cups all-purpose flour
30 Hershey's Kisses
½ cup confectioners' sugar

Caramel Nest

1 cup sugar
½ teaspoon vanilla

In a medium bowl, using an electric mixer set on medium speed, beat the butter and brown sugar until light and fluffy. Beat in the vanilla and cinnamon. Stir the flour into the creamed mixture until well blended. Cover the dough. Chill for 1 hour.

Preheat the oven to 350°F/180°C.

Shape or roll 2 tablespoons of the dough into a flat round large enough to cover a Hershey's Kiss. Place a chocolate candy in the center of each round. Roll the dough around the candy into a ball. Make sure the dough around the chocolate candy is completely sealed. Otherwise, the chocolate will melt and leak out through the dough, causing a sticky mess. Repeat with the remaining dough and candy. Place the cookies, 1 inch apart, on two ungreased baking sheets.

Bake the cookies about 20 minutes, or until golden. Transfer the baking sheets to wire racks and cool the cookies slightly, then transfer to wire racks and cool completely.

Arrange the cookies on a cutting board or other work surface. Spoon the confectioners' sugar into a strainer and shake over the cookies, dusting them evenly.

To make the caramel nest, place the sugar and vanilla in a heavy skillet over medium heat. Cook and stir with a wooden spoon until the sugar is dissolved and the caramel is golden. Cool the caramel for 5 minutes and then drizzle it very slowly over a very cold ceramic plate, trying to make solid lines. Place the plate in the refrigerator until the caramel has hardened, about 15 minutes. Remove the caramel gently from the plate and use it as a nest for about 10 cookies.

Makes about 2½ dozen cookies

Eggnog Snickerdoodles

Margie Willis, Hagerstown, Maryland

Dough

2¼ cups all-purpose flour
¼ teaspoon salt
2 teaspoons cream of tartar
1 teaspoon baking soda
1 cup (2 sticks) butter, softened
1½ cups sugar
2 large eggs
½ teaspoon brandy extract
½ teaspoon rum extract

Nutmeg Sugar

1 teaspoon grated nutmeg
¼ cup colored (or plain) sugar

Preheat the oven to 400°F/200°C. Line the baking sheets with parchment paper.

In a medium bowl, whisk together the flour, salt, cream of tartar, and baking soda; set aside. In the bowl of an electric mixer fitted with the paddle attachment, cream the butter and sugar. Add the eggs and beat well. Add the brandy and rum extracts. Gradually add in the flour mixture, beating until well blended. Combine the nutmeg and sugar in a separate bowl. Shape teaspoonfuls of the dough into 1-inch balls; roll in nutmeg sugar. Place the cookies, 2 inches apart, on the lined baking sheets.

Bake the cookies for 8 to 10 minutes, or until the edges are lightly browned, or for less time if you prefer softer cookies. Transfer the cookies to wire racks to cool.

Makes about 40 cookies

Cherry Chocolate Chippers

Louise Guard, Takoma Park, Maryland

Every year I bring a different cherry cookie recipe to Robin's cookie party.

2 cups all-purpose flour
1 teaspoon baking powder
½ teaspoon salt
¼ teaspoon baking soda
½ cup (1 stick) butter or margarine, softened
½ cup granulated sugar
½ cup firmly packed light brown sugar
1 large egg
¼ cup milk
1 teaspoon vanilla extract
½ teaspoon cherry extract
1 cup semisweet chocolate chips
1 cup maraschino cherries, drained and chopped

Preheat the oven to 375°F/190°C. Lightly grease the baking sheets or line with parchment paper.

In a medium bowl, combine the flour, baking powder, salt, and baking soda; set aside. In a separate bowl, cream together the butter and sugars. Beat in the egg, milk, and vanilla and cherry extracts. Gradually add the flour mixture to the creamed mixture. Stir in the chocolate chips and the chopped, drained cherries. Drop the dough by tablespoonfuls, 2 inches apart, onto the prepared baking sheets.

Bake the cookies for 10 to 12 minutes, or until golden brown. Transfer to wire racks to cool.

Makes about 4 dozen cookies

Santa's Whiskers

Sylvia Olson

1 cup (2 sticks) butter, softened
½ cup granulated sugar
½ cup confectioners' sugar
1 large egg
1 teaspoon vanilla extract
2¼ cups all-purpose flour plus 2 teaspoons for coating the cherries
1½ cups red and green candied cherries, quartered
¾ cup pecans, chopped
2 cups sweetened flaked coconut

Using an electric mixer, combine the butter, granulated sugar, confectioners' sugar, egg, and vanilla in a large bowl and beat well. Gradually add the flour, and continue beating until well blended. In a small bowl, coat the cherries with the 2 teaspoons of flour. Stir the cherries and pecans into the dough. Shape the dough into 3 or 4 logs, using wax paper. Roll each log in the flaked coconut, wrap tightly, and refrigerate until firm, about 2 hours or overnight.

Preheat the oven to 350°F/180°C. Line the baking sheets with parchment paper.

Cut the logs into ¼-inch slices with a sharp knife. Place the slices, 1 inch apart, on the lined baking sheets. Bake for 10 to 13 minutes, or until the edges are very lightly browned. Transfer to wire racks to cool.

Makes 5 dozen cookies

Peanut Butter and Jam Cookies

Margie Willis, Hagerstown, Maryland

Dough

> 1½ cups all-purpose flour
> 1 teaspoon baking soda
> ½ teaspoon baking powder
> ¼ cup granulated sugar
> ½ cup firmly packed light brown sugar
> ½ cup (1 stick) butter, softened
> ½ cup peanut butter
> 1 large egg

Topping

> Various colored jams, such as apricot, strawberry, grape, and raspberry jam
> Extra granulated sugar for rolling

In a small bowl, whisk together the flour, baking soda, and baking powder until combined. In a large bowl, using an electric mixer, beat the granulated and brown sugars, butter, peanut butter, and egg until light and fluffy. Slowly add the dry ingredients to the creamed mixture and beat until well combined. This dough works best completely chilled, so if the dough is too soft, chill it for half an hour before shaping into balls.

Line the baking sheets with parchment paper. Dust your hands with sugar. Roll the chilled dough into 1½-inch balls, then roll and coat in granulated sugar and place on the lined baking sheets, spacing the balls 2 inches apart. Make a deep indentation in the middle of each ball. Fill the indentation with a teaspoon of the jam of your choice. Chill the cookies on the baking sheets in the refrigerator for 15 to 20 minutes.

Preheat the oven to 350°F/180°C.

Bake the cookies for 11 to 13 minutes, or until light golden brown. Transfer to wire racks to cool. Cool thoroughly before storing in airtight containers.

Makes about 2½ dozen cookies

Spritz Cookies

Sue Callaway, Germantown, Maryland

1 cup (2 sticks) butter, softened
⅔ cup granulated sugar
2¼ cups all-purpose flour
1 teaspoon almond or vanilla extract
½ teaspoon salt
1 large egg
Food coloring (optional)
Candied fruits, icing, sprinkles (optional)
Special equipment: cookie press

Preheat the oven to 400°F/200°C.

Mix the butter and sugar in a medium bowl. Stir in the remaining ingredients. Place the dough in a cookie press. Press cookies in the desired shapes on ungreased baking sheets.

Bake the cookies for 6 to 9 minutes, or until set but not brown. Transfer to wire racks to cool. Decorate with candied fruits, icing, and sprinkles, if desired.

Makes 4 to 5 dozen cookies

Hot Cheeses aka Man Cookies

Robin Olson

This is the only cookie recipe in the collection that doesn't have sugar in it. It's cheesy, crunchy, and men just love them! The story: In 1979, when I was a waitress at a popular dinner house in Santa Barbara, this cute little elderly couple would be the first to arrive every Friday when the doors opened at 5 P.M. They'd drink martinis and the woman would always bring a little plate of these homemade cookies to nibble on while they sipped their cocktails. She would never fail to offer a cookie to me, and each time I'd rave about how great they were as if each time was the first time. This is the recipe she gave me.

½ cup (1 stick) butter, softened
½ cup grated cheddar cheese
⅓ teaspoon salt
¼ teaspoon cayenne pepper
1 cup all-purpose flour
1 cup Rice Krispies

Preheat the oven to 325°F/160°C.

In a large bowl, using your hands, combine all the ingredients together, adding the Rice Krispies last. Shape the mixture into 1-inch balls and place on ungreased baking sheets, 2 inches apart. Flatten with the back of a fork in a grid pattern.

Bake for 12 to 15 minutes. Transfer the cookies to wire racks to cool. Store in a tin or an airtight container.

Note: ¼ teaspoon cayenne pepper gives a subtle peppery flavor, which is more noticeable as an after-flavor. If you like kick, add more cayenne.

Makes 3 dozen cheese cookies

Apricot Jewels

Diane Lewis, Frederick, Maryland

Dough
    1¼ cups all-purpose flour
    ¼ cup sugar
    1½ teaspoons baking powder
    ¼ teaspoon salt
    ½ cup (1 stick) butter, softened
    1 (3-ounce) package cream cheese, softened
    ½ cup sweetened flaked coconut
    ½ cup apricot preserves

Frosting
    1 cup sifted confectioners' sugar
    1 tablespoon butter, softened
    ¼ cup apricot preserves

Preheat the oven to 350°F/180°C.

In a small bowl, whisk together the flour, sugar, baking powder, and salt; set aside. In a separate bowl, cream together the butter and cream cheese. Add the flour mixture, then add in the coconut and apricot preserves. Drop by teaspoonfuls onto ungreased or parchment paper–lined baking sheets.

Bake the cookies for 12 to 15 minutes, or until lightly browned. Immediately transfer the cookies to cooling racks.

Meanwhile, make the frosting. In a small bowl, combine the ingredients and whisk or beat together until smooth. Frost when completely cool.

Makes 36 cookies

Loaded Oatmeal Cookies

Debbie Rogers, Kent Island, Maryland

¾ cup (1½ sticks) butter, softened
¾ cup firmly packed light brown sugar
¼ cup granulated sugar
1 large egg
1 teaspoon vanilla extract
1½ cups quick-cooking oats
1 cup all-purpose flour
½ teaspoon baking soda
½ teaspoon salt
½ teaspoon ground cinnamon
1 cup semisweet chocolate chips
1 cup white chocolate chips
¼ cup sweetened flaked coconut
¼ cup dried cranberries
½ cup raisins
½ cup chopped pecans

Preheat the oven to 350°F/180°C. Line the baking sheets with parchment paper, or use ungreased baking sheets.

In a large bowl, using an electric mixer, beat together the butter and sugars until creamy. Beat in the egg and vanilla until light and fluffy. Mix in the oats, flour, baking soda, salt, and cinnamon until well blended. Stir in the chips, coconut, cranberries, raisins, and pecans. Drop the dough by rounded tablespoonfuls, 2 inches apart, onto the baking sheets.

Bake the cookies for 12 to 15 minutes, or until the edges are lightly browned. Cool 2 minutes on the baking sheets, then transfer to wire racks to cool completely.

Makes about 4 dozen cookies

Cream Cheese-Almond Pastry Cookies

Robin Olson

You will love these cookie-size, miniature Danish pastries!

Cookies

1 (8-ounce) package cream cheese, softened
3 tablespoons sugar
2 sheets frozen puff pastry, thawed
1 (8-ounce) can Solo Almond Paste

Egg Wash

1 egg
1 tablespoon milk

Icing

⅓ cup confectioners' sugar
Milk to thin

Combine the cream cheese and sugar in a small bowl until smooth; set aside.

Make the egg wash, in a small bowl, beat the egg with the milk; set aside.

Unfold 1 sheet of puff pastry on a lightly floured surface. Roll it out to make a 14×10-inch rectangle. Spread half the cream cheese mixture over the puff pastry, leaving a 1-inch border on one long side. Spread half of the can of almond paste on top of the cream cheese. Roll up the pastry, starting with the long side covered with cream cheese.

Seal the end by brushing with the egg wash. Repeat the procedure with the second sheet of pastry and the remaining filling. Lightly brush the rolls with egg wash. Cover the rolls in plastic wrap and chill for at least 1 hour.

Preheat the oven to 375°F/190°C. Line baking sheets with parchment paper.

Cut the chilled rolls, crosswise, into ¾-inch slices. Place the slices, cut side down, on the lined baking sheets. Bake the cookies for 20 to 25 minutes, or until golden brown. Cool on the baking sheets for 2 minutes, then transfer to wire racks to cool completely.

To make the icing, place the confectioners' sugar in a small bowl, and stir in enough milk to reach the desired consistency.

Drizzle the icing on the cooled cookies.

Makes 3 dozen pastry cookies

Chocolate Crackle Tops

Judy Willis, Frederick, Maryland

2 cups all-purpose flour
2 teaspoons baking powder
½ teaspoon salt
4 (1-ounce) squares unsweetened chocolate
½ cup (2 sticks) butter, softened
2 cups granulated sugar, plus additional for rolling
4 large eggs
2 teaspoons vanilla extract
Confectioners' sugar for rolling

Preheat the oven to 350°F/180°C. Lightly grease the baking sheets, or line with parchment paper.

In a small bowl, sift together the flour, baking powder, and salt; set aside. Melt the chocolate in a microwave or double boiler, cool, and then beat together in a bowl with the butter and sugar. Add the eggs one at a time, beating after each addition. Add the vanilla. Add the flour mixture to the creamed ingredients and mix until well combined. Chill the dough for 1 hour.

With sugar-coated hands, roll the dough into 1-inch balls; and roll first into granulated sugar, then confectioners' sugar. Place the balls, 2 inches apart, on prepared baking sheets.

Bake the cookies for 11 to 13 minutes. They are done when the sugar cracks and parts of chocolate cookie are visible. Transfer to wire racks to cool.

Makes about 4 dozen cookies

Robin's Favorite Gingerbread, page 44

Eggnog Logs, page 70

Santa's Whiskers, page 80

Hot Cheeses, page 83

Chocolate Crackle Tops, page 88

Sesame Thumbprint Cookies, page 90

Crisscross Peanut Butter Cookies, page 92

Peppermint Pinwheels, page 97

Espresso Shortbread Cookies, page 103

Pineapple-filled Cookies

Janet Albright, Middletown, Maryland

This recipe for Pineapple-filled Cookies came from my husband's grandmother Gram Oliver, who, bless her heart, is ninety-four and still alive and kicking! I make these every year for the holidays.

Filling

3 tablespoons cornstarch

1½ cups sugar

2 tablespoons freshly squeezed lemon juice

1 (16-ounce) can crushed pineapple in its own juice (undrained)

Dough

1½ cups sugar

¾ cup shortening

¾ cup milk

2 large eggs

5½ cups all-purpose flour

4½ teaspoons baking powder

1½ teaspoons vanilla extract

Mix together all the ingredients for the filling in a medium saucepan over medium heat and stir until thick. Set aside to cool while making the dough.

Preheat the oven to 350°F/180°C. Line the baking sheets with parchment paper.

In a large bowl, mix all the ingredients together to form a dough. Roll out the dough very thinly on a floured surface. Cut the dough into rounds, about 2½ inches in diameter, with a cookie cutter. Place them on a cookie sheet, spaced 2 inches apart. Place 1 teaspoon of the filling onto each cut-out cookie, then place another cookie on top of the filling and press the ends together gently.

Bake the cookies for 10 to 15 minutes, or until lightly brown around the edges. Transfer the cookies to wire racks to cool. These cookies can be refrigerated and are good to eat cold as well as at room temperature!

Makes about 5 dozen, using a 2½-inch cookie cutter

Sesame Thumbprint Cookies

Debby Griffith, Gaithersburg, Maryland

This is a delightful and different twist on the thumbprint cookie. The sesame seeds add a unique crunch and flavor.

2 cups (4 sticks) butter, softened
½ cup sugar
2 teaspoons almond extract
4 cups all-purpose flour
1 teaspoon salt
⅓ cup sesame seeds
About 1½ cups fruit preserves of your choice

In a large bowl, cream the butter. Gradually add the sugar and beat until light and fluffy. Add the almond extract, flour, and salt and mix well. Wrap the dough in plastic wrap and chill for at least 1 hour.

Preheat the oven to 400°F/200°C. Lightly grease the baking sheets.

Shape the dough into 1-inch balls and roll in the sesame seeds. Place the balls, 2 inches apart, on the prepared baking sheets. Flatten the cookies slightly, and make an indentation in the center with your thumb. Fill the centers with preserves.

Bake the cookies for 12 to 15 minutes. Transfer to wire racks to cool. Store in airtight containers.

Makes about 36 cookies

White Chocolate Cranberry Yummies

Ann Hallock, Gaithersburg, Maryland

½ cup (1 stick) butter, softened
½ cup margarine, softened
1 (8-ounce) package cream cheese, softened
2 cups sugar
½ teaspoon vanilla extract
2 cups all-purpose flour
⅔ cup pecan pieces
1 cup white chocolate chips
1 cup dried cranberries

Preheat the oven to 325°F/165°C.

In a medium bowl, using an electric mixer, cream the butter, margarine, and cream cheese. Gradually beat in the sugar. Add the vanilla and continue to beat well, for 2 minutes, until fluffy.

Gradually mix in the flour, blending after each addition. Add the nuts and white chocolate chips and mix until evenly distributed. Drop by rounded tablespoonful, about 1 inch apart, on ungreased baking sheets. Press about 6 dried cranberries in a desired pattern on top of each cookie.

Bake the cookies for 15 minutes, or until lightly browned. Cool a few minutes on the baking sheets, then transfer to wire racks to cool completely.

Makes about 5 dozen cookies

Crisscross Peanut Butter Cookies

Robin Olson

This is my other all-time favorite cookie, besides chocolate chip, and this cookie is the one I specifically credit for my annual five-pound winter weight gain. The recipe is from Grandma Olson and was passed down to Sylvia, my mother-in-law, in the 1940s.

2½ cups all-purpose flour
1½ teaspoons baking soda
1 cup (2 sticks) butter, softened
1 cup firmly packed dark brown sugar
1 cup granulated sugar
2 large eggs
1 cup crunchy peanut butter (I like Skippy Super Chunk)
2 teaspoons vanilla extract

In a bowl, sift together the flour and baking soda; set aside. In a separate bowl, mix the butter and sugars, then add the eggs and beat well.

Add the peanut butter and vanilla and beat until smooth and fluffy. Slowly pour the flour mixture into the creamed mixture and beat until thoroughly combined.

Chill the dough for at least 1 hour.

Preheat the oven to 375°F/190°C. Line the baking sheets with parchment paper.

Roll the chilled dough into 1-inch balls and place on the lined baking sheets. Dip the tines of a fork in flour and flatten each ball with the fork, making a crisscross pattern on each.

Bake the cookies for 8 to 10 minutes. Remove from the oven, cool on the baking sheets for 1 minute, then transfer to wire racks to cool completely.

Makes 6 dozen cookies

Cherry Cookies

Sylvia Olson

1¾ cups all-purpose flour
½ teaspoon salt
½ teaspoon baking powder
1 cup shortening (or use half butter, half shortening)
⅔ cup sugar
1 large egg
½ teaspoon vanilla extract
⅓ cup maraschino cherries, drained and chopped

In a medium bowl, sift the flour, salt, and baking powder; set aside. In a separate bowl, cream together the shortening and sugar thoroughly. Beat in the egg and vanilla and mix well. Gradually add the flour mixture to the creamed mixture. Add the cherries and mix in well. Chill the dough in the bowl, covered, for 1 hour.

Preheat the oven to 375°F/190°C. Line the baking sheets with parchment paper, or use ungreased baking sheets.

Using a teaspoon, scoop out portions of the dough and roll them into 1-inch balls. Place them on the baking sheets 2 inches apart. Flatten the balls with the bottom of a small glass.

Bake the cookies for 10 minutes, or until the edges turn golden. Transfer to wire racks to cool.

Makes 3½ dozen cookies

Butter Thins

Sylvia Olson

These delicate, buttery cookies melt in your mouth. I recommend making a double batch, because these cookies will go quickly! These are a must-have for cookie platters to be given away as gifts during the holidays.

1 cup (2 sticks) butter, softened
1 cup sugar
1 large egg
2 tablespoons evaporated milk
1 teaspoon vanilla extract
2 cups all-purpose flour
¼ teaspoon salt
1 level teaspoon baking soda
1 level teaspoon baking powder
Sprinkles for decorating

In a medium bowl, cream together the butter and sugar. Add the egg and beat well. Add the evaporated milk, continue beating, and add the vanilla. In a separate bowl, whisk together all the dry ingredients. Add to the creamed mixture; the dough will be soft. Refrigerate for 1 hour.

Preheat the oven to 375°F/190°C. Line the baking sheets with parchment paper.

Divide the chilled dough and return one-half to the refrigerator. Working quickly, as the dough gets soft fast at room temperature, roll it into ½-inch balls and place them 3 inches apart on the lined baking sheets. Dampen a tea towel, cover the bottom of a glass, and stamp the dough balls down evenly, but not too thinly, about ¼ of an inch. Decorate the cookies with the sprinkles of your choice.

Bake the cookies for 8 minutes. They are done when the faintest brown appears at the edges. The cookies will be puffed up and not look done, but they are. Remove from the oven, let cool no more than 1 minute on the baking sheets (where they continue to bake), then transfer to wire racks to cool completely.

Makes 6 dozen cookies

Candy Cane Twists

Sylvia Olson

This cookie is a pretty addition to a Christmas cookie platter.

Dough

2½ cups all-purpose flour
1 teaspoon salt
1 cup shortening (or use half butter, half shortening)
1 cup confectioners' sugar
1 large egg
1½ teaspoons almond extract
1 teaspoon vanilla extract
½ teaspoon red food coloring

Topping

3 tablespoons finely crushed red or green peppermint candies
3 tablespoons sugar

In a small bowl, mix the flour and the salt; set aside. In a separate bowl, cream together the shortening (or butter-shortening mixture), the confectioners' sugar, egg, and extracts. Add the flour mixture to the creamed mixture. Divide the dough in half. Blend red food coloring into one half and leave the other half plain. Wrap the dough in wax paper or plastic wrap and chill for 1 hour.

Preheat the oven to 375°F/190°C. Line the baking sheets with parchment paper.

Stir together the topping of crushed peppermint candy and sugar; set aside. For each candy cane, shape 1 rounded teaspoonful of dough from each half—one red, one plain—into a 4-inch rope by rolling it back and forth on a floured surface. Place the strips side by side; press together lightly and twist. Place on the lined baking sheets. Curve the top of the cookie to form the handle of the cane.

Bake the candy cane twists 9 minutes, or until lightly browned. Remove from the oven and immediately sprinkle the candy mixture over the cookies. Transfer to wire racks to cool. Cool completely before storing.

Makes about 4 dozen cookies

Oatmeal Crispies

Sylvia Olson

An old-fashioned crispy, crunchy little oatmeal cookie. It's a different version than most other oatmeal cookies, which are usually chewy.

1 cup (2 sticks) butter, softened
1 cup firmly packed light brown sugar
1 cup granulated sugar
2 large eggs
1 teaspoon vanilla extract
1½ cups all-purpose flour
½ teaspoon salt
1 teaspoon baking soda
3 cups quick-cooking oats
½ cup broken nut meats

In a medium bowl, cream the butter, then slowly add the sugars and beat until light and fluffy. Add the eggs and beat well. Stir in the vanilla. In another medium bowl, whisk the flour, salt, and soda together. Add the quick-cooking oats and nuts, then add this to the creamed mixture and mix well; the dough will be stiff, you may have to use your hands to mix it. Shape the dough into 2-inch-wide logs, using wax paper, and chill thoroughly.

Preheat the oven to 350°F/180°C. Line the baking sheets with parchment paper.

Cut the chilled logs into ¼-inch-thick slices and place them 2 inches apart on the lined baking sheets. Bake for 10 minutes. Transfer to wire racks to cool.

Makes 6 dozen cookies

Peppermint Pinwheels

Sylvia Olson

These cookies look and taste like Christmas!

Dough

    1 cup (2 sticks) butter, softened
    1 cup confectioners' sugar
    1 large egg
    1 teaspoon vanilla extract
    ¼ teaspoon peppermint extract
    2½ cups all-purpose flour
    1 teaspoon salt
    ½ teaspoon red food coloring

Topping

    1 large egg white
    2 tablespoons water

Candy Topping

⅓ cup granulated sugar

⅓ cup peppermint candy, such as candy canes

Preheat the oven to 375°F/190°C. Line the baking sheets with parchment paper.

In a medium bowl, cream together the butter, sugar, egg, vanilla, and peppermint extract. In a separate bowl, whisk together the flour and salt, then add it to the creamed mixture and blend thoroughly. Divide the dough in half. Blend red food coloring into one-half of the dough and leave the other half plain. Between sheets of wax paper, form two dough disks. Wrap and chill until firm.

On a lightly floured surface, roll the plain dough into a 12-inch square. Roll the red-colored half into a square of the same size and lay it on top of the plain dough layer. Roll out the layered sheets gently until the dough is ³⁄₁₆-inch thick, then roll up jelly-roll style. Wrap and chill again for at least 1 hour.

Cut the chilled rolls into ⅛-inch-thick slices. Place the slices on the lined baking sheets.

Bake the cookies for 8 to 10 minutes, or until lightly browned. While the cookies are baking, make the egg glaze. Using a small bowl and a fork, beat the egg white with 2 tablespoons water.

Make the candy topping: Lay candy canes between two pieces of wax paper and beat gently with a meat tenderizer mallet or a rolling pin to crush. Leave a few pieces slightly chunky. In another small bowl, combine the ⅓ cup granulated sugar and ⅓ cup finely crushed peppermint stick candy.

When the cookies are done, transfer them to wire racks and cool slightly, but while still warm, add the topping: Brush the top of each cookie with the beaten egg white and then sprinkle with about 1 teaspoon of the sugar and candy cane mix.

Makes 6 dozen cookies

Glazed Pineapple Cookies

Sylvia Olson

Dough

  2 cups all-purpose flour
  ¼ teaspoon baking soda
  1½ teaspoons baking powder
  ¼ teaspoon salt
  ½ cup (1 stick) butter, softened
  1 cup firmly packed light brown sugar
  1 large egg
  1 teaspoon vanilla extract
  1 (8-ounce) can crushed pineapple, in its own juice, drained, juice reserved

Glaze

  3 cups confectioners' sugar
  3 to 4 tablespoons reserved pineapple juice

Preheat the oven to 400°F/200°C. Lightly grease the baking sheets.

In a small bowl, sift the flour with the baking soda, baking powder, and salt; set aside. In a separate bowl, cream together the butter and sugar until fluffy. Add the egg and vanilla and beat until light and fluffy. Add the drained pineapple and mix well. Drop the dough by teaspoonfuls 2 inches apart onto the prepared baking sheets.

Bake the cookies 8 to 10 minutes, or until lightly golden.

Meanwhile, mix confectioners' sugar and 3 to 4 tablespoons of the reserved pineapple juice until smooth and the right consistency for a glaze. Transfer the cookies to wire racks and cool partially. While the cookies are still slightly warm, spread the tops with the glaze.

Make 3½ dozen cookies

Nut Jammers

Sylvia Olson

Everyone loves these cookies, even though they are a fair amount of work.

2 cups all-purpose flour
½ teaspoon baking powder
1 cup (2 sticks) unsalted butter, softened
1 (8-ounce) package cream cheese, softened
2 cups finely chopped pecans or walnuts
1 (12-ounce) jar apricot jam
2 teaspoons granulated sugar
⅓ cup confectioners' sugar

In a small bowl, whisk together the flour and baking powder; set aside. In a separate bowl, cream together the butter and cream cheese, then add the flour mixture. Chill the dough for several hours or overnight.

In a small bowl, mix together the finely chopped nuts, jam, and granulated sugar for the filling.

Preheat the oven to 350°F/180°C. Line the baking sheets with parchment paper.

Divide the dough into four equal parts, and work with one-fourth of the dough at a time. Refrigerate the remaining dough.

Roll out the dough very thinly (about ¹⁄₁₆ of an inch) on a pastry rolling mat or lightly floured work surface, then cut into 4-inch squares. Transfer the squares to the lined baking sheets. Place 1 rounded teaspoon of the nut filling on one-half of each square and fold over. Press the edges together with your fingers. For decoration, if desired, use floured or sugared fork tines to make little marks on the edges.

Bake the cookies for 15 to 20 minutes, or until lightly brown. Repeat with the remaining three-quarters of the dough, working with one-fourth at a time. Transfer to wire racks to cool. When completely cool, sprinkle with confectioners' sugar.

Makes about 5 dozen cookies

Cherry Winks

Sylvia Olson

15 cherries for "winks"
2¼ cups all-purpose flour
1 teaspoon baking powder
½ teaspoon baking soda
½ teaspoon salt
½ cup (1 stick) butter, softened
¼ cup shortening
1 cup sugar
2 large eggs
2 tablespoons milk
1 teaspoon vanilla extract
1 cup chopped pecans
⅓ cup maraschino cherries, drained and chopped
2 cups crushed cornflakes

Preheat the oven to 375°F/190°C. Line the baking sheets with parchment paper.

Cut 15 maraschino cherries in quarters to make the "winks"; set aside.

In a medium bowl, whisk together the flour, baking powder, baking soda, and salt. In a large bowl, using an electric mixer, beat the butter, shortening, and sugar until creamy. Beat in the eggs, milk, and vanilla. Add the pecans and the ⅓ cup chopped cherries and mix together. Drop the dough by teaspoonfuls into crushed cornflakes and roll them around. Place the cookies 2 inches apart on the lined baking sheets and top each with a cherry "wink."

Bake the cookies for 10 to 12 minutes. Transfer to wire racks to cool.

Makes about 5 dozen cookies

Gumdrop Cookies

Sylvia Olson

This is an old-fashioned cookie that was a part of Syl's annual baking repertoire. If you like gumdrop candies, then you'll like this cookie.

2 cups all-purpose flour
¼ teaspoon salt
1 teaspoon baking powder
1 teaspoon baking soda
1 cup sweetened flaked coconut
2 cups quick-cooking oats
1 cup (2 sticks) butter, softened
1 teaspoon vanilla extract
¾ cup granulated sugar
¾ cup firmly packed light brown sugar
2 large eggs
1 cup cut-up gumdrops (use kitchen shears)
1 cup chopped nuts
Icing (optional) made of ⅓ cup confectioners' sugar and water

Preheat the oven to 350°F/180°C. Line the baking sheets with parchment paper, or grease lightly.

In a small bowl, sift the flour and reserve one-fourth for dredging the nuts. In a separate bowl, resift the remaining flour with the salt, baking powder, and baking soda. Add the flaked coconut and oats and mix thoroughly. In a separate bowl, cream the butter, add the vanilla, and gradually add the granulated and brown sugars. Continue to cream until light and fluffy. Add the eggs one at a time, beating well after each addition. Add the dry ingredients and blend well. Fold in the gumdrops and floured nuts. Drop the dough by tablespoonfuls onto the lined or greased baking sheets.

Bake the cookies for 10 to 12 minutes. Transfer to wire racks to cool. If desired, drizzle cookies with a simple icing made with ⅓ cup confectioners' sugar mixed with a few drops of boiling water.

Makes 8 dozen cookies

Espresso Shortbread Cookies

Joelen Tan, Chicago, Illinois

½ cup (1 stick) unsalted butter, softened
⅓ cup lightly packed light brown sugar
1 teaspoon espresso powder, dissolved in 2 teaspoons water
1 teaspoon finely ground coffee or espresso beans
1¼ cups all-purpose flour
Pinch of salt

In a medium bowl, cream together the butter and sugar until well blended. Mix in the dissolved espresso powder. Add the ground espresso beans, flour, and salt and mix until the dough comes together. Turn the dough out onto a sheet of plastic wrap. Use the plastic to help form the dough into a log about 7 inches long. Wrap the log in plastic wrap and refrigerate at least 6 hours and up to 3 days.

Preheat the oven to 350°F/180°C. Line the baking sheets with parchment paper.

Cut the chilled dough into ¼-inch slices and arrange 2 inches apart on the lined baking sheets.

Bake about 12 minutes, or until the tops look dry and the edges just start to brown. Transfer to wire racks to cool.

Makes about 36 cookies

Chocolate Caramel Treasures

Teresa Brethauer, Forest Hill, Maryland

Dough

½ cup (1 stick) unsalted butter, softened
⅔ cup sugar
1 large egg, separated
2 tablespoons milk
1 teaspoon vanilla extract
1 cup all-purpose flour
⅓ cup Dutch-process unsweetened cocoa powder
¼ teaspoon salt
½ cup finely chopped hazelnuts (or other nuts)

Caramel Filling

10 (1 × ½-inch) plain caramels
2 tablespoons heavy cream

Chocolate Drizzle

3 ounces fine-quality semisweet or bittersweet chocolate (not unsweetened), finely chopped

In a large bowl, using an electric mixer, beat together the butter, sugar, egg yolk, milk, and vanilla until well blended. In a separate bowl, sift together the flour, cocoa, and salt. Add the flour mixture to the creamed mixture and beat on low speed until it forms a dough. Wrap the dough in plastic wrap, and chill until firm, at least 30 minutes.

Preheat the oven to 350°F/180°C. Lightly grease the baking sheets.

Lightly beat the egg white. Roll scant tablespoonfuls of dough into balls and coat with egg white, letting the excess drip off, then roll in the nuts to coat. Arrange the balls, as you coat them, 1½ inches apart on the prepared baking sheets. Press your thumb into the center of each ball to flatten, leaving an indentation.

Bake the cookies, in batches, in the middle of the oven until they have puffed slightly but the centers are still soft, 10 to 12 minutes. Remove from oven and immediately press the centers of cookies again (I use the handle end of a wooden spoon). Transfer to wire racks to cool.

Meanwhile, make the filling. Heat the caramels and cream in a small saucepan over moderately low heat, stirring occasionally, until melted and the mixture is smooth. Spoon about ½ teaspoon of the caramel filling into the center of each cookie and cool completely.

One hour before serving, make the chocolate drizzle. Melt the chocolate in the microwave or a double boiler, stirring until smooth. Cool to warm and pour into a heavy-duty sealable plastic bag. Seal the bag and make a small snip in one corner to form a small hole. Drizzle the chocolate over the cookies and let stand until set, about 30 minutes.

Makes about 2½ dozen cookies

Creamy Cashews

Tracy O'Connell, Sewell, New Jersey

Every year this is one of my most requested cookie recipes for my cookie exchange!

Dough

4 cups all-purpose flour
1½ teaspoons baking powder
1½ teaspoons baking soda
½ teaspoon salt (if using salted cashews, omit salt)
1 cup (2 sticks) butter or margarine, softened
2 cups firmly packed light brown sugar
2 large eggs
1 teaspoon vanilla extract
⅔ cup sour cream
3 cups roasted cashews, chopped
Whole cashews for garnish

Brown Butter Frosting

1 cup (2 sticks) butter
4 cups confectioners' sugar
6 tablespoons heavy cream
½ teaspoon vanilla extract

Preheat the oven to 350°F/180°C. Lightly grease the baking sheets.

In a medium bowl, combine the flour, baking powder, baking soda, and salt; set aside. In the bowl of an electric mixer, beat the butter and brown sugar until light and fluffy. Beat in the eggs and vanilla. On low speed, beat in the sour cream, and then the flour mixture. Stir in the chopped cashews.

Drop the dough by rounded teaspoonfuls onto the prepared baking sheets.

Bake the cookies for 12 minutes, or until lightly browned. Transfer to wire racks to cool.

While the cookies are baking, make the frosting. Melt the butter in a saucepan over medium heat, until lightly browned. Remove from heat; whisk in the confectioners' sugar, then the cream and vanilla, and continue to whisk until smooth. Spread the warm frosting on the cookies. Garnish each cookie with a whole cashew.

Makes 9 dozen cookies

Gingersnaps

Debra Tate, Riverside, California

4 cups sifted all-purpose flour
1 teaspoon baking soda
1 cup molasses
½ cup sugar
1 teaspoon ground ginger
½ cup (1 stick) butter

In a medium bowl, sift together the flour and the baking soda; set aside. In a medium saucepan, mix the molasses, sugar, ginger, and butter and stir over low heat until the butter melts. Remove from the heat. Add the flour and soda mixture, stirring quickly to incorporate. Knead the dough until it becomes smooth. Wrap in plastic wrap and refrigerate overnight.

Preheat the oven to 350°F/180°C. Line the baking sheets with parchment paper.

To make the cookies, roll out the chilled dough on a lightly floured surface, rolling it as thinly as possible, about ⅛ inch. Cut out the dough with cookie cutters. Transfer the cookies to the lined baking sheets.

Bake the cookies for 10 to 12 minutes. Transfer to wire racks to cool.

Makes 4 to 5 dozen cookies using a 2-inch cutter

Lemonade Cookies

Linda Maxwell, Porterville, California

This is an old family favorite.

1 cup (2 sticks) butter, softened
1 cup sugar, plus ¼ cup for sprinkling
2 large eggs
3 cups sifted all-purpose flour
1 teaspoon baking soda
1 (6-ounce) can frozen lemonade concentrate, defrosted

Preheat the oven to 400°F/200°C.

Cream together the butter and sugar in a medium bowl. Add the eggs one at a time, and mix well. In a separate bowl, combine the flour and baking soda, and add alternately with ½ cup of undiluted lemonade concentrate. Mix well and drop by teaspoonfuls 2 inches apart onto ungreased baking sheets.

Bake the cookies for 8 minutes. Remove from the oven and transfer to wire racks. Brush while still warm with the remaining lemonade concentrate and sprinkle with sugar.

Makes 5 dozen cookies

Peanut Butter Christmas Mice

Donna Curry, Vernon, New Jersey

These cute little cookies will scurry off the plates!

½ cup (1 stick) butter, softened
1 cup creamy peanut butter
½ cup granulated sugar
1 large egg
1 teaspoon vanilla extract
½ teaspoon baking soda
1½ cups all-purpose flour
Peanut halves
Chopped green candy decors or mini chocolate chips
Red licorice laces, cut into 3-inch lengths

In a large bowl, using an electric mixer, beat the butter and peanut butter until creamy. Add the sugar and beat until fluffy. Beat in the egg, vanilla, and baking soda until well blended. With the mixer on low speed, gradually beat in the flour just until blended. Cover with plastic wrap and chill the dough about 1 hour, until firm enough to handle.

Preheat the oven to 350°F/180°C. Grease or line baking sheets with parchment paper.

Shape level tablespoonfuls of the dough into 1-inch balls. Taper each ball at one end into a teardrop shape. Press one side flat. Place flat side down, 2 inches apart, on ungreased baking sheets. Press the sides of the balls to raise "backs of mice." (The dough will spread slightly as it bakes.) Gently push 2 peanut halves in each for ears and 2 pieces of green chopped candy or mini chocolate chips for eyes. With a wooden pick make a ½-inch deep hole at the tail end. Bake the cookies for 8 to 10 minutes, or until firm. Transfer to wire racks to cool. Insert the licorice tails and cool completely.

Makes 60 mice

Amish Cookies

Steve Henry, Upstate New York

These cookies can be sandwiched or left single. Either way they are a wonderful, old-fashioned oatmeal cookie.

Dough

1 cup (2 sticks) butter, softened

3 cups firmly packed dark brown sugar

4 large eggs, beaten

1 teaspoon salt

1½ teaspoons baking soda

2 teaspoons ground cinnamon

½ teaspoon grated nutmeg

2 teaspoons vanilla extract

3 cups all-purpose flour

3 cups old-fashioned rolled oats

Filling

1 large egg white (or use the equivalent of dry egg white powder)

½ teaspoon vanilla extract

1½ cups confectioners' sugar

½ cup shortening

Preheat the oven to 350°F/180°C.

In a medium bowl, cream together the butter and sugar. Add the eggs and beat until fluffy, then add the remaining ingredients, adding the flour and oats last. Make walnut-size balls from the dough and flatten with a glass covered with a damp towel. Place on ungreased baking sheets 2 inches apart.

Bake the cookies for 8 to 10 minutes. Transfer to wire racks to cool. When cool, fill to make sandwich cookies.

In a bowl, cream together all the ingredients for the filling. Spread the filling on the flat, bottom side of a cookie, and place another cookie, flat bottom side down, on top of the filling to form a sandwich. Repeat with the remaining cookies.

Make 4 dozen single cookies or 2 dozen sandwich cookies

Orange-Cream Cheese Chocolate Chip Cookies

Tim Dolan, Kensington, Maryland

The best cookies ever.

½ cup shortening
3 ounces cream cheese, softened
½ cup sugar
1 large egg, beaten
1 teaspoon vanilla extract
1 teaspoon grated orange zest
1 cup all-purpose flour
½ teaspoon salt
1 cup semisweet chocolate chips

Preheat the oven to 350°F/180°C. Line the baking sheets with parchment paper.

Combine the first four ingredients in a large bowl and, using an electric mixer, beat on low speed until smooth and creamy. Add the vanilla and orange zest and beat well. In a small bowl, combine the flour and salt. Add to the creamed mixture and beat until well blended. Stir in the chocolate chips.

Drop the dough by heaping teaspoonfuls onto parchment-lined baking sheets.

Bake the cookies for 12 to 15 minutes, or until the edges are just beginning to brown. Remove from the oven and cool on wire racks.

Makes 3 dozen cookies

Rolo Cookies

Joni Butler Kent, Riverton, Wyoming

Everyone falls in love with these delicious cookies!

2½ cups all-purpose flour
¾ cup unsweetened cocoa powder
1 teaspoon baking soda
½ teaspoon ground cinnamon (optional)
1 cup granulated sugar plus 1 tablespoon
1 cup firmly packed dark brown sugar
1 cup (2 sticks) butter, softened
2 teaspoons vanilla extract
2 large eggs
1 cup finely chopped nuts
1 (12-ounce) bag of Rolos or 7 rolls of Rolos (at 9 per roll)

Preheat the oven to 375°F/190°C. Lightly grease the baking sheets.

In a small bowl combine the flour, cocoa powder, baking soda, and cinnamon, if using. In a large bowl, using an electric mixer, beat 1 cup of the granulated sugar with the brown sugar and butter until light and fluffy. Add the vanilla and eggs and beat well. Add the flour mixture and incorporate. Stir in ½ cup of the nuts. To form each cookie, shape about 1 tablespoon of dough around 1 Rolo, covering it completely.

In another small bowl, combine the remaining finely chopped nuts with the remaining 1 tablespoon sugar. Press one side of each ball into the nut mixture and place, nut side up, 2 inches apart, on the prepared baking sheets.

Bake the cookies for 7 to 10 minutes until slightly cracked. Cool on the baking sheets for 2 minutes, then transfer to wire racks to cool completely. Enjoy!

Makes about 4 dozen cookies

Oat Cut-out Cookies

Linda Maxwell, Porterville, California

Our different and delicious version of cut-out cookies!

2½ cups sifted all-purpose flour
¾ teaspoon salt
½ teaspoon baking powder
1 cup (2 sticks) butter, softened
1 cup sugar
2 large eggs
½ teaspoon almond extract
2 cups old-fashioned rolled oats
Your favorite cookie frosting

In a small bowl, sift together the flour, salt, and baking powder; set aside. In a separate bowl, cream together the butter and sugar. Add the eggs and extract and beat until light and fluffy. Add the dry ingredients to the creamed ingredients and mix until combined. Stir in the oatmeal. Chill the dough for at least 1 hour.

Preheat the oven to 350°F/180°C. Line the baking sheets with parchment paper.

Roll out the chilled dough ¼ inch thick and cut into shapes with a 4-inch cutter. Place 2 inches apart on the lined baking sheets.

Bake the cookies for 8 to 10 minutes until barely browned. Transfer to wire racks to cool. Ice the cooled cookies with your favorite cookie frosting, flavored with almond extract, if desired.

Makes about 3 dozen cookies

Butter Brickle Cookies

Micki Snapp, Silver Spring, Maryland

½ cup butter, softened
1 cup firmly packed dark brown sugar
1 teaspoon vanilla extract
1 large egg
1 cup all-purpose flour
1 teaspoon baking powder
½ teaspoon salt
½ cup finely chopped pecans
½ cup Heath Bits o' Brickle Toffee Bits

Preheat the oven to 350°F/180°C.

In a medium bowl, cream the butter. Add the sugar, vanilla, and egg and beat until light and fluffy. In a separate bowl, mix together the flour, baking powder, and salt. Add the dry ingredients to the creamed mixture and mix thoroughly. Stir in nuts and brickle chips. Drop by rounded teaspoonfuls 2 inches apart onto ungreased baking sheets.

Bake the cookies for 8 to 10 minutes. Remove from the oven and let cool for 2 minutes on the baking sheets. With a broad spatula quickly transfer the cookies to wire racks to cool completely. Store in airtight containers.

Makes about 4 dozen cookies

Grandma Crane's Favorite Cookies

Sister Jean Crane, West Palm Beach, Florida

1½ cups shortening
1 cup firmly packed dark brown sugar
1 cup granulated sugar
3 large eggs
5 cups all-purpose flour
2 teaspoons baking soda
1 teaspoon salt
1 teaspoon ground cinnamon
1 cup pecans, finely chopped

Melt the shortening and mix with the sugars in a medium bowl. Beat in the eggs. In a separate bowl, sift together the flour, soda, salt, and cinnamon. Add the dry ingredients to the sugar-egg mixture. Mix in the chopped pecans. Divide the dough into four portions, shape each portion into a roll, and wrap in wax paper. Refrigerate overnight or freeze until needed.

Preheat the oven to 350°F/180°C. Lightly grease the baking sheets.

When ready to bake the cookies, cut the chilled dough into slices about ¼ inch thick. Place the slices 2 inches apart on lightly greased cookie sheets. Bake the cookies for about 10 minutes, or until brown. Transfer to wire racks to cool.

Makes 8 dozen cookies

Macadamia Nut and Coconut Pinwheels

Donna Mrotek, Child's Play Creative Learning Center, Santa Barbara, California

Dough

2 cups all-purpose flour

½ teaspoon baking powder

½ cup sugar

½ cup unsalted butter, softened

6 tablespoons cream or mascarpone cheese, softened

1 large egg

1 teaspoon vanilla extract

1 to 2 teaspoons coconut extract

Filling

6 tablespoons cream or mascarpone cheese

1 tablespoon coconut extract

2 tablespoons sugar

½ cup sweetened toasted flaked coconut

½ cup sweetened flaked coconut

½ cup chopped, toasted macadamia nuts

¼ cup chopped white chocolate chips

Glaze

1 egg

1 tablespoon shortening, melted

1 teaspoon coconut extract

1 tablespoon sugar

Topping

¼ cup finely chopped macadamia nuts

1 tablespoon sugar

In a small bowl, sift together the flour and baking powder; set aside. In a separate bowl, using an electric mixer, beat the sugar, butter, and cream or mascarpone cheese until light and fluffy. Beat in the egg, vanilla, and coconut extract. Gradually add the flour mixture to the creamed mixture and mix until thoroughly combined. Divide the dough in half, flatten into disks, and wrap each portion in plastic wrap. Chill the dough for 1 to 2 hours.

To make the filling, in a bowl, using an electric mixer, beat the cream or mascarpone cheese, coconut extract, and sugar until light and fluffy. Add the coconut, nuts, and white chocolate chips. Set aside as this needs to be at room temperature when you assemble the cookies.

To make the glaze, beat together the egg, melted shortening, coconut extract, and sugar; set aside.

Preheat the oven to 350°F/180°C. Line the baking sheets with parchment paper, or grease lightly.

To assemble the cookies, remove a dough roll from the refrigerator. Roll out one-half of the dough on a floured pastry rolling mat to a thickness of ⅛ inch. Using a biscuit-size cookie cutter (a square, rectangle, or circle—fluted looks nice) cut out the cookies and place them on the prepared baking sheets. Cut in diagonally from each corner (use a fluted pastry wheel if you have one; a knife or scissors will work, too) to about one-third into each cookie. You are leaving room in the center for the filling. Place 1 teaspoon of filling in the center of each cookie, then fold every other flap over. Brush the cookies with the glaze, and sprinkle with the topping, the combined sugar and finely chopped nuts.

Bake the cookies for 10 minutes, or until golden brown. Transfer to wire racks to cool.

Makes about 3 dozen cookies

Chocolate Dream Cookies

Helen Sturgeon, Brasstown, North Carolina

1 (11.5-ounce) bag Ghirardelli dark chocolate chips
1 cup dried cranberries, coarsely chopped
1 cup chopped pecans, toasted and cooled
1 cup (2 sticks) butter, softened
1 (3-ounce) package cream cheese, softened
2 tablespoons milk
½ cup granulated sugar
½ cup firmly packed light brown sugar
1 large egg
2 (1-ounce) squares unsweetened chocolate, melted and cooled
1½ teaspoons vanilla extract
2¼ cups all-purpose flour
½ teaspoon baking powder
½ teaspoon salt
¼ cup unsweetened cocoa powder
1 cup marshmallow cream

Preheat the oven to 325°F/165°C. Lightly grease the baking sheets.

Combine the chocolate chips, cranberries, and cooled toasted nuts in a large bowl; set aside.

Combine the butter, cream cheese, and milk in the bowl of an electric mixer. Mix until creamy and well blended. Gradually add the sugars, creaming well. Add the egg, melted chocolate, and vanilla and beat until well combined. In a small bowl, sift together the flour, baking powder, salt, and cocoa. Add to the creamed mixture, stirring well. Fold in chocolate chip mixture; the batter will be very thick. Drop the batter by tablespoonfuls 2 inches apart onto the prepared baking sheets.

Bake the cookies for 12 to 15 minutes, until puffed and the tops are firm to the touch. Cool on the baking sheets for 1 minute, then transfer to wire racks to cool completely.

Makes 4 dozen cookies

Holiday Fruit Drops

Wanda Bolin, Louisville, Kentucky

This recipe has been a must every Christmas for years in our family. The drops are like miniature fruit cakes.

1 cup shortening
2 cups firmly packed light brown sugar
2 large eggs
½ cup sour milk (see Note) or buttermilk
3½ cups all-purpose flour
1 teaspoon baking soda
1 teaspoon salt
1½ cups broken pecans
2 cups candied cherry halves
2 cups cut-up dates

In a large bowl, combine the shortening, sugar, and eggs and mix well. Stir in the sour milk. In a separate bowl, combine the flour, baking soda, and salt and whisk to blend. Add the dry ingredients to the creamed mixture and stir in. Stir in the pecans, cherries, and dates. Chill the dough for at least 1 hour.

Preheat the oven to 375°F/190°C. Lightly grease the baking sheets.

Drop the dough by rounded teaspoonfuls, about 2 inches apart, on the prepared baking sheets. Place a pecan half or piece of candied cherry on each cookie, if desired.

Bake the cookies for 8 to 10 minutes, or until almost no imprint remains when touched lightly in the center. Transfer to wire racks to cool.

Note: To make sour milk: Add 1 tablespoon of freshly squeezed lemon juice or white vinegar to a glass measuring cup. Add enough milk to equal ½ cup. Stir and let stand for 15 minutes, or until slightly curdled.

Makes 8 dozen cookies

Oatmeal Chocolate Cookies

Jo-ann Morin, Frankfort, Maine

This cookie tastes wonderful and is a family favorite.

1 cup (2 sticks) butter, softened
1 cup granulated sugar
1 cup firmly packed light brown sugar
2 large eggs
1 teaspoon vanilla extract
2 cups all-purpose flour
2½ cups oatmeal, processed in a blender to a fine powder
½ teaspoon salt
1 teaspoon baking powder
1 teaspoon baking soda
1 (12-ounce) package chocolate chips
1 (8-ounce) Hershey Bar, grated
1½ cups chopped nuts

Preheat the oven to 375°F/190°C. Line the baking sheets with parchment paper.

In a medium bowl, cream together the butter and both sugars. Beat in the eggs and vanilla. In a separate bowl, combine the flour, oatmeal, salt, baking powder, and baking soda. Add the dry ingredients to the creamed mixture and incorporate. Add the chocolate chips, grated Hershey Bar, and nuts. Roll into 1½-inch balls and place, 2 inches apart, on parchment-lined baking sheets.

Bake the cookies for 10 minutes. Transfer to wire racks to cool.

Makes 5 dozen cookies

Jelly Butter Cookies

Patti Fox, Jackson, New Jersey

I made these for my cookie exchange party and won second prize in the tasting contest out of ten entries! I shared them with many friends, teachers, and neighbors and received rave reviews on how buttery, sweet, and decadent they were. People couldn't believe I baked them and didn't buy them at a fancy bakery! I had a friend freeze hers and tell me how great it was to experience the cookie all over again. These may seem like a lot of work, but I assure you they are worth every minute you put into them once you pop this rich butter cookie into your mouth.

1 cup (2 sticks) unsalted butter
2 cups all-purpose flour
¾ teaspoon baking powder
Pinch of fine salt
1 large egg yolk
¾ cup granulated sugar
1 teaspoon vanilla extract
Good-quality seedless raspberry jelly or jam
Confectioners' sugar for decoration

Preheat the oven to 325°F/165°C. Line the baking sheets with parchment paper.

Melt the butter in a saucepan over medium heat. Cook the butter, swirling it as it melts, until it becomes slightly brown and smells nutty, about 15 minutes. (It's very important to smell the nuttiness; it makes all the difference in the taste!) Transfer the butter to a medium bowl, scraping all brown bits into the bowl. Cool slightly.

In another medium bowl, mix together the flour, baking powder, and salt. Whisk the egg yolk, granulated sugar, and vanilla into the cooled browned butter. Stir the dry ingredients into the butter mixture to make a crumbly dough that looks slightly wet. Scoop out the dough with a small teaspoon and scrape the spoon against the side of the bowl to make a spoon-shaped cookie. Slide the cookie out onto the lined baking sheet, retaining its spoon shape. Remember this is a sandwich cookie, so make enough to have equal pairs.

Bake the cookies until just browned, about 12 to 15 minutes. Cool on the baking sheets for 3 to 5 minutes and then transfer to wire racks to cool completely. When cool, spread approximately ½ teaspoon of jelly on the flat side of one cookie, and then gently sandwich together with another cookie, placing it flat side down over the jelly. Lightly dust the sandwiched cookies with confectioners' sugar.

Makes 4 dozen single cookies or 2 dozen sandwich cookies

Chocolate-Almond Cream Sandwich Cookies

Kelly Zarate, Leopold, Indiana

You'll need two hands to eat this delicate, crumbly cookie. One hand to eat the cookie, the other to catch the rich, dark, chocolatey crumbs! This cookie was the winner of Cookie-Exchange.com's 1st Original Recipe Contest.

Cookie

2 cups all-purpose flour

1¾ cups sugar

1 cup unsweetened cocoa powder

2 teaspoons baking powder

1 teaspoon salt

¼ cup shortening

2 large eggs

½ cup vegetable oil

¼ cup water

½ teaspoon almond extract

Almond Cream Filling

½ cup sugar

⅔ cup shortening

1 teaspoon vanilla extract

1 teaspoon almond extract

⅓ cup milk

¼ teaspoon salt

1 cup confectioners' sugar

Preheat the oven to 350°F/180°C. Line the baking sheets with parchment paper.

In a large bowl, whisk together the flour, sugar, cocoa powder, baking powder, and salt; set aside. In another large bowl, using an electric mixer, beat together the shortening, eggs, oil, water, and extract until well combined. Slowly add the dry ingredients to the creamed mixture; the dough should come together quickly and will be soft.

Use a 1¼-inch scoop to make uniform balls. If you don't have a scoop, roll pieces of the dough into 1¼-inch balls. Flatten the dough balls with the bottom of a drinking glass dipped in sugar. Place the cookies on the lined baking sheets.

Bake the cookies for 8 to 10 minutes. Transfer to wire racks and cool completely. Meanwhile, make the filling. Combine all the ingredients and beat with an electric mixer for 3 to 5 minutes, or until firm and spreadable. Sandwich the desired amount of filling between 2 cookies, or use to frost the tops of each cookie.

Variations: Drizzle the tops of the cookies with melted chocolate. Substitute other flavored extracts such as orange, mint, or raspberry for the almond extract in the dough and icing.

Makes 6 dozen single cookies, or 36 sandwich cookies

Raspberry-Almond Oatmeal Cookies

Susan J. Sias, Wilton Instructor, Lafayette, Colorado

This cookie took second place in Cookie-Exchange.com's 1st Original Recipe Contest—it's a fragrant oatmeal thumbprint cookie.

1 cup (2 sticks) unsalted butter, softened
¾ cup firmly packed light brown sugar

½ cup granulated sugar

2 large eggs

1 teaspoon vanilla extract

2 cups all-purpose flour

1 teaspoon ground cinnamon

1 teaspoon baking soda

½ teaspoon salt

2 cups old-fashioned rolled oats

1 cup sliced almonds with ½ cup reserved

1 jar seedless raspberry jam (or jam of your choice)

In a large bowl, using an electric mixer, cream together the butter and sugars. Add the eggs and beat until light and fluffy. Add the vanilla and mix until just combined. Add the flour, cinnamon, baking soda, salt, rolled oats, and ½ cup of the sliced almonds and mix until well combined. Cover the bowl with plastic wrap and refrigerate the dough for several hours. (The dough needs to be very well chilled in order to hold a shape.)

Preheat the oven to 350°F/180°C. Line baking sheets with parchment paper.

Roll the chilled dough, by large teaspoonfuls, into 1½-inch balls and place 2 inches apart on parchment-lined baking sheets. Make a small indentation in the center of each dough ball with the tip of your thumb. To ensure proper shape, chill the cookies on the baking sheets in the refrigerator for 30 minutes before baking.

When well chilled, remove from the refrigerator and fill each indentation with a small bit of raspberry jam. Sprinkle the remaining ½ cup sliced almonds over the tops of the cookies. Bake for 9 minutes. Transfer to wire racks to cool.

Variation: Use any seedless jam that you please. The flavor change is wonderful and does not alter the baking time or make-up of the cookie itself. A mix of strawberry and apricot is my favorite! This recipe is so very easy to make and so very easy to consume! Enjoy!

Note: This recipe was created at high altitude. If baking at sea level you may have to add a little more flour to prevent cookies from spreading.

Makes 6 dozen cookies

Dreamsicle Cookies with Glaze

Kristy Dean, Flat Lick, Kentucky

This cookie came in third in Cookie-Exchange.com's 1st Original Recipe Contest. It also won "Best Cookie" and "Best Overall" at our county fair as well as in a local newspaper contest, and is always a hit at my annual cookie exchange. Enjoy!

Dough

¾ cup shortening

1½ cups firmly packed light brown sugar

2 large eggs

1 teaspoon vanilla extract

1 teaspoon baking soda

½ cup buttermilk

½ teaspoon salt

3 tablespoons powdered orange drink mix, such as Tang

3 cups all-purpose flour

1½ teaspoons baking powder

1 cup white chocolate chips

Glaze

1 teaspoon butter or margarine

1 tablespoon powdered orange drink mix, such as Tang

1 cup confectioners' sugar

Milk

Preheat the oven to 375°F/190°C. Lightly grease the baking sheets.

In a large bowl, cream together the shortening and the sugar until light and fluffy. Add the eggs and vanilla and mix well. Dissolve the baking soda in the buttermilk. Add the buttermilk mixture, salt, Tang, flour, and baking powder to the shortening mixture and mix well. Stir in the white chocolate chips. Drop the dough, by teaspoonfuls, onto the prepared baking sheets.

Bake the cookies for 10 to 12 minutes.

Meanwhile, make the glaze. Combine the butter, Tang, confectioners' sugar, and enough milk to reach a thick, yet still pourable, consistency. Beat until smooth.

Frost cookies while still hot with the Tang glaze.

Makes 4 dozen cookies

Nutmeg Cookie Logs

Ava Marney, Humboldt, Kansas

I've made this recipe at Christmastime for many years and it's my husband's favorite.

Dough

3 cups all-purpose flour
1 teaspoon grated nutmeg, plus more for sprinkling
1 cup (2 sticks) butter, softened
2 teaspoons vanilla extract
1 large egg
2 teaspoons rum flavoring
¾ cup sugar

Frosting

3 tablespoons butter
½ teaspoon vanilla extract
1 teaspoon rum flavoring
2½ cups confectioners' sugar

2 to 3 tablespoons cream
Nutmeg for sprinkling

Preheat the oven to 350°F/180°C.

In a bowl, mix together the flour and nutmeg; set aside. In a separate bowl, thoroughly cream the butter, sugar, vanilla, egg, and rum flavoring until light and fluffy. Gradually add the dry ingredients and mix until well blended. On a lightly floured board, shape pieces of dough into long rolls, about ½ inch in diameter. Cut the rolls into 3-inch-long logs. Place the logs on ungreased baking sheets.

Bake the cookies for 12 to 15 minutes. Transfer to wire racks to cool.

Meanwhile, make the frosting. Cream the butter, vanilla, and rum flavoring. Add the confectioners' sugar alternately with the cream, a tablespoon at a time, beating until of a spreading consistency.

When the cookies are cool, frost, and mark the frosting with the tines of a fork to resemble bark. Sprinkle with nutmeg.

Chocolate Surprises

Dawn Stribling, McDonough, Georgia

This is an old recipe that I've tweaked a bit, and I think it is really good. You bite into the caramel topping and find a pecan piece hidden inside, at the bottom of the cookie. Chocolately, gooey, and crunchy . . . Surprise!

1½ cups all-purpose flour
¼ cup unsweetened cocoa powder
¼ teaspoon baking powder
⅛ teaspoon salt

½ cup (1 stick) unsalted butter, softened
½ cup firmly packed dark brown sugar
¼ cup granulated sugar
1 large egg
2 teaspoons vanilla extract
36 pecan halves
10 caramels, coarsely chopped

Preheat the oven to 350°F/180°C. Line baking sheets with parchment paper or nonstick silicone baking mats and set aside.

In a bowl, whisk together the flour, cocoa powder, baking powder, and salt; set aside. In a stand mixer fitted with the paddle attachment, cream the butter and sugars on medium speed for 1 minute. Beat in the egg and vanilla. Turn the mixer to low speed, add the flour mixture, and beat to combine.

Using a 1¼-inch ice cream scoop, form a ball of dough. Place a pecan in the dough ball, pressing lightly to secure. Place the ball, pecan side down, onto a prepared baking sheet. Repeat with the remaining dough and pecans. Using the back of a teaspoon, or your thumb, create an indentation in the top of each cookie and fill with ¼ teaspoon of chopped caramels.

Bake the cookies until firm, about 15 minutes. Transfer to wire racks to cool completely.

Makes 3 dozen cookies

Toasted Almond and Blueberry Shortbread Squares

Jill St. Claire, Ferndale, California

⅓ cup sliced almonds
1 cup all-purpose flour
⅛ teaspoon salt
¼ cup sugar
¾ cup (1½ sticks) unsalted butter, cut into pieces
¼ cup dried blueberries

Preheat the oven to 350°F/180°C. Spray an 8 × 8 × 2-inch baking dish with cooking spray.

Place the almonds in a single layer in a dry skillet, over medium heat. Toast, stirring occasionally, until the almonds are fragrant and golden brown, about 2 minutes.

Combine the flour, salt, and sugar in a large bowl. With your fingertips, crumble in the butter until the dough resembles coarse meal. Add the almonds and blueberries. Press the dough into the prepared dish. Bake for 20 minutes, or until golden brown. Let cool to room temperature, then cut into eight equal pieces. Store in an airtight container until ready to serve.

Makes 8 shortbread squares

Cranberry-Orange Oatmeal Dreams

Jill St. Claire, Ferndale, California

2 cups all-purpose flour
½ teaspoon salt
½ teaspoon ground cinnamon
1 teaspoon baking powder
1 teaspoon baking soda
1 tablespoon vanilla extract
½ teaspoon orange extract
1 tablespoon grated orange zest
¼ teaspoon ground cloves
3 tablespoons milk
2 large eggs
1 cup (2 sticks) unsalted butter, softened
1 cup firmly packed light brown sugar
½ cup granulated sugar
3 cups old-fashioned rolled oats
1 cup dried cranberries

In a medium bowl, whisk together the flour, salt, cinnamon, baking powder, and baking soda; set aside. In a small bowl, whisk together the vanilla and orange extracts, orange zest, ground cloves, milk, and eggs; set aside.

In the bowl of an electric mixer fitted with the paddle attachment, combine the butter with the sugars, and beat on medium speed until light and fluffy. Reduce the speed to low, gradually add milk-egg mixture, and beat well. Add the flour mixture, and beat until just combined. Remove the bowl from the mixer, and stir in the rolled oats and dried cranberries. Place the dough, covered with plastic wrap, in the refrigerator until firm, at least 2 hours or overnight.

Preheat the oven to 350°F/180°C. Line the baking sheets with parchment paper and set aside.

Shape 2 tablespoons of the dough into a ball; place on one of the lined sheets. Repeat with the remaining dough, placing the balls 3 inches apart. Press each dough ball with the bottom of a glass to flatten the dough into 2-inch-diameter rounds.

Bake the cookies for 16 to 18 minutes until golden but still soft in the center, rotating the baking sheets halfway through the baking time. Remove from the oven; transfer on the parchment paper to wire racks to cool.

Makes 2 dozen cookies

Chocolate, Vanilla, and Cream Cheese Crescents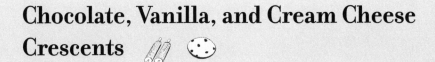

Rose Friedrich

2½ cups all-purpose flour
1 teaspoon baking powder
1 cup butter, softened
1 (8-ounce) package cream cheese, softened
2 cups sugar
1 large egg
1 teaspoon vanilla extract
1 teaspoon almond extract
1 cup semisweet chocolate chips
¼ cup crushed nuts

Preheat the oven to 350°F/180°C. Line the baking sheets with parchment paper.

In a medium bowl, mix or whisk together the flour and baking powder. Place the butter and cream cheese into a large bowl, and, using an electric mixer, beat the mixture until light and fluffy. Beat in the sugar and the egg, and then add the vanilla and almond extracts. Beat well. Slowly add the flour mixture until well combined.

Divide the dough in half. Add ½ cup of the chocolate chips to one portion of the dough. Leave the other portion plain. Use 2-tablespoon portions to form crescents with the plain dough and with the chocolate chip dough. Place the crescents 2 inches apart on the lined baking sheets.

Bake the cookies for 12 to 15 minutes, or until lightly browned. Transfer to wire racks to cool.

For the plain crescents, melt the remaining ½ cup of chocolate chips in the microwave or in a double boiler. Dip one end in the melted chocolate chips and sprinkle the finely crushed nuts over the chocolate. Place the crescents on wax paper until the chocolate sets.

Makes 4 dozen crescents

Sour Cream Cardamom Cookies

Helen Mueller, Westchester, Illinois

These cookies are very cake-like.

2 cups sifted all-purpose flour
½ teaspoon ground cardamom, or substitute grated nutmeg or allspice
¼ teaspoon baking soda
2 teaspoons baking powder
½ cup (1 stick) butter, softened
1 cup firmly packed light brown sugar
1 large egg
1 teaspoon grated orange zest
1 cup chopped nuts
½ cup sour cream

Preheat the oven to 400°F/200°C. Lightly grease the baking sheets.

In a small bowl, sift the first four ingredients together; set aside. In a separate bowl, cream the butter with the brown sugar. Add the egg and beat until fluffy. Stir in orange zest and nuts. Add the sifted dry ingredients alternately with the sour cream to the creamed mixture. Drop the dough batter by teaspoonfuls 2 inches apart onto the prepared baking sheets.

Bake the cookies for 12 minutes. Transfer to wire racks to cool.

Makes 4 to 5 dozen cookies

Orange Delight Cookies

Linda Maxwell, Porterville, California

Dough
3 cups all-purpose flour
2 teaspoons baking powder
¼ teaspoon salt
¾ cup shortening
1½ cups firmly packed dark brown sugar
2 teaspoons grated orange zest
1 teaspoon vanilla extract
2 large eggs
½ teaspoon baking soda
½ cup sour milk (see Note on page 120) or buttermilk
¾ cup chopped nuts

Glaze
2 teaspoons grated orange zest
⅓ cup orange juice
1 cup confectioners' sugar

Preheat the oven to 350°F/180°C. Lightly grease the baking sheets.

In a medium bowl, sift together the flour, baking powder, and salt; set aside. In a separate bowl, cream the shortening, sugar, orange zest, and vanilla until smooth. Beat in the eggs. Add the baking soda to the sour milk. Add the flour mixture alternately with the sour milk to the creamed mixture. Stir in the nuts. Drop the dough by tablespoonfuls 2 inches apart onto the prepared baking sheets.

Bake the cookies for 10 minutes. Meanwhile, mix the ingredients for the glaze. When the cookies are done, remove them from the oven. Transfer to wire racks. While still hot, spread thinly with the glaze to form a thin, sugary coating over the cookies.

Makes about 5 dozen cookies

White Chocolate Candy Cane Drops

Sandy Granger, Petaluma, California

I'd like to share a recipe that was brought to one of my first cookie exchange parties. I don't know where the recipe came from, but these cookies are now on my must-have list of cookies to bake for the holidays. This recipe calls for chocolate-filled peppermint candy canes that can be found at specialty candy shops or online at hammonds candies.com. I have also made these cookies with plain peppermint candy canes, but the flavor is a little different.

8 ounces white baking chocolate with cocoa butter (I use Ghirardelli white baking chocolate)
½ cup (1 stick) butter, softened
1 cup sugar
1 teaspoon baking powder

½ teaspoon salt

2 large eggs

1 teaspoon vanilla extract

2¾ cups all-purpose flour

⅔ cup finely crushed chocolate-filled peppermint candy canes or peppermint candy canes

Preheat the oven to 375°F/190°C. Line the baking sheets with parchment paper.

Chop 4 ounces of the white chocolate; set aside. In a small saucepan, cook the remaining 4 ounces of white chocolate over low heat, stirring, until melted. Set the saucepan aside off the heat to allow the chocolate to cool slightly.

In a large mixing bowl, beat the butter with an electric mixer on medium to high speed for 30 seconds. Add the sugar, baking powder, and salt and beat until combined. Beat in the eggs and vanilla. Beat in the cooled, melted white chocolate. Beat in as much of the flour as you can with the mixer, then stir in any remaining flour. Stir in the chopped white chocolate and crushed candy canes. Drop the dough by rounded teaspoonfuls, 2 inches apart, on the lined baking sheets.

Bake the cookies for 8 to 10 minutes, or until lightly browned around the edges. Transfer to wire racks to cool.

Makes about 50 cookies

Child's Play "Throw It In" Surprise Cookies

Donna Mrotek, Child's Play Creative Learning Center, Santa Barbara, California

One rainy day someone suggested we make cookies. The only thing we had in abundance was oatmeal, and no one wanted oatmeal cookies except me. So we invented these cookies using the little bits of everything we had and a lot of oatmeal. You can double the sugar to make a sweeter cookie or leave it as is and be healthier. We add a bit of chocolate if we are feeling bad.

Base

3½ cups quick-cooking oatmeal, finely ground (see Note)
1 cup whole wheat flour
1 teaspoon salt
1 teaspoon baking powder
1 cup butter, softened
½ cup granulated sugar
½ cup firmly packed dark brown sugar
2 large eggs, at room temperature
2 tablespoons vanilla extract
½ cup (4 ounces) grated semisweet dark chocolate

Preheat the oven to 350°F/180°C. Grease the baking sheets.

In a medium bowl, whisk together the finely ground oatmeal, flour, salt, and baking powder; set aside. In a large bowl, using an electric mixer, beat the butter and sugars together until light and fluffy. Add the eggs and vanilla to the creamed mixture and beat in well. Add the grated dark chocolate. Add the dry ingredients to the creamed mixture and incorporate.

Throw-ins

⅛ cup slivered almonds

¼ cup pecans

1/16 cup pine nuts

¼ cup chopped dried cherries

¼ cup dried cranberries

⅛ cup Rice Krispies

⅛ cup cornflakes

⅛ cup high-fiber cereal with 9 grams of protein (okay, I snuck that one in by calling it dried worms)

⅛ cup sweetened toasted flaked coconut

1 raisin (not popular with the group)

2 banana chips

1 chopped dried apple slice

1 potato chip (from someone's lunch)

1 vitamin to make it extra healthy (Also from someone's lunch. I had to appreciate the gesture but I feared what a vitamin would become or smell like at high temperatures, so I dug it out when no one was looking.)

Now for the fun part. "Throw-it-in" measurements are optional. We used a child's hand, which is about ⅛ cup because we literally were "throwing it in." More than ⅛ cup means more than one child picked it to throw in. Less then ⅛ cup means that it was not a popular choice among the group and much negotiating took place to get it accepted. Drop the dough by tablespoonfuls onto the prepared baking sheets. Bake the cookies for 10 to 12 minutes. Cool slightly on the baking sheets and eat with a cold glass of milk.

Note: We blended all but ½ cup of the oatmeal. Magically, it transformed into the *secret ingredient*. We used a hand grinder and it took a very, very long time. For those of you who are not trying to entertain a group of preschoolers on the third consecutive rainy day, use a food processor or blender, they are faster and will blend the oatmeal to a fine powder.

Makes 6 to 7 dozen cookies

Date-Nut Pinwheels

Linda Gavin, Fairbanks, Alaska

I've had this recipe for over twenty-five years, it was given to me by my good friend Patty Zmuda. I made it every Christmas for my father as it was his favorite cookie in the world. It is rather time-consuming. The trick is in the chilling of the dough before rolling it out.

1 (8-ounce) package dates, chopped
1 cup granulated sugar
1 cup hot water
1 cup finely chopped walnuts
2 cups firmly packed light brown sugar
1 cup butter, softened
2 large eggs
3½ cups all-purpose flour
½ teaspoon baking soda
½ teaspoon salt
½ teaspoon cream of tartar
1 teaspoon vanilla extract

Combine the dates, sugar, and hot water in a saucepan and cook over medium heat until thickened, stirring constantly. Remove from heat, stir in the nuts, and set aside to cool.

In a large bowl combine the brown sugar and butter and beat until fluffy. Add the eggs and beat until blended. Combine the dry ingredients and stir into the creamed ingredients. Add the vanilla. Chill the dough until stiff enough to work with. Divide the dough into thirds. On wax paper, roll each third into a 12-inch square. Spread each with one-third of the date mixture, roll up, and chill 2 hours or overnight.

Preheat the oven to 350°F/180°C. Line the baking sheets with parchment paper.

Cut each chilled roll into approximately ¼-inch slices and place on the lined baking sheets.

Bake the cookies for 10 to 12 minutes. Transfer to wire racks to cool.

Note: Definitely use parchment paper–lined baking sheets because these cookies are rather sticky little devils, especially if you spread the filling on thick in spots. I usually put small pieces of wax paper in between the finished cookies before storing—a lot of trouble, I know, but they were for my dad so I didn't mind a bit.

Makes about 4 dozen cookies

Butterscotch Cookies

Jo-ann Morin, Frankfort, Maine

When my children were little and my mother was alive and baking, the kids told Mom that these cookies were their favorite, so she'd bake them often.

1 cup plus 2 tablespoons all-purpose flour
½ teaspoon baking soda
½ teaspoon salt
¼ cup firmly packed light brown sugar
½ cup shortening
1 large egg
1 teaspoon vanilla extract
½ cup granulated sugar
1 (11-ounce) package butterscotch chips

Preheat the oven to 375°F/190°C.

In a small bowl, whisk together the flour, baking soda, and salt; set aside. In a large bowl, using an electric mixer, beat together the brown sugar, shortening, egg, vanilla, and granulated sugar until well combined. Gradually add the flour mixture, and when incorporated, add the butterscotch chips. Drop by tablespoonfuls 2 inches apart on ungreased cookie sheets.

Bake the cookies for about 10 minutes. Transfer to wire racks to cool.

Makes 2½ dozen cookies

Gram's Pecan Crescents

Jenny Grimaud, Crofton, Maryland

3¼ cups all-purpose flour
¾ teaspoon ground cinnamon
1½ cups (3 sticks) butter, softened
¾ cup light corn syrup
1 tablespoon vanilla extract
2¼ cups ground pecans or walnuts
1½ cups confectioners' sugar

In a bowl, mix together the flour and cinnamon; set aside. Using an electric mixer, beat the butter, corn syrup, and vanilla in a large bowl on medium speed until well blended. Gradually stir in the flour mixture and pecans. Cover the bowl with plastic wrap and refrigerate the dough until chilled and easy to handle, at least 3 hours.

Preheat the oven to 350°F/180°C.

Shape the dough, by rounded teaspoonfuls, into 2-inch-long rolls. Place 2 inches apart on ungreased baking sheets, shaping to form crescents.

Bake the cookies until light brown on the bottom, 15 to 18 minutes. Transfer to wire racks to cool. Roll in confectioners' sugar.

Makes about 6 dozen cookies

Anise Cut-out Cookies

Sharon Erhart, Lake Mary, Florida

This is my family recipe for Christmas cut-out cookies. We make these cookies every year, and they keep very well in an airtight container. I have not taken them to a cookie exchange yet because people either love them or do not care for them at all! I ship some to my brother in Cincinnati every year because his wife and kids don't care for them and she won't make them for him. So it's a love-it-or-hate-it cookie, but if you love anise, it's worth trying!

Dough

1 cup (2 sticks) butter, softened

1 cup sugar

3 large eggs

2 teaspoons anise extract

4 cups all-purpose flour

1 teaspoon baking soda

½ teaspoon salt

2 teaspoons cream of tartar

Frosting

3 large egg whites

1 teaspoon cornstarch

1 teaspoon vinegar

1 pound confectioners' sugar

2 teaspoons anise extract or more to taste
Food coloring (optional)

Preheat the oven to 400°F/200°C.

In a large bowl, cream together the butter and sugar. Beat in the eggs and anise. Sift in the flour, soda, salt, and cream of tartar and mix together. Roll out the dough on a floured surface and cut it out with 2-inch cookie cutters. Place the cookies on ungreased baking sheets 2 inches apart.

Bake the cookies for 9 to 10 minutes. Transfer to wire racks to cool.

To make the frosting, beat the egg whites until stiff. Add the cornstarch, vinegar, confectioners' sugar, and anise. The frosting will be runny but will dry firmly and nicely on the cookies. When the cookies are cool, frost and decorate as desired.

Makes 4 dozen cookies

Chocolate Crackles

Linda Maxwell, Porterville, California

This cookie is the most requested by my family, who call them chocolate snicker-doodles.

1 cup semisweet chocolate chips, melted
1¾ cups all-purpose flour
¼ teaspoon salt
2 teaspoons baking soda
1 teaspoon ground cinnamon
⅔ cup (1 stick plus 2⅔ tablespoons) butter, softened

½ cup sugar, plus sugar for rolling
1 large egg
¼ cup light corn syrup

Melt the chocolate chips in the microwave or a double boiler; set aside. In a small bowl, sift together the flour, salt, baking soda, and cinnamon; set aside. In a large bowl, beat the butter, sugar, and egg until creamy. Blend in the melted chocolate and corn syrup. Gradually stir in the sifted dry ingredients. Chill the dough for at least 1 hour.

Preheat the oven to 350°F/180°C.

Shape the dough into 1½-inch balls. Roll the balls in sugar. Place 2 inches apart on ungreased baking sheets.

Bake the cookies for 10 minutes, or until barely browned. Transfer to wire racks to cool.

Makes 3 dozen cookies

Orange-Nut Pinwheels

Susan Gebhardt, Bel Air, Maryland

1 cup ground walnuts
½ cup orange marmalade
⅓ cup raisins, finely chopped
3 tablespoons plus 1 cup firmly packed light brown sugar
½ teaspoon ground allspice
1¾ cups all-purpose flour
½ cup shortening
1 large egg

In a food processor fitted with the metal blade, combine the walnuts, marmalade, raisins, 3 tablespoons of the brown sugar, and allspice; set aside.

In a large bowl, combine the flour, shortening, egg, and 1 cup brown sugar. Knead until the dough holds together, or use the food processor.

On wax paper, roll half of dough into a 14 × 6-inch rectangle and spread with half of the nut mixture. Starting with the 6-inch side, roll the rectangle up tightly. Wrap in wax paper. Repeat with the remaining dough. Refrigerate the rolls for 2 hours, or until firm enough to slice.

Preheat the oven to 350°F/180°C. Lightly grease the baking sheets.

Unwrap the chilled rolls and cut them into ¼-inch slices. Place them 1 inch apart on the prepared baking sheets.

Bake the cookies for 10 minutes, or until lightly browned. Transfer to wire racks to cool.

Makes 3 to 4 dozen cookies

Banana-Chocolate Chip Cookies

Jamie Rice, Cumberland, Maryland

These cookies are always in high demand and never last long (unless I hide them!).

Dough

1⅛ cups all-purpose flour
½ cup sugar
1 teaspoon baking powder
⅛ teaspoon baking soda
½ teaspoon salt
⅓ cup lard
1 large egg
½ cup mashed ripe banana

½ teaspoon vanilla extract

½ cup chocolate chips

Topping

¼ teaspoon ground cinnamon

1 teaspoon sugar

Preheat the oven to 400°F/200°C.

Sift together the flour, sugar, baking powder, soda, and salt into a mixing bowl. Cut in the lard. Add egg, mashed banana, and vanilla and beat until thoroughly blended. Fold in the chocolate chips. Drop by teaspoonfuls, about 1½ inches apart, onto ungreased baking sheets.

Combine the cinnamon and sugar and sprinkle the top of each cookie with the mixture. Bake the cookies for about 12 minutes, until they are golden brown. Transfer to wire racks to cool.

After the cookies are completely cool, store in gallon-size tie bags with a slice of white bread to keep the cookies soft. Then put them into a cookie tin—and hide them!

Makes about 2½ dozen cookies

International Cookies

Viennese Chocolate Fingers

Iris Grundler, Gaithersburg, Maryland

½ cup (1 stick) unsalted butter, softened
6 tablespoons confectioners' sugar
1½ cups self-rising flour, sifted
3 tablespoons cornstarch
1 cup semisweet chocolate chips

Preheat the oven to 375°F/190°C. Line the baking sheets with parchment paper.

Beat the butter and sugar in a medium bowl until light and fluffy. Gradually add the flour and cornstarch. Melt ¼ cup of the semisweet chocolate in the microwave or a double boiler. Beat the melted chocolate into the cookie dough.

Place the dough in a pastry bag fitted with a large star tip and pipe fingers about 2 inches long on baking sheets, spacing them 2 inches apart, to allow for spreading. If the cookie dough is too thick to pipe, beat in a little milk to thin it out before you place it in the pastry bag. Bake for 12 to 15 minutes. Transfer to wire racks to cool.

Melt the remaining ¾ cup of chocolate chips and dip one end of each cookie in the chocolate. Allow the excess to drip back into the bowl. Place the dipped cookies on a sheet of parchment paper and let the chocolate set.

Makes 30 cookies

Hertzog Koekies: A True South African Tradition

Elsie van Rooyen, Theunissen, South Africa

Affectionately known as "Hertzoggies," these cookies or jam and coconut tartlets are known as Hertzog koekies in South Africa and are part of every South-African home-maker's traditional recipes. They were named after General J. B. M. Hertzog, prime minister of the South Africa Union in 1924. Every family has their own variation, I hope you enjoy mine!

Dough

    5 cups cake flour
    1 teaspoon baking powder
    ¼ teaspoon salt
    ½ cup (1 stick) margarine or butter, softened
    1 cup sugar
    4 extra-large eggs

Filling

    1 jar smooth apricot jam, mixed with 1–2 teaspoons flour
    5 large egg whites
    1 cup sugar
    ¾ cup desiccated coconut, plus 1 tablespoon (see Resources, page 329)

Preheat the oven to 350°F/180°C. Lightly grease muffin pans.

In a medium bowl, sift together the flour, baking powder, and salt. In a large bowl, cream the margarine or butter and sugar until light and fluffy. Add the eggs one by one, beating thoroughly after each addition.

Add the dry ingredients to the creamed mixture and mix to form a soft dough. Add a little more flour if the dough is too moist, or a little water if the dough is too dry. If you use large or jumbo eggs, this is normally not a problem.

Roll out the dough thinly, ⅛ to ¼ inch thick, and cut out 3-inch circles. Line the base of the prepared muffin pans with the dough circles.

Spoon a teaspoonful of the apricot jam into the middle of each circle of dough. (To prevent the apricot jam from leaking out during the baking process, add a teaspoon or two of flour to it.)

Beat the egg whites to soft peak stage, adding the sugar gradually while still beating. Add the coconut. Spoon the meringue mixture on top of the apricot jam filling.

Bake the tartlets for 20 to 25 minutes. Remove from the pans and place on wire racks to cool.

Variation: For a festive touch, cut red or green candied cherries into small pieces and add to the coconut mixture.

Makes 60 to 72 Hertzoggies

Russian Torte

Nancy Wert, Olney, Maryland

The Russian Torte is a much beloved Pennsylvania tradition. At weddings, not only is cake served, but each table at the reception is heaped with luscious cookies made by family and friends. Each cookie is the family's favorite and is then shared by all who attend. The Russian Torte is my husband's personal favorite and we always serve it at Christmas and Easter.

4 cups ground nuts
1 cup sugar, plus ½ cup
2 teaspoons ground cinnamon
1 package active dry yeast
¼ cup warm water
4 cups all-purpose flour
1 cup (2 sticks) butter, cold
4 large eggs, separated
¼ cup milk
2 jars store-bought apricot filling or make your own (see Note)

Preheat the oven to 350°F/180°C.

In a small bowl, mix together 3½ cups of the nuts, 1 cup of the sugar, and the cinnamon. Reserve ½ cup of nuts for topping the meringue.

In a measuring cup, combine the yeast and warm water; set aside.

Sift the flour into a large bowl, add the butter, and mix until the texture is like pie dough, blending until it comes away from the sides of the bowl. Slightly beat the egg yolks. Add the egg yolks, milk, and yeast to the flour mixture. Place the dough on a floured board and knead. Divide the dough into thirds.

Roll the first portion of the dough to fit a large glass 15½ × 10½-inch casserole dish, allowing the dough to come up the sides of the dish (the pastry can be patched if it tears during this process). Spread the nut mixture over the dough.

Roll out the second portion of the dough and place it over the nut mixture. Spread the apricot filling on top.

Roll out the third portion of the dough and place it on top of the apricot filling. Using a large fork, prick through all the layers.

Bake the torte for 35 minutes. While the torte is baking, in a clean bowl, with clean beaters, beat the egg whites until frothy. Gradually add the remaining ½ cup of sugar, continuing to beat to form a meringue.

When the torte is baked, remove it from the oven. Spoon the meringue over the top and sprinkle with the remaining nuts. Return the torte to the oven for 10 minutes to brown the meringue.

Cut the torte while warm into 1½-inch squares. Cool on wire racks and store in airtight containers and refrigerate, or freeze for up to 1 month.

Note: To make your own apricot filling, cook 24 ounces of dried apricots, covered in water, until soft and plump. Drain. Mash while still hot with a potato masher, or blend in a food processor. Add about 1 cup sugar while the mixture is still hot.

Makes 24 to 30 cookies

Polish Chrusciki aka Angel's Wings

Nancy Wert, Olney, Maryland

Chrusciki, or Angel's Wings, are best served the same day as they are prepared. They are often made during the holidays. This recipe has been in my family for years.

¼ cup (½ stick) unsalted butter, softened

¼ cup sugar

3 to 4 large egg yolks

1 large egg

2½ cups all-purpose flour, sifted, plus more if needed

½ teaspoon baking soda

¼ teaspoon salt

2 tablespoons honey or orange honey

½ cup sour cream

2 teaspoons white vinegar

3 tablespoons rum

Canola oil for deep-frying, about 3 to 4 cups

1 tablespoon honey for glaze

2 cups confectioners' sugar for dusting

In a large mixing bowl, with an electric mixer, beat the butter and sugar until well combined. Add the egg yolks and the egg, flour, baking soda, salt, honey, sour cream, vinegar, and rum. Mix well.

The mixture should form a dough much like bread dough.

Roll out the dough on a floured pastry mat, into a rectangle about 4 inches wide and ¼ inch thick. Cut into 1 × 4-inch strips. Cut the ends of the strips off on the diagonal. Make a slit in the center of each strip, and take the bottom of the strip and, working from bottom to top, pull the bottom corner through the middle slit in an upward direction on one side and reverse on the other side, pulling the dough downward. Repeat the procedure until the cookies are all prepared.

Use a deep soup pot to prevent splashing, filling only to a depth of about 6 inches with the oil. Preheat the oil to 350°F/180°C. Deep-fry each cookie (you can do more than one as long as they do not touch) until they rise to the surface and are golden brown. Remove from the oil and place on a brown paper bag or paper towels to drain.

Lightly glaze the cookies with the honey, using a pastry brush (do not coat them heavily or they will turn mushy). I normally apply the glaze if I am serving these the same day I make them; if not, I skip this step and just dust them with confectioners' sugar.

Makes 12 cookies

Pierniki: Polish Honey Almond Cookies

Nancy Wert, Olney, Maryland

This is a traditional Polish spice cookie that is made at Christmastime. It is also made at Easter, but then you omit the meringue-like topping and use a light confectioners' sugar icing and top with almonds.

Dough

4 large eggs
1 cup orange or clover honey
3 cups all-purpose flour
1 teaspoon baking soda
½ teaspoon ground cinnamon
½ teaspoon grated nutmeg
½ teaspoon ground ginger
¼ teaspoon ground cloves

Topping

> 3 large egg whites
> Slivered almonds

In a large bowl, beat the 4 whole eggs and honey together until light and fluffy. In a separate bowl, sift together the flour, baking soda, and all the spices. Slowly add the dry ingredients to the egg-honey mixture and mix until it forms a pie crust–looking dough. Roll the dough into a ball, wrap in plastic wrap, and chill for 1 hour.

Preheat the oven to 225°F/110°C. Line the baking sheets with parchment paper.

Beat the egg whites until they are light and form soft peaks like meringue.

Roll out the chilled dough ¼ inch thick. Cut out the dough with shaped or round cookie cutters approximately 1½ to 2 inches in diameter and place the cookies 2 inches apart on the lined baking sheets. Brush the cookies with the beaten egg whites and top with 3 to 4 slivered almonds, applying the almonds in a flower-like pattern.

Bake the cookies for 15 to 18 minutes, until they are a light golden brown. Transfer to wire racks to cool. When completely cool, store in airtight tins.

Makes 2 dozen cookies

Bulgarian Maslenki

Svetla Encheva, Ocean City, Maryland

These traditional maslenki from my homeland of Bulgaria will melt in your mouth.

Dough

> 2 cups all-purpose flour
> ½ teaspoon baking powder
> ½ cup lard, at room temperature (can substitute butter, but lard is traditional; see Note)

1 cup confectioners' sugar
½ teaspoon grated lemon zest
2 large egg yolks
1 teaspoon vanilla extract
2 tablespoons Greek-style yogurt

Fillings

Jams of your choice: apricot, raspberry, strawberry

Preheat the oven to 375°F/190°C. Line the baking sheets with parchment paper.

In a small bowl, whisk together the flour and baking powder; set aside.

In a large bowl, mix the softened (or melted and cooled) lard with the confectioners' sugar until incorporated. Add the grated lemon zest, egg yolks, and vanilla and mix together. Add the yogurt and stir until smooth. Gradually add the dry ingredients. The mixture will form a crumbly, soft dough.

Divide the dough in half. Between two pieces of wax paper, roll out the dough to a thickness of ⅛ inch. You'll need two different cookie cutters. Use a 2½-inch cutter for all of the dough, then go back, and use a 1-inch cutter to make holes in half of the cut-out circles, for the top pieces that the jam peeks through. Transfer the cut-out dough to the lined baking pans. The cookies do not spread so you can place them closely together on the pan.

Bake the cookies for 8 minutes. Transfer to wire racks to cool. When cool, spread each bottom (full) half with a heaping teaspoon of jam and place top piece over the filling to make a sandwich. Sprinkle lightly with confectioners' sugar.

Note: Look for high-quality, pure, nonhydrogenated lard at finer groceries. If you use cheaper hydrogenated lard, your house will smell like bacon when the cookies are baking!

Variations: Popular additions and variations of Bulgarian Maslenki include: jams or preserves, prunes, sour cherries, walnuts, pecans, almonds, Turkish Delight, and a dusting of confectioners' sugar.

Makes 36 plain or 18 (2½-inch) sandwich cookies

Peruvian Alfajores

Iris Grundler, Gaithersburg, Maryland (Originally from Peru!)

After Robin served an Americanized version of alfajores for her cookie exchange party, I called my relatives in Peru and had them send me a true Peruvian Alfajore cookie recipe. Enjoy!

For my CE party, I'd found a recipe on the Internet from a well-known media doyenne that called for 100 percent all-purpose flour. *Everyone loved the cookies*—except for Iris, who declared she would procure a real alfajores recipe. Iris's recipe calls for 100 percent cornstarch, which makes the cookies melt in your mouth. However, it might be too much "melt in your mouth" for the average American taste, therefore I suggest a 50/50 ratio of cornstarch and all-purpose flour.—Robin

Dough

4 cups of cornstarch (or substitute 2 cups all-purpose flour and 2 cups cornstarch)

6 tablespoons confectioners' sugar

1½ cups (3 sticks) butter, softened

½ teaspoon grated lemon zest

½ teaspoon almond extract

5 to 8 tablespoons milk

Filling

1 (14-ounce) can La Lechera dulce de leche (I use Nestlé brand) or make your own (see Note)

Confectioners' sugar for dusting

Preheat the oven to 350°F/180°C. Line the baking sheets with parchment paper.

In a large bowl, sift together the cornstarch (and/or flour) and confectioners' sugar at least once; set aside. In a separate bowl, cream the butter until light and fluffy. Add the remaining ingredients slowly and mix until a soft dough is formed. (Add a little milk, a tablespoon at a time, only if necessary, to soften the dough.) Lightly flour a smooth, clean surface. Divide the dough for ease of handling and lay out a piece of the dough on the floured surface. Roll out the dough to a thickness of ⅛ inch. Cut out the cookies with a round cutter, approximately 2½ inches in diameter. Place the cookies on the lined baking sheets.

Bake the cookies for 7 to 9 minutes. Transfer to wire racks to cool. When the cookies have completely cooled, carefully spread some of the *manjarblanco* (dulce de leche) on the bottom side of a cookie and top with another cookie. Dust the cookie sandwiches with confectioners' sugar on both sides.

Note: To make your own dulce de leche filling: Place an unopened 14-ounce can of condensed milk on a rack or steamer in a pot, so the can isn't touching the bottom of the pot. Cover with water and boil for 3 hours, checking the water level and adding water as needed. *Important warning: The can could explode if it's set on the bottom of the pan! Be sure to use a raised rack!*

Variation: After filling the cookies, roll the sides in coconut. Desiccated coconut is preferred; however, flaked sweetened coconut works well, too. (See Resources, page 329, for dessicated coconut.)

Baklava Cookies

Robin Olson

Have someone stand behind you before you take your first bite. That way when you keel over with joy, you won't hit the floor. Baklava is a sticky and lusciously sweet Middle Eastern pastry, made with layers of phyllo dough, filled with chopped nuts and a sweet, lemon-scented honey syrup. I've adapted this traditional bar recipe into individual cookies. The crunch profile is outstanding as one bites down on the dozens of layers of phyllo. These are to die for!

Pastry

1 roll (½ pound) from one box Athens phyllo dough, thawed (see box, page 159)
1 cup (2 sticks) butter, melted

Nut Filling

2 cups pecans
1 cup slivered almonds
1 cup sugar
1 level teaspoon ground cinnamon

Nectar of the Gods Honey Syrup

1 cup water
¾ cup sugar
¾ cup honey
½ teaspoon vanilla extract
1 teaspoon freshly squeezed lemon juice
½ teaspoon finely grated lemon zest

Working with Phyllo Dough

Phyllo dough is sold in the frozen foods section of grocery stores and comes in rolls: there are 2 rolls per 1-pound box. The dough should be thawed for 2 hours before working with it. Follow the package directions. If you try to unroll the dough while it is still frozen, the phyllo will break into pieces. Once the phyllo is thawed, the roll should relax and each phyllo sheet should peel off easily. Phyllo dries out quickly, so when you are working with it, keep the layers you haven't used yet covered with a barely damp dish towel. Use a plastic pastry mat or parchment paper as your work surface.

Make the syrup first. In a small saucepan, combine the water, sugar, honey, vanilla, lemon juice, and lemon zest and stir. Bring the mixture to a boil, then turn down the heat to medium. Gently boil the syrup for 15 to 20 minutes, stirring occasionally. The liquid should reduce by almost half, and become thick and syrupy. Remove from the heat. Cool in the pan, then refrigerate to chill even further.

Make the nut filling. While the syrup is gently boiling, preheat the oven to 350°F/180°C. Spread out the nuts on a baking sheet and bake for 7 to 9 minutes to toast lightly, which releases the oils and enhances the nut flavor. Let the nuts cool for several minutes, then grind finely in a food processor. Transfer to a medium bowl, add the sugar and cinnamon, and stir to combine; set aside.

Spread out one sheet of phyllo dough on your work surface and lightly brush it with melted butter. Add another layer of phyllo and brush with melted butter. Repeat this once more, using a 3-2-1 method for each roll.

Sprinkle ¼ cup of the nut filling lightly on the third buttered sheet of phyllo. Place another sheet of phyllo dough on top and lightly brush with butter. Repeat with another sheet of phyllo. Sprinkle another ¼ cup of nut filling on top. Add another piece of phyllo, and brush with melted butter. (Do not add nuts to this layer.)

Gently, but firmly, tightly roll the sheets up lengthwise as you would a jelly roll. (Large chunks of nuts will break the phyllo, so make sure the nuts have been finely ground.) Brush melted butter on the top and sides of the log to make sure it holds together. Take the log and set it on another 1 piece of phyllo and roll it up. Butter the roll lightly, especially along the edge; set aside. Repeat this procedure of making the rolls until all the phyllo and nuts are used.

Preheat the oven to 350°F/180°C. Line the baking sheets with parchment paper.

Using a large, sharp knife, slice the phyllo rolls into 1-inch pieces. Slice in a downward motion, and when the blade hits the bottom, tilt the bottom of the blade away from you and use it as a spatula to place the cookies on the lined baking sheets. Place the cookies close together but not touching. Use your free hand to hold the cookie in a round shape as you move it from the cutting surface to the baking sheet. Brush the tops of the baklava cookies with melted butter.

Bake the cookies for 20 to 22 minutes, or until lightly browned. Remove the baking sheets from the oven and cool the cookies on the sheets. Drizzle half the syrup over the completely cooled cookies. Let the syrup absorb for about 15 minutes, then turn each cookie over. Pour the remaining syrup on the cookies. Store in a sealed container, if they last that long. These cookies refrigerate and freeze well. There will be a lot of toasty nuts, phyllo bits, and honey left on the baking sheets. Scoop it all up and put in a sealed container, label, and freeze. Use it as a topping for vanilla ice cream. To swap Baklava Cookies for a cookie party, present them in paper muffin cups.

Make about 4 dozen cookies

Italian Pizzelles

Sandy Pingatore, Adamstown, Maryland

6 large eggs
2 cups sugar
1 cup (2 sticks) butter, melted
2 teaspoons vanilla extract

½ teaspoon anise extract

7 cups all-purpose flour

4 tablespoons baking powder

In a large bowl, cream together the eggs and sugar. Add the cooled butter and beat to incorporate. Add the vanilla and anise extracts. Sift together the dry ingredients in a separate bowl and add to the creamed mixture to make a stiff dough. Drop by teaspoonfuls onto a pizzelle maker. Store the cooled cookies in an airtight container.

Note: Pizzelle makers can be found online or at kitchen specialty stores. It's a type of waffle-maker with embedded patterns that look like snowflakes.

Makes about 60 pizzelles

Czech Elephant Ear Cookies

Rose Friedrich

Dough

1 package active dry yeast

¼ cup warm water

3 cups all-purpose flour

1½ tablespoons sugar

½ teaspoon salt

1 cup (2 sticks) butter

¼ cup scalded milk, cooled

1 large egg yolk

Middle Layer

2 tablespoons butter, melted

2 cups sugar

1 tablespoon or more ground cinnamon

Topping

¼ cup (½ stick) butter, melted
½ cup chopped pecans or walnuts

In a small bowl or glass measuring cup, dissolve the dry yeast in the warm water and let stand 5 minutes. In a large bowl, combine the flour, sugar, and salt. Cut in the butter as for a pie crust. Combine the cooled scalded milk, egg yolk, and yeast mixture. Add to the flour mixture and mix well. Chill the dough for 2 hours.

Preheat the oven to 400°F/200°C.

Turn out the chilled dough onto a floured surface and knead 1 to 2 minutes. Cover with a clean towel and let rest 10 minutes. Roll out the dough into an 18 × 10-inch rectangle on a lightly floured surface. Brush with the 2 tablespoons of melted butter. Combine the sugar and cinnamon. Sprinkle 1 cup of the cinnamon-sugar mixture over the dough, then roll it up jelly-roll style. Starting on the long side, pinch the long edge down. Cut the roll into 18 crosswise slices.

Sprinkle some of the remaining cinnamon-sugar mixture lightly on a sheet of wax paper. Roll each slice to a thickness of ⅛ inch, turning once. Carefully transfer the slices to un-greased baking sheets. Spread each cookie slice with the remaining cinnamon-sugar and some of the melted butter. Sprinkle the chopped nuts on top.

Bake the cookies for 10 minutes until lightly browned. Transfer to wire racks to cool.

Makes 1½ dozen cookies

Italian Anisette Cookies

Angel Vick, Jacksonville, Florida

My mother made these cookies every year during the holidays and I always looked forward to them. Now I make these and sometimes substitute lemon extract for the anise flavoring, and they are just as good.

Cookies

    1 cup (2 sticks) butter, softened
    1 cup sugar
    2 large eggs, beaten
    2 tablespoons vanilla extract
    4 cups all-purpose flour
    2 tablespoons baking powder

Icing

    ½ box confectioners' sugar
    1 tablespoon anise extract
    2 tablespoons milk

Preheat the oven to 375°F/190°C. Line the baking sheets with parchment paper.

In a large bowl, cream together the butter and sugar. Add the eggs and vanilla and mix well. Blend in the flour and baking powder and work to form a soft, pliable dough. Using a cookie press, press out in the desired shape, or make 1-inch balls. Place 2 inches apart on prepared baking sheets.

Bake the cookies for 15 to 20 minutes, until lightly brown. Transfer to wire racks to cool.

Meanwhile, make the icing. Blend together the confectioners' sugar and anise, adding the milk slowly to make a soft, smooth icing. Ice cookies when they are cool.

To decorate for the holidays, divide the icing between two bowls and tint with red and green food coloring.

Makes 4½ dozen cookies

Russian Tea Cakes

Calie Kenyon, Santa Barbara, California

I make these every year for our annual cookie exchange Christmas party. I've discussed making something else, but everyone always complains because they look forward so much to these very simple but delicious cookies. I usually triple this recipe because these go so fast.

1 cup (2 sticks) butter, softened
½ cup confectioners' sugar, plus more for rolling
1 teaspoon vanilla extract
2¼ cups all-purpose flour
¼ teaspoon salt
¾ cup finely chopped pecans or walnuts

In a medium bowl, cream together the butter and confectioners' sugar. Stir in the vanilla. In a separate bowl, sift together the flour and salt and mix into the creamed mixture until well combined. Mix in the finely chopped nuts. Chill the dough thoroughly for 12 to 24 hours.

Preheat the oven to 400°F/200°C. Line the baking sheets with parchment paper or use ungreased sheets.

Using a spoon, scoop out portions of the chilled dough and roll it into 1-inch balls. Place the balls closely together on the baking sheets.

Bake the cookies for 10 to 12 minutes until they are set, but not brown. While still hot, roll carefully in confectioners' sugar and transfer to wire racks to cool. When cool, roll again in confectioners' sugar.

Makes about 4 dozen cookies

Lemon Ricotta Cookies

Mary Beth Guba, Scotch Plains, New Jersey

I got the recipe for these cookies from a sweet older Italian lady named Maria. They are one of my family's favorites: soft, lemony, and cake-like—yum!

Dough

1 cup (2 sticks) butter, softened
2 cups sugar
2 large eggs
1 (15-ounce) container ricotta cheese (use part skim, if desired)
1 tablespoon lemon extract
1 teaspoon salt
2 teaspoons baking powder
4 cups all-purpose flour

Icing

2 cups confectioners' sugar
Juice of 1 lemon
1 to 2 tablespoons water or milk

Preheat the oven to 350°F/180°C. Line the baking sheets with parchment paper, or use ungreased sheets.

In a large bowl, mix the butter, sugar, eggs, and ricotta. Then mix in the lemon extract, salt, and baking powder. Slowly add the flour, a cup at a time. If the mixture seems too mushy, add a little more flour. Drop the dough by tablespoonfuls 2 inches apart onto the baking sheets, or roll them into 1½-inch balls, whichever you prefer.

Bake the cookies for approximately 10 minutes; they should be slightly golden.

While the cookies are baking, make the icing. Mix together the confectioners' sugar and lemon juice, adding a little water or milk, if desired, to achieve a spreading consistency. Icing should be glaze-like, not a thick frosting. When the cookies are done, remove them from the oven and transfer to wire racks to cool. When cool, spread the tops with the frosting. I use a pastry brush to do this, which works very well.

Makes about 4 dozen cookies

Mandelbrot

Sheila Lyon, Marysville, Washington

1 cup sugar
3 large eggs
¾ cup melted shortening, cooled but still liquid
¼ teaspoon salt
1 teaspoon anise seeds
3 cups all-purpose flour
1 cup finely chopped walnuts

Preheat the oven to 350°F/180°C. Line the baking sheets with parchment paper.

In the bowl of an electric mixer beat the sugar and eggs on medium speed, until well blended. Beat in the melted, cooled shortening and beat until light and fluffy. Add the salt and anise seeds and beat until well mixed. Add the flour a cup at a time and mix until well blended. Stir in the walnuts. The dough will be very stiff.

Divide the dough in half. With lightly greased hands, shape each half into a 12 × 3-inch loaf. Place the loaves on a lined baking sheet, about 3 inches apart.

Bake the loaves 20 to 25 minutes, until light brown. Remove from the oven and immediately cut each loaf crosswise into ½-inch diagonal slices. Turn each slice on its side. Return the slices to the baking sheets and place back in the oven. Bake for 15 to 20 minutes more, until lightly browned and toasted. Turn at least once during the baking to ensure even browning.

Makes about 4 dozen cookies

Grandma Ida's Mandel Bread

Robin Olson

This is the only cookie my maternal grandmother ever baked, and the recipe had been in her family since the 1800s. Grandma Ida died in 2000, at age ninety-two. I was her only granddaughter and the apple of her eye. When I bite into a piece of Mandel Bread, it is as if Grandma were standing right next to me.

Dough

2¾ cups unbleached flour
2 teaspoons baking powder
¾ cup sugar
3 large eggs
¾ cup (1½ sticks) unsalted butter, melted
2 teaspoons vanilla extract
1 cup crushed nuts (I use pecans—you could use walnuts)
½ cup mini chocolate chips (optional)

Topping

    ½ teaspoon ground cinnamon
    ⅓ cup sugar

Preheat the oven to 350°F/180°C. Line the baking sheets with parchment paper.

In a small bowl, whisk together the flour and baking powder; set aside. In a large bowl, using an electric mixer, beat the sugar and eggs until light and lemon colored, then add the melted butter and keep beating until light and fluffy. Add the vanilla. Gradually add in the flour mixture. Stir in the nuts and optional mini chocolate chips by hand. The dough will be stiff.

Divide the dough into 3 loaves, and place them on a lined baking sheet.

Bake the loaves for 25 minutes, or until light brown. Cool for 5 minutes, then slice thinly into ½-inch pieces (and not a centimeter more!). Meanwhile, mix together the cinnamon and sugar. Sprinkle the slices with the cinnamon-sugar. Return the slices to the baking sheets and place back in the oven. Bake for 15 minutes more. Remove the sheets from the oven, flip each piece over, sprinkle with cinnamon-sugar, and bake another 20 minutes, until golden brown.

Variation: Add ½ cup mini semisweet chocolate chips. (Grandma always put them in, but I make half the batch without the chips and nuts as this cookie can stand on its own.)

Note: My grandmother always made this recipe with vegetable oil. I prefer butter, but both work fine.

   Makes about 4½ dozen cookies

Monte Carlos

Biancamaria Duke, Adelaide, Australia

These were my late grandpa's favorite biscuits, as we call cookies in Australia, and my sister used to make this recipe for him.

Dough

¾ cup (1½ sticks) butter, softened

½ cup firmly packed dark brown sugar

1 large egg

1 teaspoon vanilla extract

2 cups all-purpose flour

1½ teaspoons baking powder

½ teaspoon salt

½ cup desiccated coconut (see Resources, page 329)

Raspberry or other jam

Filling

¼ cup (½ stick) butter, softened

¾ cup confectioners' sugar, sifted

½ teaspoon vanilla extract

2 teaspoons milk

Preheat the oven to 375°F/190°C. Lightly grease the baking sheets.

In a medium bowl, cream together the butter and sugar until light and fluffy. Add the egg and vanilla and beat well. Sift the dry ingredients into another bowl, add the coconut, and mix well. Add the dry ingredients to the creamed mixture and mix until well blended. Roll teaspoonfuls of the dough into balls, shape the balls into ovals, and place on the prepared baking sheets. Rough up the surface of the ovals with the back of a fork.

Bake the cookies for 10 to 15 minutes, or until golden brown. Remove from the oven and cool on wire racks.

Meanwhile, prepare the filling. In a bowl, cream together the butter and sifted confectioners' sugar until light and fluffy. Add the vanilla, then gradually add the milk and beat well.

To assemble the biscuits: Put a teaspoon of jam and a teaspoon of the filling in the center of half of the biscuits. Top with the remaining halves and press together lightly.

Makes about 25 sandwich cookies

Anzac Biscuits I

Anita Jeavons, Carrum Downs, Victoria, Australia

ANZAC stands for the Australian and New Zealand Army Corps, which was established in World War I. The ingredients do not spoil easily, so the biscuits (cookies) kept well for those who were fighting abroad.

1 cup old-fashioned rolled oats
1 cup all-purpose flour
1 cup sugar
¾ cup desiccated coconut (see Resources, page 329)
½ cup (1 stick) butter
2 tablespoons Lyle's Golden Syrup (see box, page 171)
½ teaspoon baking soda
1 tablespoon boiling water

Preheat the oven to 300°F/150°C. Lightly grease the baking sheets.

In a mixing bowl, combine the oats, sifted flour, sugar, and coconut. In a saucepan, combine the butter and golden syrup; stirring over gentle heat until melted. Mix the baking soda with the boiling water, add to the melted butter mixture, then stir into the dry ingredients. Place tablespoonfuls of the mixture 2 inches apart onto the prepared baking sheets, allowing room for spreading.

Bake the biscuits for 20 minutes. Remove from the oven and loosen with a spatula while warm, then cool on the baking sheets. These Anzac biscuits are delicious! The trick is to bake a chewy biscuit by underbaking them ever so slightly.

Makes 3 dozen biscuits

Golden syrup is an amber-colored liquid sweetener that is popular among British, Australian, and Caribbean Creole cooks. (See Resources, page 330.) It's made by evaporating sugarcane juice until it's thick and syrupy. If you're unable to find Lyle's Golden Syrup, make a substitute by combining two parts light corn syrup with one part molasses.

Anzac Biscuits II

Terri Good, Brisbane, Australia

This is my favorite Anzac biscuit recipe—with every good wish!

2 cups all-purpose flour

1 cup sugar

2 cups old-fashioned rolled oats

1½ cups desiccated coconut (see Resources, page 329)

1 cup (2 sticks) butter

3 tablespoons Lyle's Golden Syrup (see Resources, page 330)

3 teaspoons baking soda
4 tablespoons boiling water

Preheat the oven to 325°F/160°C. Lightly grease the packing sheets.

In a medium bowl, mix the flour, sugar, oats, and coconut together. Melt the butter with the golden syrup in the microwave in a good-sized microwave-safe bowl, or in a pan on the stovetop. Dissolve the baking soda in the boiling water, and add to the butter; it will froth up—that is why you need a good-sized container! Add the butter mixture to the dry ingredients and mix to combine. Roll the dough into small (1-inch) balls. Put on the prepared baking sheets, spacing them 2 inches apart; they will spread in the oven.

Bake the biscuits for 7 minutes. Transfer to wire racks to cool.

Makes about 6 dozen biscuits

Caramel Cornflake Cookies

Anita Jeavons, Carrum Downs, Victoria, Australia

¼ cup (½ stick) butter
½ cup lightly packed brown sugar
½ cup castor sugar or superfine sugar (see box, page 173, and Resources, page 329)
½ cup desiccated coconut (see page 329; can substitute sweetened flaked coconut)
3 cups cornflakes
½ cup chopped mixed nuts
1 large egg, lightly beaten

Preheat the oven to 350°F/180°C. Lightly grease the baking sheets.

In a saucepan, combine the butter and sugars. Heat until the butter is melted, and gently stir in the coconut, cornflakes, nuts, and lightly beaten egg. Drop teaspoonfuls of the mixture onto the prepared baking sheets, about 2 inches apart.

Bake the cookies for about 10 minutes, or until golden brown. Let sit a few minutes on the baking sheets before transfering to wire racks to cool completely.

Makes about 30 cookies

Castor sugar is a very fine sugar that is sold in the U.K., Europe, and Australia; it gets its name from the fact that the grains are small enough to fit though a sugar caster. If you can find it, it's sold as superfine sugar in the U.S. Because of its fineness, it dissolves more quickly than regular granulated sugar; however, it's not as fine as 10X confectioners' sugar, which also has cornstarch added. If you can't find any castor or superfine sugar, make your own by grinding regular granulated sugar in a food processor. Let the dust cloud settle for a few moments before removing the lid.

Australian Chocolate Wheaties

Anita Jeavons, Carrum Downs, Victoria, Australia

I fell in love with this cookie when I baked it and just couldn't stay away from them. I think it would make a great lunch-box cookie, plus it has healthy wheat germ in it, which gives it a hearty flavor.—Robin

¾ cup white whole wheat flour (preferably King Arthur brand)
½ cup all-purpose flour
½ teaspoon baking powder

¼ teaspoon salt

⅛ teaspoon baking soda

¼ cup (½ stick) butter

½ cup firmly packed dark brown sugar

1 large egg

¼ cup desiccated coconut (see Resources, page 329)

¼ cup wheat germ

¼ cup bittersweet baking chocolate

Preheat the oven to 350°F/180°C. Lightly grease the baking sheets, or line with parchment paper.

In a medium bowl, sift together the wheat and white flours, along with the baking powder, salt, and baking soda; set aside. In a separate bowl, cream together the butter and sugar until light and fluffy. Add the egg and beat well. Stir in the coconut and wheat germ, then fold in the dry ingredients. Roll the dough into 1-inch balls and place them 2 inches apart on the prepared baking sheets. Flatten each ball slightly with a fork.

Bake the cookies for 15 to 20 minutes, or until golden brown. Transfer to wire racks to cool. Melt the chocolate in a double boiler or microwave. Dip half of each cooled cookie into the melted chocolate; allow to set on wire racks in the refrigerator.

Makes about 2¼ dozen cookies

Mexican Wedding Cookies

Maria Moreno, Takoma Park, Maryland

1 cup (2 sticks) butter, softened

2 cups confectioners' sugar

2 cups all-purpose flour, divided in half

2 teaspoons vanilla extract

$\frac{1}{8}$ teaspoon salt

1 cup pecan pieces or halves, finely ground

Beat the butter and $\frac{1}{2}$ cup of the confectioners' sugar in a large bowl with an electric mixer at medium speed until light and fluffy. Gradually add 1 cup of the flour, the vanilla extract, and the salt. Beat at low speed until well blended. Stir in the remaining 1 cup flour and the ground nuts. Shape the dough into a ball; wrap in plastic wrap. Refrigerate 1 hour or until firm.

Preheat the oven to 350°F/180°C. Shape the dough into 1-inch balls. Place the balls 1 inch apart on ungreased baking sheets.

Bake 12 to 15 minutes, or until golden brown. Let cookies stand on the baking sheets 2 minutes. Meanwhile, place 1 cup sugar in a 13 × 9-inch glass dish. Transfer hot cookies to the sugar. Roll the cookies in the sugar, coating well. Let the cookies cool in the sugar. Sift the remaining $\frac{1}{2}$ cup confectioners' sugar over the sugar-coated cookies before serving. Store tightly covered or freeze up to 1 month.

Makes about 4 dozen cookies

Spicy Mexican Chocolate Cookies

Robin Olson

Serve these delightfully spicy hot cookies as a garnish to cold and creamy vanilla bean ice cream.

1 cup unbleached or all-purpose flour
$\frac{1}{4}$ cup cornstarch
$\frac{1}{4}$ teaspoon baking soda
$\frac{2}{3}$ cup unsweetened dark cocoa powder (I like Ghirardelli brand)
$\frac{1}{2}$ teaspoon cayenne pepper

1 teaspoon ground cinnamon
¼ teaspoon salt
½ teaspoon ground black pepper
¾ cup (1½ sticks) butter, softened
½ cup firmly packed dark brown sugar
½ cup confectioners' sugar
1 large egg white
1½ teaspoons vanilla extract

In a medium bowl, sift together the flour, cornstarch, baking soda, cocoa powder, cayenne, cinnamon, salt, and pepper; set aside.

In a large bowl, using an electric mixer, cream together the butter, brown sugar, and confectioners' sugar. Add the egg white and vanilla and mix on high speed for 2 minutes until light and fluffy. Turn the mixer speed down to medium-low and gradually add the cocoa-flour mixture and mix until fully blended. The dough will come together and be soft.

Divide the dough in half and roll each half into a 10-inch log 1½ inches in diameter. Wrap each log tightly in wax paper and chill for 2 hours, or until firm.

Preheat the oven to 350°F/180°C. Line the baking sheets with parchment paper.

Using a sharp knife, cut the chilled logs into ¼-inch rounds. Place on the lined baking sheets.

Bake the cookies for 10 minutes, or until the edges are firm. Allow the cookies to cool 30 seconds to 1 minute on the baking sheets, then transfer to wire racks to cool.

Variations: After the dough is chilled, remove the wax paper, and roll the logs in about ½ cup of Demerara sugar. Slice and bake as directed above. A sprinkling of confectioners' sugar is another option after baking. Do this when the cookies are slightly cool.

Makes about 4½ dozen cookies

Palet aux Raisins

Charlene Clark, Charlene Clark Studios, Baltimore, Maryland

I'm not a baker; I'm an artist. Luckily, my husband is a chef who was born in the south of France. He baked the cookies for Robin's cookie exchange party for me! The literal translation of palet *is "quoit," a small iron disc used to play a game.*

¾ cup (1½ sticks) plus 2 tablespoons butter, softened
1 cup plus 1 tablespoon confectioners' sugar
4 large eggs
1 tablespoon rum or rum extract
1⅓ cups unbleached flour
⅔ cup raisins

Preheat the oven to 350°F/180°C. Lightly butter the baking sheets.

In a medium bowl, cream together the butter and 1 cup of the confectioners' sugar. Add the eggs, one at a time, and then add the rum. Slowly add the flour and fold it in with a spatula. Put the mixture into a pastry bag fitted with a medium-size cone tip. Pipe out about a tablespoon's worth per cookie onto the prepared baking sheets. Put about four raisins on the top of each cookie and push them in slightly so they adhere.

Bake the palets for 8 to 12 minutes. Remove from the oven and transfer the cookies to wire racks to cool. Finish with a light sprinkling, 1 tablespoon, of confectioners' sugar to give the cookies some depth and interest.

Makes 4 dozen cookies

Spumoni Slices

Lisa Molampy, Murray, Kentucky

This is my own take on the classic Neapolitan cookie.

½ cup shortening
½ cup (1 stick) butter or margarine, softened
3 cups all-purpose flour, divided in half
1 cup sugar
1 large egg
2 tablespoons milk plus 4 teaspoons
1 teaspoon vanilla extract
½ teaspoon baking soda
¼ teaspoon salt
1 (1-ounce) square semisweet chocolate, melted and cooled
½ cup chopped macadamia nuts
⅓ cup chopped candied red cherries
½ cup chopped pistachio nuts
¼ teaspoon rum flavoring
A few drops green food coloring
Confectioners' sugar icing or melted chocolate for decorating (optional)

In a large bowl, beat together the shortening and butter or margarine about 30 seconds, or until soft and creamy. Add half the flour, and the sugar, egg, 2 tablespoons milk, vanilla, baking soda, and salt. Beat until thoroughly combined, scraping down the sides of the bowl occasionally. Stir in the remaining flour.

Divide the dough into thirds. Mix the melted, cooled chocolate and 2 teaspoons of milk into one portion. Add the macadamia nuts to the chocolate layer. Mix the cherries into the second portion. Mix the pistachios, remaining 2 teaspoons milk, rum flavoring, and enough green food coloring to tint dough into the third portion.

To shape the dough, line the bottom and sides of an 8 × 4 × 2-inch loaf pan with plastic wrap. Press the cherry dough evenly into the lined pan. Top with the chocolate dough, then top with the green dough. Cover and chill for 4 to 24 hours.

Preheat the oven to 375°F/190°C.

Invert the pan and remove the dough. Remove the plastic wrap. Cut the dough into ¼-inch-thick slices; then cut each slice crosswise into three pieces. Place the pieces, 2 inches apart, on ungreased baking sheets. Bake the cookies for 8 to 10 minutes, or until the edges are lightly browned. Transfer to wire racks to cool. Drizzle with confectioners' sugar icing tinted green, or with melted chocolate.

Makes 7 dozen cookies

Neapolitan Cookies

Susan Gebhardt, Bel Air, Maryland

I have had this recipe for years, it's a favorite of mine and a little different from regular cookies.

1 cup (2 sticks) butter, softened
1½ cups sugar
1 large egg
1 teaspoon vanilla extract
2½ cups all-purpose flour
½ teaspoon salt
¾ teaspoon baking powder
½ teaspoon almond extract
5 drops red food coloring
½ cup chopped nuts
1 (1-ounce) square unsweetened chocolate

In a bowl, cream the butter and gradually add the sugar. Beat in the egg and vanilla. Add the dry ingredients to a separate bowl and whisk to combine. Add the dry ingredients to the creamed mixture and beat just until blended.

Line 9 × 5 × 3-inch pan with plastic wrap. Spoon one-third of the dough into a small bowl and add the almond extract and 5 drops of red food coloring. Mix well and spread evenly onto the plastic wrap. Spoon half of the remaining dough into a small bowl and stir in the nuts. Spread over the bottom layer in the pan. Melt the chocolate and mix into the remaining dough to make the third layer. Cover and chill overnight.

Preheat the oven to 350°F/180°C.

Lift the plastic wrap and remove the dough from the pan. Peel off the plastic wrap and cut the dough in half lengthwise. Slice each half crosswise into ⅛-inch slices. Place the slices on ungreased baking sheets, 1 inch apart.

Bake the cookies for 10 to 12 minutes. Do not overbake. Cool on wire racks.

Makes 5 to 6 dozen cookies

Czech Nut Butter Ball Cookies

Rose Friedrich

Orechove Kuli'cky *translates as Walnut Marbles.*

⅔ cup (1 stick plus 2⅔ tablespoons) butter, softened
1 cup ground walnuts, pecans, or almonds
1 cup sifted all-purpose flour
2 tablespoons sugar
1 teaspoon vanilla extract
Confectioners' sugar for coating

Preheat the oven to 350°F/180°C. Lightly butter the baking sheets.

In a bowl, cream the first five ingredients well, using your hands. Pinch off pieces of dough and roll into balls the size of marbles. Place the balls 1 inch apart on the prepared baking sheets.

Bake the cookies for 10 minutes, or until lightly browned. Roll while slightly warm in confectioners' sugar.

Makes 2 dozen cookies

Bohemian Butter Cookies

Rose Friedrich

2 cups (4 sticks) butter, softened
1 cup sugar
4 large eggs (1 egg divided, and the white lightly beaten)
½ teaspoon grated lemon zest
1 teaspoon vanilla extract
4 cups all-purpose flour

Preheat the oven to 350°F/180°C. Line the baking sheets with parchment paper.

In a medium bowl, cream together the butter and sugar until light and fluffy. Add the 3 whole eggs plus 1 egg yolk, lemon zest, and vanilla, mixing continuously. Add the flour, reserving a small amount for rolling the dough. If the dough is too soft to handle, refrigerate it for 1 hour. Do not overwork the dough. Roll out the dough very thinly and make cut-out cookies in your favorite shape or use a simple round cookie cutter. Place the cut-outs 2 inches apart on the lined baking sheets. Just before baking, brush each cookie with the beaten egg white and sprinkle with finely chopped nuts or sugar mixed with cinnamon, and for the holidays top with a piece of red or green candied cherry. Bake the cookies for 8 to 9 minutes. Transfer to wire racks to cool.

Variations: Make a vanilla, chocolate, or lemon glaze. To make a glaze: combine 1 cup confectioners' sugar and 1 tablespoon desired flavoring. Add boiling water drop by drop, mixing until smooth and of a spreading consistency.

Makes 8 dozen cookies

Orechove Dorticky: Czech Walnut Tarts

Tatjana Pavlovicova Andrew, San Diego, California

Dough

    1 cup (2 sticks) unsalted butter, softened
    ⅔ cup sugar
    1 teaspoon grated lemon zest
    1 tablespoon vanilla extract
    4 large egg yolks
    ½ cup ground walnuts
    2¼ cups all-purpose flour
    1 tablespoon unsweetened cocoa powder (if you like things really chocolatey)
       (optional)

Filling

    ¼ cup sugar
    1 tablespoon unsweetened cocoa powder
    1 teaspoon vanilla extract
    2 large egg yolks
    ½ cup (1 stick) unsalted butter, softened

Topping

    1 (4-ounce) bar Ghirardelli dark chocolate for baking

    1 cup walnut halves

In a large bowl, mix together the butter, sugar, lemon zest, vanilla, egg yolks, and ground walnuts. Slowly mix in 1¾ cups of the flour and the cocoa powder, if using. Work the mixture into a dough. Chill at least 2 hours or overnight.

Remove the dough from the refrigerator and let it come to room temperature, about 1 hour.

Preheat the oven to 325°F/160°C.

Use the remaining flour to coat the surface you will roll out the dough on. Roll out the dough until it is ¼ inch thick. As you work, coat the rolling pin with flour, and keep sprinkling your work surface with a little bit of flour to prevent sticking. Use your favorite cookie cutters to cut out various shapes of cookies; keep in mind that the final product is going to be quite filling so the smaller the cookie, the better.

Place the cut-out cookies 1 inch apart on ungreased baking sheets.

Bake the cookies for 10 to 12 minutes. Let cool on a plate or on a baking sheet lined with parchment paper.

Meanwhile, make the cookie filling. In a medium bowl, whisk together the sugar, cocoa powder, vanilla, and egg yolks. Add the softened butter, and whisk everything together until the mixture appears smooth and creamy.

Spread the cream on the bottom side of a cookie and cover it with another cookie, placing it bottom side down, to make a cookie sandwich. The cream layer should be thick, about ¼ inch. If possible, use a pastry bag to layer the filling so that the sides of the cookie sandwiches don't get messy.

Melt the chocolate bar according to the directions on the package. Dip one side of each cookie sandwich into the chocolate. Top each cookie with a walnut half.

Makes about 2½ dozen tarts

Ausukai: Lithuanian "Little Ears"

Wendy-Ann Antanaitis, Mission Viejo, California

I'm a second-generation Lithuanian gal, and Ausukai was a given at every family gathering. Because I love to bake, I decided in 1984, when I was twenty-two, that I would make Ausukai for the first time for Christmas, as my grandmothers had before me. So I asked my mom, who had only made them as a young girl, if she knew how. She couldn't remember, but she mentioned that my eldest brother's wife knew, since she decided to learn how to make all the Lithuanian goodies once she married into our family. I got the recipe from her, and over the years I made it my own, using hints from others who baked Ausukai. Now it's a tradition every Christmas, when I make them for my family, friends, and neighbors. I don't have any children, but I hope one day to pass on the recipe to my nieces, who call them Teta's (Aunt's) Cookies.

6 large eggs
Pinch of salt
1 cup (2 sticks) butter
1 cup sugar
1 teaspoon vanilla extract
1 jigger of rum (optional but suggested)
2 cups flour, approximately (more as needed)
2 teaspoons baking powder
2 tablespoons milk
½ cup whipping cream
Vegetable oil for frying
Confectioners' sugar for sprinkling

In a large bowl, beat the eggs. Add the salt. Melt the butter and add it to the egg batter. Add the sugar and vanilla and beat until combined. Add the rum.

In a separate bowl, sift the flour with the baking powder, then slowly fold the flour mixture into the egg-sugar mixture, alternating with the milk and cream.

Chocolate Caramel Treasures, page 104

Peanut Butter Christmas Mice, page 109

Peruvian Alfajores, page 156

Russian Torte, page 150

Neapolitan Cookies, page 179

Egyptian Asbusa, page 186

Lemon Bars, page 212

Cherry Coconut Bars, page 213

Rocky Road Bars, page 218

Coconut Key Lime Bars, page 223

Irish Chocolate Mint Squares, page 231

Tiger Nut Sweets, page 252

Bird's Nests (Easter version made with white chocolate), page 235

Keep adding flour until the dough is no longer sticky, and is firm enough to handle. Turn the dough out onto a well-floured board. Be sure to flour your hands and continue to keep your hands floured as you work with the dough. When the dough is floured just enough to be of a good consistency, take a small portion and roll it out thin—as thin as possible (but not paper-thin).

Cut the dough into small diamonds. Cut a small slit, about ½ inch, in the middle of each diamond shape and pull an end through the slit and back out the other end. Or just use your favorite cookie cutter.

Pour oil into a large pot to a depth of 4 to 6 inches. Heat the oil. (It is ready when a small piece of dough dropped into it browns quickly. The oil is hot enough when a test cookie sizzles and rises to the top.)

Fry the cookies in the hot vegetable oil until golden crisp, flipping each over. The cookies should fry near the top of the oil.

Drain the Ausukai on paper towels or paper bags—paper bags work best.

Place the cookies on wax paper and sift confectioners' sugar liberally over the tops. These are best eaten within a few hours since they are fried. If storing, line a cookie tin with wax paper, and add the cookies but only loosely cover the tin, or the cookies will become soggy.

Makes dozens, depending on size

Egyptian Asbusa

Robin Olson

Asbusa, also called basbousa, is a very old Egyptian sweet cake (bar cookie!) that has been found recorded on ancient pottery shards, called ostraca, *dating back to antiquity. It's still commonly enjoyed today in Egypt with afternoon tea and usually soaked with a light lemon sugar syrup; however, I enjoy it plain, since I really like cream of wheat. In the last year I've made this recipe every way possible. I've tried low-fat plain yogurt and vanilla yogurt as well as Greek yogurt. Variations I've added are raisins, dates, coconut, almonds, and the lemon syrup. I've also made different heights using large or small baking pans (9 × 9 or 9 × 13), yielding either a 2-inch-high bar or a 1-inch bar. It's a really good adaptable recipe that's impossible to screw up. I enjoy eating this bar for breakfast with my morning coffee. If you decide to add the syrup, it becomes less barlike and more cakelike, a dessert to eat with a spoon. A suggestion would be to send the kids to school with Asbusa to nibble on while riding the bus. My dog, Bear, got into a batch that was cooling on the counter and broke my fifteen-year-old, well-seasoned stoneware baking pan, and he ate every last crumb. Bad dog!*

Dough

1¼ cups sugar

2 cups Cream of Wheat cereal

¾ cup (1½ sticks) butter, softened

1 cup plain or Greek-style yogurt, at room temperature

Water, if necessary

Almonds, whole, halved, or sliced, for decoration

Lemon Sugar Syrup (Optional)

1½ cups water

2 cups sugar

½ to 1 teaspoon lemon juice (depending on your taste)

Preheat the oven to 375°F/190°C.

In a large bowl, using an electric mixer, combine the sugar and Cream of Wheat. Add the butter and beat for 2 minutes. Add the yogurt and mix for 3 to 5 minutes, until velvety smooth.

Alternatively, use the old-school method and mix by hand, rubbing the butter, sugar, and Cream of Wheat between the palms of your hands for 10 minutes, or until the mixture is very well blended. Add the yogurt and mix with your hands until the dough feels smooth. If it feels dry, add a little water until it becomes cohesive and holds together like a thick batter.

To make a 2½-inch-high bar, butter an 8 × 8-inch baking pan. To make a 1-inch-high bar, butter a 13 × 9-inch pan. Add the batter. Put one almond half onto the surface of each piece, or sprinkle sliced almonds over the top, covering the batter.

For either pan size, bake for 30 to 40 minutes, or until golden brown.

Cool the bars thoroughly, then slice into 2-inch squares if using a 13 × 9-inch pan, or smaller squares if using an 8 × 8-inch pan. If desired, drizzle with lemon sugar syrup. To make the syrup: Boil the water and sugar, stirring constantly until sugar dissolves, about 2 minutes. Let it continue to boil until it becomes clear and syrup-like. Cool slightly, add the lemon juice, and pour on the Asbusa.

Makes about 2 dozen pieces

Ghorayebah: Arabic Cardamom Shortbread Cookies

Aparna Balasubramanian, Panaji, Goa, India

Ghorayebah, also sometimes known as the "Queen's Bracelets," are fragile shortbread-like cardamom cookies with a rich buttery texture and taste. They derive their rather quaint name from their shape. Each cookie is shaped from a strand of dough. The two ends are joined together, and a blanched almond is pressed in at this joint. Thus, the finished cookie looks like a bracelet with an almond "gem." These cookies are sometimes served during Purim and thought to represent Queen Esther's bracelets. Ghorayebah are made throughout the Middle East and there are many variations of the recipe. Some recipes use orange-flower water or rosewater, while some use pistachios instead of almonds. Some recipes call for almond extract and even suggest that cardamom is optional. While I have no idea which of these is most authentic, I make these delicious cookies using the following recipe. I also shape them into flat rounds rather than "bracelets."

½ cup ghee (clarified butter; see box, page 189)
½ cup confectioners' sugar
¾ teaspoon ground cardamom
⅛ teaspoon salt
¼ teaspoon baking soda
¾ cup plus 1½ tablespoons all-purpose flour
15 blanched, halved almonds

Heat the ghee in a small saucepan. Add the sugar and keep mixing until the sugar dissolves. Remove from heat. When it has cooled, add the cardamom, salt, baking soda, and flour and knead everything gently to a soft, non-sticky dough. If the dough is sticky, add a little more flour. The dough may seem a bit crumbly, but this is all right as long as it holds its shape.

Preheat the oven to 350°F/180°C. Lightly grease the baking sheets.

Shape the dough into walnut-size balls, flatten gently, and press an almond half in the center of each cookie. Place the cookies on the prepared baking sheets.

Bake the cookies for about 20 minutes. The cookies are done when they have lost their whitish color and are just becoming faintly golden. It is very important that the cookies do not brown or they will overbake on the inside and become hard. Cool on wire racks.

Makes about 15 cookies, approximately 2 inches in diameter

Ghee: A Clarified Butter with a Nutty Aroma

The ghee in these cookies gives them their characteristic aroma and flavor, which would be missing if just plain butter were used. In keeping with the spirit of these cookies, please try to use ghee. In India, many of us still make homemade butter and homemade ghee and it really has the best flavor. Ghee is usually available in Indian stores in the U.S. but might be a bit expensive. It is quite easy to make at home. You will just need to watch the pan to ensure the ghee does not burn, and it should not take more than 20 to 30 minutes to do this. If your butter has a high percentage of water, it will take a little longer as the water has to evaporate. I notice many Western recipes these days using clarified or browned butter, including recipes for spaghetti, ice cream, cakes, and frosting.

Homemade Ghee

4 sticks good-quality unsalted butter

Using a heavy-bottomed wok, saucepan, or double boiler, melt the butter over medium heat, stirring frequently. Once the butter has melted, lower the heat and allow the butter to cook further; a froth will form on the top.

(continued)

Keep stirring occasionally, until the yellow butter turns clear and golden in color. The froth should have disappeared and given way to some bubbles on the surface. The color will start deepening and the butter will give off a nutty aroma. The milk solids that have settled at the bottom of the pan will also start browning. At this point, remove the pan from the heat; do not allow the milk solids to blacken and burn. Allow the ghee to cool a bit. Then slowly decant the liquid, or strain it through a fine-mesh or cheesecloth-lined strainer into a clean glass jar. Once the ghee has cooled to room temperature, it will solidify to a pale yellow color. Seal the jar. Ghee keeps at room temperature for several months. Always a use a fresh, dry spoon to remove ghee from the jar.

To liquefy the ghee, place the jar in a small pan of hot, not boiling, water for 5 to 10 minutes.

This recipe makes a small jar of ghee, about 1¼ cups. You can use larger amounts of butter to make more ghee if you wish, as ghee has a long shelf life. You do not need to refrigerate ghee.

Madeleines

Rose Friedrich

A French creation, this buttery, spongy, lemon-flavored, cake-like cookie is made in traditional shell-shaped molds. There are two conflicting histories of the Madeleine. It was invented either by Madeleine Paulmier, a nineteenth-century pastry cook, or by Madeleine Paulmier who was a cook in the eighteenth century for Stanisław Leszczyński, whose son-in-law, Louis XV of France, named them for her. Either way, we've all been able to enjoy these special, shell-shaped little cookies for hundreds of years! Vive la France!

2 large eggs
¼ teaspoon salt
⅓ cup granulated sugar

1 teaspoon grated lemon zest

¼ teaspoon lemon extract

½ cup all-purpose flour

¼ cup (½ stick) butter, melted and cooled

In a medium bowl, using an electric mixer, beat the eggs with the salt until frothy. Gradually add the sugar. Beat the mixture on high speed until thick and lemon colored; don't be impatient with this step, beat for 12 to 15 minutes. Fold in the grated lemon zest and lemon extract. Sift the flour into the egg mixture and gently fold until incorporated. Add the melted and cooled butter, a tablespoon or two at a time, and quickly fold it into the mixture. Prepare a madeleine pan, thoroughly greasing and flouring each shell in the pan.

Preheat the oven to 400°F/200°C.

Fill the shells of the prepared pan about three-quarters full with the batter. Bake for 8 to 10 minutes, or until golden brown. Remove the Madeleines from the pan and cool on wire racks. Serve plain, dusted with sifted confectioners' sugar, or glaze with your favorite chocolate glaze.

Makes 12 Madeleines, each about 3¾ × 2 inches

Cinnamon–Hazelnut Biscotti

Donna Dlubac, Gaithersburg, Maryland

¾ cup (1½ sticks) butter, softened

1 cup sugar

2 large eggs

1½ teaspoons vanilla extract

2½ cups all-purpose flour

1 teaspoon ground cinnamon

¾ teaspoon baking powder
½ teaspoon salt
1 cup chopped hazelnuts

Preheat the oven to 350°F/180°C. Grease the baking sheets, or line with parchment paper.

In a medium bowl, cream together the butter and sugar until light and fluffy. Beat in the eggs and vanilla. In a separate bowl, sift together the flour, cinnamon, baking powder, and salt and mix it into the egg mixture. Stir in the hazelnuts. Shape the dough into two equal logs approximately 12 inches long. Place the logs on the prepared baking sheets and flatten them out to a thickness of about ½ inch.

Bake the logs for about 30 minutes, or until the edges are golden and the center is firm. Remove from the oven and cool on the baking sheets. When the logs are cool enough to handle, using a serrated knife, slice the loaves on a slight diagonal into ½-inch-thick slices. Return the slices to the baking sheets.

Bake for an additional 10 minutes, turning them over once. Cool the biscotti completely, and store in an airtight container at room temperature.

Makes about 3 dozen

Almond-Chocolate Biscotti

Mamie Godfrey Bartlett, Rochester, New York

Everyone loves my Almond-Chocolate Biscotti, and it is hard to stop eating them once you start. I find these to be much less dense than other biscotti I have eaten; these are light and crispy. An Italian friend from Argentina gave me the base recipe. She always used a fruit and nut combination, but people seem to prefer the almond and chocolate version best.

2½ cups all-purpose flour
1 teaspoon baking soda
1 teaspoon baking powder
1 cup slivered almonds
½ cup (1 stick) unsalted butter, softened
1 cup granulated sugar
2 extra-large or jumbo eggs
1 teaspoon vanilla extract
2 ounces milk chocolate or semisweet chocolate, for drizzling or dipping

Preheat the oven to 350°F/180°C. Lightly grease two noninsulated baking sheets.

In a large bowl, combine the flour, baking soda, baking powder, and almonds; set aside. It is important to add the nuts to the flour mixture. The flour coats the almonds and prevents them from sinking to the bottom during baking.

In a separate bowl, using an electric mixer, mix together the butter and sugar and beat on high speed until pale and creamy, 3 to 5 minutes. Add the eggs one at a time; then add the vanilla. Add the dry ingredients to the creamed mixture in three parts; mix thoroughly but try not to overmix. If the mixture seems too dry, add a teaspoonful of water. The dough should be dense, on the dry side, and not too sticky. Separate the dough into two equal portions.

Form each portion into a log 8 to 9 inches long and 3 to 4 inches wide, with a uniform thickness. It does *not* have to be perfect but if the edges are too thin or irregular, they will crack and break off. Place the logs on the prepared baking sheets.

Bake the logs for 20 to 22 minutes, or until light golden brown; do not overbake. Remove from oven and let rest on a rack on the countertop for 2 minutes, then, using a spatula, transfer each log to a cutting board. Let cool 5 minutes.

Using a serrated knife (it is absolutely essential that the knife is serrated) slice the logs into ½-inch pieces, using a sawing motion; this will reduce breakage. (Any broken pieces are for the cook!) Return the slices to the same baking sheets and place on their sides. Return to the oven and bake 5 to 7 minutes, or until golden. Remove from the oven and turn them over. Bake an additional 4 to 6 minutes, or until done. These will go from perfect to burnt very quickly so watch them carefully toward the end of each baking time. Transfer to a cutting board or tea towels and cool for 10 minutes.

Melt the chocolate in a double boiler or microwave. Place the cookies on racks and drizzle or dip one side of each cooled biscotti with melted chocolate. Allow the chocolate to set. Store in an airtight container for up to 1 week—if they last that long!

Variations: You can substitute any nut for the almonds. You can add dried cranberries or other dried fruit, or a combination of fruit and nuts. Keep the additions to about 1 cup total, and be sure the additions go into the dry ingredients. For the holidays use pistachios and dried cherries for a festive look. If you don't care for nuts or dried fruit you could just make a mildly flavored biscotti, adding the zest of an orange or lemon (about 1 teaspoon) to the dry ingredients and 2 teaspoons of the juice to the wet ingredients.

Makes about 3 dozen biscotti

Irish Lace Cookies

Leslie Jackson Kelly, Laurel, Maryland

This is a simple recipe that gives great results. These cookies are thin, light, crunchy, and delish!

½ cup (1 stick) unsalted butter, softened
1 cup firmly packed brown sugar
1 tablespoon vanilla extract
4 tablespoons all-purpose flour
2 tablespoons milk
1 cup old-fashioned rolled oats

Preheat the oven to 350°F/180°C. Line the baking sheets with parchment paper.

In a large bowl, using an electric mixer, cream together the butter, sugar, and vanilla. Add the flour, milk, and rolled oats and stir to combine. Drop the batter by tablespoonfuls onto the lined baking sheets about 3 inches apart to allow room for the cookies to spread.

Bake the cookies for 9 to 11 minutes, or until flat and golden. Let the cookies cool on the baking sheets for 1 to 2 minutes, or until firm enough to be moved with a metal spatula.

Using a spatula, lift the edges of the cookies, then roll into cylinders or horn-shapes while still on the warm baking sheets. If the cookies become too hard to roll, return them to the oven for about 10 to 15 seconds to soften. After rolling, transfer the cookies to wire racks and let them cool completely. If you wish to omit the rolling part, just use less batter and make a flat 2-inch cookie.

Variations: Dip the ends in melted white chocolate, or add the filling of your choice to the rolled cylinders or horns.

Makes 2 dozen rolled cookies

Yorkshire Parkin Pigs

Kathryn Hey, West Yorkshire, England

The Parkin Pig biscuit is the northern English version of gingerbread and is a taste of English history. Parkin Pigs are traditionally eaten on Guy Fawkes Night, or Bonfire Night, although they can be eaten year-round. Guy Fawkes Night is celebrated annually on the evening of November 5 to commemorate the foiling of the Gunpowder Plot, which took place on November 5, 1605. In London, Catholic conspirators, including Guy Fawkes, were alleged to be attempting to blow up the Houses of Parliament. The name derives from the wooden parkin boxes (a type of old box) that the cakes were originally stored in.

⅓ cup plus 1 teaspoon butter (lard is traditional)
1 tablespoon Lyle's Golden Syrup or substitute light molasses (see Resources, page 330)
2½ cups all-purpose flour
1¼ cups sugar
¼ teaspoon salt
1 teaspoon ground ginger
½ teaspoon ground cinnamon
1 teaspoon baking soda, scalded with 2 tablespoons boiling water
Water (or milk) by the teaspoonful if needed to make dough come together

Preheat the oven to 350°F/180°C. Line the baking sheets with parchment paper.

Melt the butter with the golden syrup (or molasses) and allow to cool.

In a large bowl, stir together the flour, sugar, salt, ginger, and cinnamon. Pour the melted butter and syrup into the flour mixture. In a measuring cup mix the baking soda and boiling water, then pour it into the flour mixture.

Traditional Parkin can be made according to a cake recipe or a biscuit (cookie) recipe, and both the cake and the biscuit pigs are made with some oatmeal (oat flour) added. This is what makes Parkin special and different from plain old gingerbread. Additionally, what Americans call oatmeal, we call porridge. If you want to create a completely authentic version of Parkin, grind some rolled oats in your food processor until you get a flour-like consistency and substitute the ground oat flour for a quarter to a half of the all-purpose flour. Adjust the liquids as necessary to form a dough.

On a floured surface, roll the dough out to a thickness of ¼ inch and then cut into shapes—preferably pigs. Transfer the cookies to the lined baking sheets.

Bake the cookies for 12 to 14 minutes, or until golden brown. Transfer to wire racks, and cool thoroughly. Decorate with raisins, nuts, or icing, if desired.

Makes about 3½ dozen biscuits

Nussecken: German Nut Triangles

Kerstien Matondang, Gothenburg, Sweden

I was raised in Hamburg, Germany and grew up with Nussecken. This popular cookie has a shortbread base and a moist, nutty topping and is found in most German bakeries. They are triangle-shaped nut bars, with the corners, and often the sides, dipped in dark chocolate. Guten Appetit!

Dough

1¾ cups all-purpose flour
2 heaping teaspoons baking powder
1 cup (2 sticks) butter, softened
¾ cup sugar

1 large egg
1½ teaspoons vanilla extract
1 teaspoon rum extract
½ cup apricot jam

Topping

⅔ cup butter
1 cup sugar
1½ teaspoons vanilla extract
1 cup ground hazelnuts
1 cup ground almonds
½ cup dark chocolate, melted, for dipping corners

Preheat the oven to 350°F/180°C. Line a 13 × 9 × 2-inch baking pan with parchment paper.

In a small bowl, mix together the flour and baking powder; set aside. In a large bowl, cream together the butter and sugar. Add the egg and vanilla and rum extracts and continue to beat. Add the flour mixture to the creamed mixture and blend well. The dough will become firm and form a ball.

Using your fingers, flatten the dough, and spread it into the prepared baking pan. Spread the jam over the dough in a thin layer.

To make the topping, melt the butter in a medium saucepan, add the sugar and vanilla, and stir until dissolved. Take off the heat and stir in the ground nuts. Pour the nut mixture over the dough and jam and spread it out until it covers the whole panful and has an even thickness.

Bake for 30 minutes, or until the topping is set.

Remove from the oven and cool for 10 minutes.

While the cake is still warm, using a sharp knife, cut it into 2-inch- or 3-inch-long triangles, by first cutting it into squares and then cutting the squares diagonally. When completely cool, dip the corners (and side edges, if you wish) of each triangle into the melted chocolate. Place on wire racks to cool until set.

Makes about 16 3-inch-long triangles, or 2 dozen 2-inch-long triangles

Swedish Coconut Cookies

Sylvia Olson

A buttery, shortbread-like cookie that melts in your mouth!

3½ cups all-purpose flour
1 teaspoon baking soda
1 teaspoon baking powder
½ teaspoon salt
2 cups (4 sticks) butter, softened (or 1 cup [2 sticks] butter and 1 cup lard)
2 cups sugar
1 teaspoon vanilla extract
1 cup sweetened flaked coconut

In a large bowl, using an electric mixer, beat all the ingredients together, except for the coconut, for 3 to 5 minutes; the dough will be crumbly like shortbread or pie crust. If the dough is too dry to work with, add a little milk, a teaspoon at a time. Stir in the coconut last.

Make three 8 × 2-inch rolls, wrap in wax paper, and chill for 2 hours.

When ready to bake the cookies, preheat the oven to 350°F/180°C. Line the baking sheets with parchment paper. Cut the chilled rolls into ¼-inch-thick slices and place the cookies on the lined baking sheets.

Bake the cookies for 8 to 12 minutes, or until the edges are golden brown. Cool on the baking sheets for a few minutes, then transfer to wire racks to cool completely.

Makes about 8 dozen cookies

Greek Kourambiedes

Toni Ann Ebert, Gaithersburg, Maryland

This is a traditional Greek almond shortbread cookie.

2 cups (4 sticks) unsalted butter
½ cup confectioners' sugar, plus more for sprinkling
1 large egg yolk
1 teaspoon vanilla extract
1 teaspoon almond extract
2 tablespoons ouzo (anise-flavored spirit, like Sambuca) or ½ teaspoon anise extract
2 cups all-purpose flour
1 teaspoon baking powder
¾ cup almonds, toasted

Preheat the oven to 350°F/180°C.

In a large bowl, cream the butter until light and fluffy. Add the ½ cup confectioners' sugar and beat well. Add the egg yolk, extracts, and ouzo. Sift together the flour and baking powder and blend into the butter mixture. Stir in the toasted almonds. Shape the dough into small crescent shapes. Place the cookies on ungreased baking sheets.

Bake the cookies for 15 to 20 minutes. Place the hot cookies on a sheet of wax paper sprinkled with confectioners' sugar, then sift additional confectioners' sugar over the tops of the hot cookies.

Makes about 4½ dozen cookies

YiaYia's Koulourakia: Greek Twists

Stella Lintzeris, Ocean City, Maryland

Koulourakia is a slightly sweet Greek cookie with a texture like shortbread. This recipe was lovingly transcribed via a telephone conversation between twenty-two-year-old Zoe and her ninety-one-year-old YiaYia, Stella. *YiaYia*, the Greek word for grandmother, is pronounced "yah YAH." (I love how recipes link the generations together. Stella does not top her Koulourakia with sesame seeds, however; I added that because it's quite common to do so.)—Robin

Dough

4½ cups all-purpose flour, plus more as needed
¼ teaspoon baking soda
4½ teaspoons baking powder
1 cup (2 sticks) butter
1 cup shortening
1½ teaspoons vanilla extract
3 large eggs
3 cups sugar
½ cup orange juice

Topping

Egg wash made with 1 egg beaten with a little milk or cream
Sesame seeds (optional)

Preheat the oven to 350°F/180°C. Line the baking sheets with parchment paper.

In a bowl, sift together the flour, baking soda, and baking powder; set aside. Melt the butter and shortening together in a saucepan or in the microwave.

In a large mixing bowl, combine the melted fat and vanilla. Let cool for a bit. Beat in the eggs. Slowly add the sugar and orange juice and beat well until "real nice and frothy."

Make sure the sugar is melted and incorporated into the mixture. Slowly add the flour mixture and blend together to form a dough.

To test the proper consistency of the dough, scoop out a little piece of dough, roll it out to resemble a long cord, and twist it. If the twist retains its shape and does not flatten, you have used enough flour. If you don't use enough flour, the Koulourakias won't retain their shape; if you use too much flour, the cookies will be hard. Start with 4½ cups and add more flour as needed.

To shape the cookies, make some into a tight *S* shape, and/or others into small braids by rolling them out like a pencil into 6-inch-long-strips, then bending each at the center so that both ends are the same length, and twisting the ends together. Brush the cookies with the egg wash and sprinkle with sesame seeds, if desired. Place the cookies on the lined baking sheets.

Bake the cookies for approximately 15 minutes, or until golden brown. Transfer to wire racks and cool thoroughly before storing.

Makes 125 to 150 cookies. The smaller you make the cookies, depending on your preference, the more cookies you'll get!

Bars, Tartlets, and Turtles

Butter Pecan Turtle Bars

Suzie Troia, Hilton Head, South Carolina

Crust

2 cups all-purpose flour
1 cup firmly packed dark brown sugar
½ cup (1 stick) butter, softened
1 cup whole pecan halves

Caramel Layer

1 cup firmly packed light or dark brown sugar
1⅓ cups (2 sticks plus 5 tablespoons) butter
1⅓ cups milk chocolate chips

Preheat the oven to 350°F/180°C. Line a 13 × 9 × 2-inch baking pan with parchment paper.

In a 3-quart bowl, using an electric mixer, combine the first three ingredients for the crust. Mix on medium speed for 2 to 3 minutes, or until well mixed and the particles are fine. Pat the dough firmly into the lined baking pan. Sprinkle the pecans evenly over the unbaked crust.

To make the caramel layer, combine the brown sugar and butter in a 1-quart saucepan. Cook over medium heat, stirring constantly, until the entire surface bubbles. Boil 30 seconds to 1 minute, stirring constantly. Pour the caramel evenly over the pecans and crust.

Place the pan in the center of the oven on the middle rack. Bake for 18 to 22 minutes. Remove from the oven and immediately sprinkle with the chocolate chips. Allow the chips to melt for 2 to 3 minutes. Gently swirl the chips with the bottom of a spoon or with a knife as they melt. Cool completely. Cut into bars.

Makes about 3 dozen 1½ × 1½-inch bars

Mudsling Bars

Debra Tate, Riverside, California

Bars

　4 large eggs
　2 cups sugar
　1 cup (2 sticks) butter, melted
　1½ cups all-purpose flour
　⅓ cup unsweetened cocoa powder
　1 teaspoon vanilla extract
　1 cup sweetened flaked coconut
　½ cup chopped nuts

Topping

　1 cup marshmallow cream

Frosting

　½ cup (1 stick) butter
　6 tablespoons milk
　½ cup unsweetened cocoa powder

1-pound box confectioners' sugar
1 teaspoon vanilla extract
½ cup chopped nuts

Preheat the oven to 350°F/180°C. Grease and flour a 13 × 9 × 2-inch baking pan.

In a large bowl, combine the eggs and sugar and beat until thick. Add the melted butter, flour, cocoa powder, vanilla, coconut, and nuts. Pour into the prepared baking pan.

Bake the bars 30 minutes. As soon as you take the bars out of the oven, spread the marshmallow cream over the top, let cool, and then frost.

To make the frosting, beat the first five ingredients together well in a bowl. Stir in the nuts, by hand, last. Drizzle the frosting on the bars.

Makes 2½ dozen bars

Fudge Sweetarts

Susan DeBay, East Granby, Connecticut

This recipe is from the 1960s and was given to my mother by a neighbor. My mom made Fudge Sweetarts when I was a kid, and now I try to make them every year, but only at Christmas time!

Dough
1 cup sifted all-purpose flour
¼ teaspoon baking powder
¼ teaspoon salt
⅓ cup (5⅓ tablespoons) butter
2 large eggs, beaten

Filling

    1 cup semisweet chocolate chips, melted
    ⅓ cup sugar
    1 tablespoon milk
    1 tablespoon butter
    1 teaspoon pure vanilla extract
    1 large egg, beaten
    Pecan or walnut halves (optional)

In a medium bowl, sift together the flour, baking powder, and salt.

Cut in the butter until the mixture resembles fine crumbs. Sprinkle 3 to 4 tablespoons of the beaten eggs over the flour mixture, stirring with a fork to form a dough.

Roll out the dough on a floured surface to a thickness of ⅛ inch. Cut into 3-inch rounds. Fit the rounds into ungreased mini muffin pans. You do not need to use muffin papers.

Preheat the oven to 350°F/180°C.

Mix together the ingredients for the filling, except for the nuts. Place a scant teaspoonful of filling into each dough cup. Top with half a pecan or walnut if desired. Bake for 20 minutes, or until done.

Note: I've used premade pie shells instead of making the crust. You lose a little in flavor but it's sometimes worth the convenience. I have a wooden tamper tool that is ideal for getting the dough to fit into the pan.

The original recipe states that a double batch yields 56, but it can vary

Raspberry-Walnut Shortbread Bars

Debby Griffith, Gaithersburg, Maryland

Shortbread Base

1¼ cups all-purpose flour
½ cup sugar
½ cup (1 stick) butter, softened
½ cup raspberry jam

Topping

½ cup firmly packed dark brown sugar
2 large eggs
1 teaspoon vanilla extract
2 tablespoons all-purpose flour
⅛ teaspoon salt
⅛ teaspoon baking soda
1 cup chopped walnuts

Preheat the oven to 350°F/180°C. Lightly grease a 9 × 9-inch baking pan.

Mix together the ingredients for the shortbread base, except for the raspberry jam. Press into the bottom of the prepared pan. Bake for 20 minutes, until the edges are a light golden brown. Remove from the oven, and spread with the raspberry jam.

Make the topping: In a small bowl, combine brown sugar, eggs, and vanilla. Beat until well mixed. Add the flour, salt, baking soda, and walnuts, and beat again until well combined. Spread over the jam layer. Return to the oven and bake for 20 to 25 minutes. Cool and cut into 2-inch bars.

Makes 2 dozen bars

Nanaimo Bars

Wendy Hunt, Ontario, Canada

A delicious and popular refrigerated bar cookie invented in Nanaimo, Canada, in the 1950s.

Bottom Layer

½ cup (1 stick) butter

¼ cup granulated sugar

⅓ cup unsweetened cocoa powder

1 large egg, beaten

1¾ cups graham cracker crumbs (or 1½ packages of graham crackers, crushed with a rolling pin)

½ cup finely chopped nuts

1 cup sweetened flaked coconut

Middle Layer

½ cup (1 stick) butter, softened

3 tablespoons light cream or half and half

2 tablespoons Bird's custard powder

2 cups confectioners' sugar

Top Layer

4 ounces semisweet chocolate

2 tablespoons butter

To make the bottom layer, in a double boiler, melt the butter, granulated sugar, and cocoa. Add the egg and cook until thickened. Add the crumbs, nuts, and coconut. Press into an ungreased 9 × 9-inch baking pan. Chill in the refrigerator.

To make the middle layer, beat together the butter, cream, custard powder, and confectioners' sugar. Spread over the base and chill.

To make the top layer, melt the chocolate with the butter; cool slightly. Pour over the second layer. Let it set. Cut into bars.

Variations: There are many variations of this recipe, including the addition of mint extract, or Grand Marnier and mocha.

Makes 16 2½-inch bars

Christmas Jewel Bars

Steve Henry, Upstate New York

My dear friend Pauline Raymon shared this recipe with me. She had a terrific sweet tooth, and this was one of her favorite Christmas cookies, although I doubt there was one she would turn away. She was a centenarian and a good friend. If you enjoy fruitcake, these are worth the effort.

Crust

2 cups Bisquick mixed with 2 tablespoons sugar
¼ cup (½ stick) butter

Topping

2 cups candied mixed fruit
1 cup chopped nuts
1 cup sweetened flaked coconut
1 cup chopped dates
1 can sweetened condensed milk

Preheat the oven to 325°F/165°C. Mix the Bisquick, sugar, and butter together like a pie crust dough and press the mixture into a 13 × 9 × 2-inch baking pan. Bake for 8 to 10 minutes.

Increase the oven temperature to 350°F/180°C.

Place the dry ingredients for the topping in layers on top of the slightly cooled crust.

Evenly pour the sweetened condensed milk over the fruits.

Bake the bars for 25 to 30 minutes. Cut into 2½-inch squares while still warm.

Makes 3 dozen bars

Petite Almond Pies

Glenda Tharp, Santa Barbara, California

Crust
    1 (3-ounce) package cream cheese, softened
    1 cup all-purpose flour
    ½ cup (1 stick) butter or margarine

Filling
    1 large egg
    ¾ cup firmly packed dark brown sugar
    1 tablespoon butter, melted
    1 teaspoon almond extract
    ⅔ cup almonds, chopped (can substitute pecans)

To make the crust, combine the softened cream cheese, flour, and butter. Chill the dough for 1 hour. Shape it into small balls, about ¾ inch in diameter. Press the balls into ungreased 1¾-inch mini muffin pans.

Preheat the oven to 325°F/160°C.

Make the filling: Beat the egg, add the brown sugar, melted butter, and almond extract and cream well. Stir in the chopped almonds. Fill each crust with a scant teaspoon of the mixture.

Bake the pies for 25 minutes. Cool, and then remove from the pan.

Makes 2 dozen petite pies

U.S. Navy Crisp Toffee Bars

Robin,
I am a cook in the submarine force of the United States Navy. One of the best liked cook-ies that we bake while at sea are the Crisp Toffee Bars. We have about 150 men onboard and usually end up making about 400 portions to satisfy their appetites. Try these, and serve them with the knowledge that the United States submarine community loves them and would probably not know what to do if we stopped baking them.
Mark Adams (1999)

1 cup (2 sticks) butter, softened
1½ cups lightly packed dark brown sugar
1½ teaspoons vanilla extract
2 cups all-purpose flour
¾ cup semisweet chocolate chips
½ cup finely chopped pecans
1 cup coarsely chopped pecans

Preheat the oven to 350°F/180°C.

Place the butter in the bowl of an electric mixer and cream it at medium speed. Add the brown sugar and vanilla and continue beating for 3 minutes, or until light and fluffy. Add the flour to the creamed mixture. Mix 1 minute on low speed, or until thoroughly blended; the mixture will be thick! Fold in the chocolate chips and nuts.

Spread the mixture evenly into an ungreased 13 × 9 × 2-inch baking pan. Press out the dough to approximately ¼ inch in thickness, covering the entire bottom of the pan. Use a sheet of wax paper to push the dough into the corners.

Bake the bars for 25 to 30 minutes, or until lightly browned. Cut into 1½ × 2-inch bars while still warm from the oven. Cool, and then remove from the pan.

Makes about 4 dozen bars

Lemon Bars

Robin Olson

Lemony and luscious. I've always loved Lemon Bars. In recent years, it's become one of my husband's most requested bar cookies, so I always end up making them several times throughout the holiday season—I think I just gained a pound by thinking about them!

Crust
    1 cup (2 sticks) butter
    2 cups all-purpose flour
    ½ cup confectioners' sugar

Lemon Layer
    4 large eggs, beaten
    2 cups granulated sugar
    ⅓ cup freshly squeezed lemon juice

¼ cup all-purpose flour
½ teaspoon baking powder
1 teaspoon freshly grated lemon zest (optional)
Confectioners' sugar

Preheat the oven to 350°F/180°C.

To make the crust, combine the butter, flour, and confectioners' sugar. Press the dough into a 13 × 9 × 2-inch baking pan. Bake for 20 minutes, or until light brown.

For the lemon layer, using an electric mixer, beat together the eggs, sugar, and lemon juice until light and foamy. Add the flour and baking powder and beat until incorporated. Add lemon zest, if you like. Pour over the baked crust.

Return the pan to the oven and bake for about 25 minutes, or until the liquid does not move when the pan is slightly tipped; it should have formed a golden crust. Let cool slightly, then sift confectioners' sugar over the top while warm and cut into 2-inch squares.

Makes 24 bars

Cherry Coconut Bars

Sylvia Olson

Of all the bars that my mother-in-law made, this one is my favorite!—Robin

Crust
1 cup all-purpose flour
½ cup (1 stick) butter
¼ cup confectioners' sugar

Filling

 ¼ cup all-purpose flour
 1 cup sugar
 ½ teaspoon baking powder
 ¼ teaspoon salt
 2 large eggs, lightly beaten
 1 teaspoon vanilla extract
 ½ cup sweetened flaked coconut
 ½ cup maraschino cherries, drained and cut in quarters
 ¾ cup chopped pecans
 Confectioners' sugar for sprinkling

Preheat the oven to 350°F/180°C.

To make the crust, combine the flour, butter, and confectioners' sugar. Cut the butter into the dry ingredients using your hands or a pastry blender until the mixture is smooth. Press into an 8 × 8-inch ungreased baking pan. Bake for 20 to 25 minutes, or until golden.

Make the filling: In a medium bowl, combine the flour, sugar, baking powder, and salt. Add the eggs and the vanilla extract and mix well. Stir in the coconut, cherries, and nuts. Spread the filling over the crust; no need to cool the crust first.

Return the pan to the oven and bake for 25 to 30 minutes more, or until golden brown on top. When cool, sprinkle with confectioners' sugar, and then cut into 2-inch squares.

Makes 16 bars

Peanut Butter and Jam Bars

Sylvia Olson

Better than a PB and J sandwich.—Robin

Bars

½ cup granulated sugar
½ cup firmly packed brown sugar
½ cup (1 stick) butter, softened
½ cup peanut butter
1 large egg
1¼ cups all-purpose flour
¾ teaspoon baking soda
½ teaspoon baking powder
½ cup raspberry jam (or jam of your choice)

Glaze

2 tablespoons butter
1 cup confectioners' sugar
1 teaspoon vanilla extract
1 to 2 tablespoons hot water

Preheat the oven to 350°F/180°C.

Mix together the white and brown sugars, butter, peanut butter, and egg. Stir in the flour, baking soda, and baking powder. Reserve 1 cup of the dough. Press the remaining dough in an ungreased 9 × 9-inch baking pan. Spread with the jam. Crumble the 1 cup of reserved dough and sprinkle it over the jam.

Bake until golden brown, about 20 minutes. Set aside to cool.

Meanwhile make the glaze: Melt the butter in a small saucepan over low heat, then add the confectioners' sugar and the vanilla. Beat in hot water, a tablespoon at a time, until smooth.

When the baked bar is cool, drizzle with the glaze. Cut into 2-inch squares once the glaze has set.

Makes 16 bars

Butterscotch Bars

Jackie Thomas, Chula Vista, California

Mmmmm, butterscotch. A simple-to-make, very rich bar cookie, cut into small pieces.

Jackie is my sister-in law. She bakes all the same Olson family recipes that I do.—Robin

½ cup (1 stick) butter
1½ cups graham cracker crumbs (from about 1½ packets of graham crackers)
1 cup chopped pecans
1 cup butterscotch chips
1½ cups sweetened flaked coconut
1 (14-ounce) can sweetened condensed milk

Preheat the oven to 350°F/180°C.

Melt the butter in a medium bowl in the microwave. Sprinkle the crumbs over the melted butter and mix with your fingertips to combine. Press the mixture into an 8 × 8-inch baking pan, then sprinkle the base with the nuts, butterscotch chips, and coconut. Pour the sweetened condensed milk evenly over the base.

Bake for 25 minutes, or until golden brown. Cool in the pan, then cut into 1½-inch squares.

Makes about 2 dozen bars

Date Bars

Beth Diesner Gee, Tuff Luck Ranch, Dayton, Nevada

I have a few memories of the baking days with Mom. I would always get the job of cutting the gumdrops and then get in trouble because I'd cut one and eat two. This date bar recipe was one of my favorites. Every Christmas since we moved away from Mom and Dad, my kids would anxiously wait for the box of Christmas cookies to arrive from Grandma. The box was always easy to spot at the bus depot as Dad just about covered it totally with duct tape.

Beth is my husband's sister.—Robin

Filling
    1 pound pitted dates, chopped finely
    1 cup firmly packed dark brown sugar
    ⅔ cup water
    1 teaspoon vanilla extract

Crust
    1½ cups old-fashioned rolled oats
    1½ cups all-purpose flour
    1 cup firmly packed dark brown sugar
    ½ teaspoon baking soda
    1 cup (2 sticks) butter, cut into pieces

Make the filling: Put all the filling ingredients in a medium saucepan and stir to combine. Bring to a low boil and when the mixture starts to boil, reduce to a simmer. Let simmer for 8 to 10 minutes, stirring often. Take off the heat and let the mixture cool.

Preheat the oven to 350°F/180°C. Lightly grease a 9 × 9-inch baking pan.

Make the crust: Mix the oats, flour, sugar, and baking soda in a medium bowl. Add the butter and use a pastry blender or your fingers to cut in the butter until the mixture resembles coarse crumbs. (You can also do this in a food processor.) Press half of the crumb mixture into the bottom of the prepared baking pan. Spread the filling over the crust. Sprinkle the remaining crumb mixture over the filling.

Bake until the top is golden brown, 25 to 30 minutes. Cool in the pan. When cool, cut into 1¾-inch squares.

Makes 2 dozen bars

Rocky Road Bars

Sylvia Olson

This is another bar that Syl used to make.—Robin

¼ cup all-purpose flour
¼ teaspoon baking powder
⅛ teaspoon salt
⅓ cup firmly packed dark brown sugar
1 large egg
1 tablespoon butter
½ teaspoon vanilla extract
1 cup chopped walnuts or pecans, halved
1 cup miniature marshmallows
1 cup semisweet chocolate chips

Preheat the oven to 350°F/180°C. Lightly grease a 9 × 9-inch baking pan.

In a small bowl, sift or whisk the flour with the baking powder and salt; set aside. In the bowl of an electric mixer, beat the sugar, egg, butter, and vanilla until smooth. Stir in the flour mixture and ½ cup of the walnuts.

Pour the batter into the prepared pan.

Bake for 15 to 20 minutes, or until the top is light brown. Remove from the oven, and sprinkle with the marshmallows, the remaining ½ cup walnuts, and the chocolate chips.

Return the pan to the oven for 2 minutes. Remove from the oven and swirl the melted chocolate over the bars. Cool the bars and then cut into 2½-inch squares.

Makes 16 bars

Raspberry Delights

Nancy Wert, Olney, Maryland

Bottom Layer

    1¼ cups sifted all-purpose flour
    ½ teaspoon salt
    1 teaspoon sugar
    1 teaspoon baking powder
    ½ cup (1 stick) butter, softened
    1 large egg yolk
    2 tablespoons brandy or milk

Middle Layer

½ cup thick, seedless red raspberry jam

Top Layer

2 large eggs

1¼ cups sugar

2 teaspoons vanilla extract

4 tablespoons melted butter

2½ cups sweetened flaked coconut

Preheat the oven to 350°F/180°C.

Sift together the flour, salt, sugar, and baking powder. Blend in the butter. Mix in the egg yolk and brandy. Pat the mixture gently into an ungreased 11 × 7 × 2-inch baking pan.

Spread the jam over the bottom layer.

Make the top layer. Beat the eggs until thick and lemon colored. Beat in the sugar, vanilla, and melted butter. Add the coconut and mix well. Spoon the mixture over the jam layer.

Bake 35 minutes. Cool in the pan on a wire rack. Cut into 1½-inch squares.

Makes about 2½ dozen bars

Pecan Tartlets

Becky Campbell, Founder and CEO, Children of Fallen
Soldiers Relief Fund, Gaithersburg, Maryland

Becky brought these to the first cookie exchange I held in Maryland, in 1994.
They're delectable and easy!—Robin

Shell

1 cup (2 sticks) butter, softened
6 ounces cream cheese, softened
2½ cups all-purpose flour

Filling

4 large eggs
2 cups firmly packed light brown sugar
2 teaspoons butter, melted
1 teaspoon vanilla extract
½ cup light corn syrup
4 tablespoons all-purpose flour
1½ cups chopped pecans

Beat together the butter and cream cheese. Add the flour and mix well. Chill the dough for
at least 1 hour.

Shape the chilled dough into balls and, using your fingers, form tartlets in a mini cupcake
pan. (You could use a tartlet presser or the handle of a wooden spoon.) Chill until ready to
fill.

Preheat the oven to 375°F/190°C.

Make the filling. Beat the eggs and then add the sugar, butter, vanilla, and corn syrup. Add the flour and mix well. Fold in the nuts. Fill the tartlets.

Bake the tartlets for 20 to 22 minutes. Cool on wire racks, then remove from pans.

Makes 36 tartlets

Chocolate Pecan Crumb Bars

Anne Van Deventer Wheeler, Myrtle Beach, South Carolina

1 cup (2 sticks) butter, softened
2 cups all-purpose flour
½ cup sugar
¼ teaspoon salt
2 cups semisweet chocolate chips
1 (14-ounce) can sweetened condensed milk
1 teaspoon vanilla extract
1 cup coarsely chopped pecans

Preheat the oven to 350°F/180°C. Lightly grease a 13 × 9 × 2-inch baking pan, or line it with parchment paper.

In a large bowl, mix the softened butter, flour, sugar, and salt until crumbly. Press 2 cups of the crumb mixture onto the bottom of the prepared pan, reserving the remaining mixture.

Bake the crust for 10 to 12 minutes, or until the edges are golden brown.

Melt 1½ cups of the chocolate chips and the sweetened condensed milk in a small heavy saucepan over low heat, stirring until smooth. Stir in the vanilla. Spread over the hot crust.

Add the pecans and the remaining ½ cup chocolate chips to the reserved crumb mixture. Sprinkle over the chocolate filling. Return to the oven for 25 to 30 minutes, or until the center is set. Cool in the pan. When cool, cut into 2-inch squares.

Makes about 2½ dozen bars

Coconut Key Lime Bars

Mimi Cummins, La Sarre, Quebec
Owner of the popular Web site Christmas-Cookies.com
and co-author of *Christmas Cookies Are for Giving*

These cookie bars are my own invention . . . they're a cross between your basic magic bar and my favorite lemon bars. I found out that animal crackers make crispier crusts than graham crackers—love them!

Crust

    Nonstick cooking spray
    2½ cups animal crackers
    ½ cup (1 stick) butter

Coconut Layer

    1¼ cups sweetened condensed milk
    ¾ cup white chocolate chips
    2 cups sweetened flaked coconut

Key Lime Layer

    4 large eggs
    2 cups granulated sugar
    ¼ cup all-purpose flour

1 teaspoon baking powder

6 tablespoons key lime juice

⅓ cup confectioners' sugar (optional)

Preheat the oven to 350°F/180°C.

Place a 13×9×2-inch baking pan upside down on the countertop. Make a foil liner for your baking pan by first shaping a piece of aluminum foil over the pan. Remove the foil, turn the pan over, and place a few drops of water in the bottom of the pan (this helps hold the liner in place). Place the aluminum foil inside the pan so that it lines the interior of the pan. Generously spray the sides of the lined pan with nonstick cooking spray.

Process the animal crackers in a food processor until they form uniformly fine crumbs. Place the butter in the pan and melt it in the oven, about 3 minutes for room-temperature butter or 7 minutes for cold butter. Using a pastry brush, spread the melted butter evenly over the bottom of the pan. Sprinkle the crumbs evenly over the butter. Pour the sweetened condensed milk evenly on top of the crumbs. Top with the white chocolate chips and the coconut. Press down firmly with the back of a fork.

Bake the crust for 20 minutes, or until golden.

Meanwhile, prepare the lemon layer. In a bowl, using an electric mixer, beat together the eggs, granulated sugar, flour, baking powder, and key lime juice. Pour the key lime mixture on top of the coconut layer.

Return the pan to the oven for 25 to 30 minutes, or until the key lime mixture is set and does not jiggle when the pan is gently shaken. Cool completely before cutting into 2-inch bars with a sharp knife. Just before serving, sift confectioners' sugar over the bars.

Makes 2 dozen bars

Marzipan Squares

Steve Henry, Upstate New York

These unique cookies are one of my favorites, anytime.

Pastry Base

    1 cup all-purpose flour
    1 teaspoon salt
    ⅓ cup shortening
    2½ tablespoons cold water

    Raspberry jam

Filling

    ½ cup (1 stick) butter
    ⅔ cup sugar
    2 large eggs, beaten
    ⅔ cup rice flour (see Note)
    ¼ teaspoon salt
    Red and green food coloring

Icing

    1½ cups confectioners' sugar
    3 tablespoons butter
    2 tablespoons milk
    1 teaspoon almond extract

Preheat the oven to 325°F/160°C.

Mix the pastry base ingredients (except for the jam) together in a bowl, using your fingers or a pastry cutter, then press into an 8 × 8-inch baking pan. Bake for 10 minutes. Remove from the oven.

Increase the oven temperature to 350°F/180°C.

Spread the jam on top of the baked pastry base. Mix all the filling ingredients (except food coloring) together. Divide in half; add food coloring, making one half red, the other half green. Drop pieces of this, evenly mixed, over the jam layer. Bake for 35 to 45 minutes. Meanwhile, make the icing: Blend all the ingredients together. Cool the squares, then spread the icing on top before cutting them.

Note: Rice flour is gluten-free and all-purpose flour shouldn't be substituted. You'll find rice flour in finer grocery stores and Asian markets (see Resources, page 330).

Makes 32 bars

Magic Bars

Debbie Rogers, Kent Island, Maryland

Who doesn't like magic?

1½ cups graham cracker crumbs (from about 1½ packets of graham crackers)
½ cup (1 stick) butter, melted
2 cups (12 ounces) semisweet chocolate chips
1⅓ cups sweetened flaked coconut
1 cup chopped walnuts or pecans
1 (14-ounce) can sweetened condensed milk

Preheat the oven to 350°F/180°C.

In a small bowl, combine the graham cracker crumbs and butter and mix well. Press the crumb mixture into a 13 × 9 × 2-inch baking pan. Evenly layer the chocolate chips, coconut, and nuts over the crust. Press the layers down firmly with a spatula. Pour the sweetened condensed milk evenly over the mixture.

Bake 25 minutes, or until lightly browned. Cool in the pan. Cut into 1½-inch squares. Store leftovers, covered, at room temperature.

Variations: Experiment with different combinations of peanuts, mini marshmallows, toffee chips, raisins, craisins, and butterscotch chips.

Makes about 3 dozen bars

Apple Butter Brickle Tartlets

Robin Olson

This is an original recipe I created. Even though you've never had this exact recipe before, you'll find it features familiar flavors. The tarts are like chewy little apple pies with a nutty crust. My husband says: "It tastes like the holidays!"

Crust

    1 packet (8) graham crackers
    ½ cup pecans
    ⅓ cup firmly packed light brown sugar
    ¼ cup melted butter

Filling

    ½ cup light corn syrup
    ½ cup apple butter
    2 teaspoons cornstarch
    ¼ teaspoon salt
    ¼ teaspoon ground cinnamon
    ½ cup chopped, toasted pecans (toasted on baking sheets in 350°F/180°C oven for 7 to 9 minutes)
    ¼ cup Heath Bits o' Brickle Toffee Bits

Preheat the oven to 350°F/180°C.

Place the graham crackers, pecans, and brown sugar in a food processor and grind until fine. When finely ground, add the melted butter and pulse a few times to combine. The crust should stick together when you crush it in your hand. If it doesn't, add a little more melted butter until it holds together firmly.

Spray mini muffin pans with cooking spray. Add 1 heaping tablespoon of graham crust dough per muffin cup. Fill all the cups first, then take a piece of wax paper and press down with your fingers over the wax paper in each cup, to make tart shells. If you have a wooden tartlet presser, use that over a piece of wax paper. Slowly peel the wax paper away from each cup.

Bake the shells for about 12 minutes; they're done when the nuts are fragrant when you open the oven door.

Meanwhile, as the crusts bake, start the filling.

In a medium saucepan, over medium-high heat, bring the corn syrup to a gentle boil. Add the apple butter, cornstarch, salt, and cinnamon. Stir with a wooden spoon. Turn the heat to medium-low and boil gently for 10 minutes, stirring occasionally; the mixture will reduce by about one-fourth and will get thicker. Remove from the heat and let cool for 5 minutes. Stir in the toasted pecans and toffee bits.

Spoon the filling into the tartlets, using a little less than a full tablespoon per tartlet. Make sure the crust is a bit higher than the filling so the sugar won't glue the edges of the tartlets to the pan. If you like, you can sprinkle a few toffee bits on top before baking.

Bake the tartlets for 15 minutes. Cool thoroughly in the pan. Before removing tartlets, place the pans in the freezer for 5 minutes to firm up; they'll pop out easier.

Makes 24 tartlets

Caramel-Chocolate Pecan Bars

Margie Willis, Hagerstown, Maryland

Crumb Base

2 cups all-purpose flour
1 cup firmly packed dark brown sugar
½ cup (1 stick) butter, softened

Second Layer

1½ cups pecans halves

Third Layer

⅔ cup butter
½ cup firmly packed dark brown sugar

Topping

1 cup chocolate chips

Preheat the oven to 350°F/180°C.

Mix the crumb base ingredients and combine until well blended. Press firmly into an un-greased 13 × 9 × 2-inch baking pan.

Press the pecans into the base crumb mixture, covering completely.

In a saucepan, heat the butter and brown sugar on medium heat until the entire surface boils. Boil for 1 minute, stirring constantly. Remove from the heat, cool slightly, about 2 minutes, then pour the hot butter and sugar sauce evenly over the pecans and crust.

Bake for 18 to 22 minutes, or until the entire top layer is bubbly. Sprinkle immediately with the chocolate chips. Allow to melt slightly, and then swirl the melting chocolate pieces to spread over the top. Cool before slicing into squares.

Makes about 30 pieces

Frosted Pumpkin Bars

Becky Campbell, CEO, Children of Fallen Soldiers
Relief Fund, Gaithersburg, Maryland

Bars

1½ cups sugar

¼ cup (½ stick) butter, softened

1 (16-ounce) can pumpkin

4 large eggs

2¼ cups all-purpose flour

2 teaspoons baking powder

1 teaspoon baking soda

½ teaspoon salt

½ teaspoon ground cinnamon

1 teaspoon pumpkin pie spice

1 cup walnuts

Frosting

3 cups confectioners' sugar

⅓ cup (½ stick plus 1½ tablespoons) butter, softened

1 (3-ounce) package cream cheese, softened

Preheat the oven to 350°F/180°C. Lightly grease a 15 × 10 × 1-inch jelly-roll pan.

In a large bowl, combine the sugar, butter, pumpkin, and eggs. Beat at medium speed, scraping down the sides of the bowl often, until well mixed, 1 to 2 minutes. Reduce the speed to low, add the flour, baking powder, soda, salt, cinnamon, and pumpkin pie spice, and mix well, 1 to 2 minutes. Stir in the walnuts by hand. Pour the mixture into the $15 \times 10 \times 1$-inch jelly-roll pan.

Bake for 20 to 25 minutes, or until the bar springs back lightly when touched in the center. Cool completely.

In a small mixing bowl, combine all the frosting ingredients. Beat at medium speed until light and fluffy, 1 to 3 minutes. Frost and cut into 1½-inch squares.

Makes 4 dozen bars

Irish Chocolate Mint Squares

Krista FitzGerald, Olney, Maryland

1½ cups (3 sticks) plus 6 tablespoons butter
2 cups granulated sugar
2 teaspoons vanilla extract
4 large eggs
1 cup all-purpose flour
¾ cup unsweetened cocoa powder
½ teaspoon baking powder
2⅔ cups confectioners' sugar
1 tablespoon plus 1 teaspoon water
1 tablespoon mint extract
4 drops green food coloring
1 cup semisweet chocolate chips

Preheat the oven to 350°F/180°C. Lightly grease a 13 × 9 × 2-inch baking pan.

Place 2 sticks of the butter in a large microwave-safe bowl and cover. Microwave on high for 2 minutes, or until melted. Stir in the granulated sugar and vanilla. Add the eggs and beat well. Add the flour, cocoa, and baking powder; beat until well blended. Pour the batter into the prepared pan.

Bake the brownies 30 to 35 minutes, or until a wooden toothpick inserted in the center comes out clean. Cool completely in the pan on a wire rack.

Prepare the mint cream center by combining the confectioners' sugar, 1 stick of the butter, water, mint extract, and food coloring in a large bowl. Beat until smooth. Spread evenly on the brownies. Cover and refrigerate until cold.

Prepare the chocolate glaze. Place the remaining 6 tablespoons butter and the chocolate chips in a covered small microwave-safe bowl. Microwave on high 1 minute, or until the mixture is smooth when stirred. Cool slightly; pour over the chilled bars. Cover and refrigerate at least 1 hour before serving. Cut into 2½-inch squares before serving.

Makes 24 bars

Easy Treats

This section includes no-bakes, more-candy-than-cookies, boiled, cake-mix cookies, and cookies from pre-made dough. They are all super-easy recipes great for quick snacks, lunch boxes, and year-round treats, and all are things that kids can make, too. The cookie exchange should endeavor to be inclusive rather than exclusive. If your whole circle of friends are non-bakers, you could easily start an exchange party featuring easy treats from this section, and simply hand out recipes with the invitations.

Chocolate Oatmeal Cookies

Pamela Sharp, Hyattsville, Maryland

These cookies were popular with children in the 1960s. These are easy to make and great to pack with a lunch. This cookie makes a wonderful summertime dessert, best enjoy these with a tall glass of cold milk!

½ cup (1 stick) butter

2 cups sugar

½ cup milk

6 tablespoons unsweetened cocoa powder (the better the quality of the cocoa, the better the taste!)

2 teaspoons vanilla extract

3½ cups quick-cooking oatmeal

Melt the butter in a heavy-bottomed pot. Add the sugar and milk and bring to a rolling boil. Boil for 2 minutes. Remove the pan from heat. Add the cocoa and vanilla and mix well with a wooden spoon. Add the oatmeal and stir well. Drop the dough by tablespoonfuls onto wax paper. Allow 1 to 2 hours for the cookies to harden.

Makes about 2 dozen cookies

Gooey Butter Cookies

Leslie Jackson Kelly, Laurel, Maryland

When you need cookies in a snap, this one is tickety-boo!

1 box yellow cake mix

1 (8-ounce) package cream cheese, softened

1 large egg

½ cup (1 stick) butter, softened

¼ teaspoon vanilla extract

Confectioners' sugar

Preheat the oven to 350°F/180°C.

Mix the first five ingredients (except sugar) together, then chill the dough at least 2 hours. Roll into 1-inch balls and roll in the confectioners' sugar. Place 2 inches apart on ungreased baking sheets.

Bake the cookies for 10 to 12 minutes. Partially cool on the baking sheets. When slightly cool, roll again in confectioners' sugar and finish cooling. Or decorate these with your favorite icing and colored sprinkles.

Makes about 5 dozen cookies

Bird's Nests aka Peanut Chow Mein or Haystacks

Robin Olson

This is a sweet treat that I've always called Bird's Nests. It's been a favorite of mine since childhood, and it's one of the few cookies or treats from my non-baking mother's baking repertoire. The main cookie my mom baked was Chocolate Chip Toll House Cookies (no complaints from me). The other cookie was a meringue cookie with chocolate chips. Make these on the small side, as they're very sweet.

¾ cup butterscotch chips, melted
½ cup crunchy peanut butter (I use Skippy Super Chunk)
1 (5-ounce) can La Choy Chow Mein Noodles
1 cup mini marshmallows
½ cup salted cocktail peanuts
1 small jar maraschino cherries, drained, quartered

Melt the butterscotch chips in a double boiler on the stovetop or in the microwave. (Make sure the bowl is microwave-safe and don't overcook.) Stir the peanut butter by hand into the melted butterscotch; it should blend easily and be nice and creamy.

Put the chow mein noodles, mini marshmallows, and peanuts in a large bowl. Pour the melted peanut butter–butterscotch mixture on top and quickly stir with a wooden spoon to incorporate.

Lay wax paper on the baking sheets. Using two spoons, drop by tablespoonfuls onto the wax paper. Top with the quartered cherries and chill until set.

Variation: For an Easter treat, substitute white chocolate chips for the butterscotch chips.

Makes 60 treats

Cathedral Windows

Charlene Dillingham, Gaithersburg, Maryland

Kids love this treat!

½ cup (1 stick) butter or margarine
1½ cups semisweet chocolate chips
1½ cups colored mini marshmallows
1 cup chopped walnuts
1 cup sweetened flaked coconut

Heat the butter and chocolate chips in the top of a double boiler over low heat, stirring occasionally, until melted and smooth. Cool slightly.

Toss the marshmallows and nuts in a large bowl; stir in the melted chocolate.

Tear five 9-inch sheets of wax paper and sprinkle each generously with coconut. Divide the dough into fifths and place each fifth on a sheet of the wax paper. Roll up tightly into 2-inch-diameter logs and refrigerate overnight, or until firm. Before serving, unwrap the rolls and remove the wax paper. Cut into ½-inch slices.

Variation: Substitute white chocolate for the semisweet at Eastertime!

Makes about 60 treats

Crème de Menthe Brownies

Jenny Grimaud, Crofton, Maryland

I made these for Robin's cookie exchange the year we were filmed by the Food Network. They're so good, no one will know that you didn't slave over them!

Bottom Layer

1 package brownie mix (family size)
Crème de menthe for brushing bottom layer

Middle Layer

2 cups confectioners' sugar
½ cup (1 stick) butter, melted
3 teaspoons crème de menthe

Topping

1 container creamy-style canned chocolate frosting

Follow the package directions for cake-like brownies, adding nuts if desired. Bake as directed in a 13 × 9 × 2-inch baking pan. Cool in the pan. While cooling, brush with crème de menthe.

In a medium bowl, mix the confectioners' sugar with the melted butter and crème de menthe. Spread on the brownies and refrigerate 2 hours or overnight.

Frost the brownies with the chocolate frosting.

Makes about 2 dozen brownies

White Christmas

Biancamaria Duke, Adelaide, Australia

White Christmas is a staple in everyone's house over the holiday season. People have been known to play around with the ingredients and add things such as marshmallows, sultanas or other raisins, candied cherries, candied ginger, or even dried cranberries to the mix. These treats also freeze very well. Here's a variation of the Australian recipe that will work for those in the U.S., where one of our common main ingredients, Copha, cannot be found (see headnote, page 239).

1¾ cups white chocolate, chopped
½ cup heavy cream
1½ cups Rice Krispies
½ cup slivered almonds, toasted
½ cup dried cranberries
1 cup desiccated coconut (see Resources, page 329)
1 cup mini marshmallows
Red and green candied cherries (optional)
⅓ cup candied ginger (optional)

Melt the chocolate and heavy cream in a heatproof, microwave-safe bowl, or in a double boiler. Cool for 5 to 10 minutes.

In a large bowl, combine the Rice Krispies, toasted almonds, dried cranberries, coconut, and mini marshmallows. Add candied cherries and/or ginger if desired. Pour the white chocolate mixture over the ingredients in the bowl and mix well.

Spoon the mixture into paper cups placed on baking sheets. Refrigerate until set.

Makes 2 dozen treats

White Christmas International

Biancamaria Duke, Adelaide, Australia, and Robin Olson

If you like no-bake cookies and you like coconut, then this is the treat for you!

This is a new recipe that we accidentally created together. Biancamaria has named it White Christmas International. We e-mailed back and forth trying to overcome the lack of availability in the U.S. for the main binding ingredient, Copha, which is a shortening made from hydrogenated coconut oil. Copha is a common ingredient in many cookies and confections in Australia and New Zealand (also marketed under the name Kremelta). Because Copha is made of coconut, I assumed the flavor was coconut and so I decided to use the closest ingredient I could find, which is canned cream of coconut and which is sold in most grocery stores in the States. After Biancamaria tested my recipe, she informed me that Copha does not impart a coconut taste, it's flavorless—but she loved the recipe anyway (her sister loved it, too). Biancamaria declared she would be serving this version at her next cookie exchange!—Robin

¼ cup shortening
¼ cup canned sweetened coconut cream
¼ cup confectioners' sugar
2½ cups Rice Krispies
1 cup milk powder (dehydrated milk)
½ cup slivered almonds, toasted
1 cup dried cranberries
1 cup unsweetened desiccated or sweetened flaked coconut
1 cup mini marshmallows
Red and green candied cherries (optional for holidays)

In a small microwave-safe bowl, heat the shortening and the coconut cream for 15 seconds, or until just melted. Add the confectioners' sugar, stir to combine, cool, and set aside.

In a large bowl, add the Rice Krispies, milk powder, toasted almonds, dried cranberries, coconut, and mini marshmallows. Pour the coconut cream mixture over the ingredients in the bowl and mix well.

Spoon the mixture into paper cups on baking sheets. Refrigerate until set.

Note: Desiccated coconut versus sweetened shredded or flaked coconut. Desiccated coconut has a subtle coconut flavor, is unsweetened, and adds more of a texture than a coconut flavor. It's a common ingredient outside of the U.S. but rather uncommon in regular U.S. grocery stores. I was able to find desiccated coconut at a local international grocery store. Also look in health food stores or see the Resources section, page 329. If you can't find desiccated coconut, use shredded coconut or omit it entirely.

Makes 2 dozen treats

Mamie's Million-Dollar Fudge

Robin Olson

Mamie Eisenhower was the First Lady of the United States from 1953 until 1961. This was Mamie's favorite treat and she often gave this recipe out to newspapers and magazines.

4½ cups sugar
Pinch of salt
2 tablespoons butter
1½ cups (12-ounce can) evaporated milk
1½ cups semisweet chocolate chips
12 (1-ounce) squares German's Sweet Chocolate (Bakers brand)
2 cups marshmallow cream
2 cups chopped nuts

Butter (or spray with Pam) an 18 × 13-inch baking pan. Boil the sugar, salt, butter, and evaporated milk together for 6 minutes.

Put the chocolate chips, German's chocolate, marshmallow cream, and nuts in a bowl. Pour the boiling syrup over the ingredients. Beat until the chocolate is all melted, then pour into the baking pan. Let stand a few hours before cutting into 2-inch squares. Remember, this is better the second day. Store in a tin box lined with wax paper.

Makes about 5 dozen pieces

Lemon Whippersnappers

Emily Korber, Gaithersburg, Maryland

I'm one of those non-bakers that Robin talks about!

1 package lemon cake mix
2 cups frozen whipped topping, thawed
1 large egg, beaten
½ cup confectioners' sugar

Preheat the oven to 350°F/180°C. Lightly grease the baking sheets.

Combine the cake mix, whipped topping, and egg in a large bowl and stir until well combined. Drop large teaspoonfuls of dough into the confectioners' sugar and roll to coat. Place the cookies on the prepared baking sheets 1½ inches apart.

Bake the cookies for 10 to 12 minutes, until golden brown. Cool on wire racks.

Makes about 3½ dozen whippersnappers

Rolo Turtles

Micki Snapp, Silver Spring, Maryland

This is a candy so addictive and yummy that I'll betcha can't eat just one!

1 package mini pretzels (honey mustard pretzels work great, too)
1 (13-ounce) package Rolo Candies (63 pieces, unwrapped)
1 (6-ounce) package pecan halves (1½ cups)

Preheat the oven to 250°F/120°C.

Put 1 Rolo on top of each pretzel. Bake for 4 to 5 minutes, or until the candy is soft. Remove from the oven and quickly place a pecan half on top of the softened candy. Push down and squish the chocolate into the pretzel.

Let set and cool for 10 to 15 minutes, then put the whole baking sheet in the refrigerator to harden the candies. Store the candies in an airtight container—if there are any left! The hardest part of making this treat is taking the wrappers off the Rolos—they're so easy to make, yet so good!

Makes 63 turtles

Seafoam Cookies aka Meringue Cookies or Forgotten Cookies

Robin Olson

These cookies were a part of my childhood. We called them Seafoam Cookies back in the '60s and '70s.

4 large egg whites, at room temperature
1 teaspoon cream of tartar
Dash of salt
1 cup sugar
2 teaspoons vanilla extract
½ cup chopped pecans
1 cup milk chocolate chips

In a large bowl, using an electric mixer, beat the egg whites until foamy. Add the cream of tartar and salt and continue to beat until the whites form soft peaks. Add the sugar a little at a time, and continue beating until the meringue holds stiff peaks and the sugar is dissolved. Add the vanilla. Gently fold in the pecans and chocolate chips by hand with a spatula.

Line baking sheets with parchment paper. Using two teaspoons, scoop and drop the meringue in small mounds on the baking sheets.

Here are two baking methods: My old family recipe says: Bake at 300°F/150°C for 25 minutes. However, to make them Forgotten Cookies, you have to leave them in the oven overnight. Preheat the oven to 350°F/180°C degrees and place the cookies on the baking sheets into the oven, shut the door, and turn the oven off. Let the cookies sit in the oven overnight.

Variations: I always make these with chocolate and nuts, but you could also make them plain. For the holidays, you could add food coloring; some red, some green, and leave some white. To make them look fancy, pipe them onto the parchment paper using a large star-shaped pastry tip.

Makes about 2 dozen

German Chocolate Thumbprint Cookies

Diane Lewis, Frederick, Maryland

Filling

1 cup sugar
1 cup evaporated milk
½ cup (1 stick) butter, softened
1 teaspoon vanilla extract
3 large egg yolks, beaten
1½ cup sweetened flaked coconut
1½ cups chopped pecans

Cookies

1 package German chocolate cake mix
⅓ cup butter, melted

In a heavy-bottomed saucepan, combine the sugar, milk, butter, vanilla extract, and egg yolks and blend well. Cook over medium heat until thickened and bubbly, stirring frequently. Stir in the coconut and pecans. Remove from heat and cool to room temperature.

Reserve 1¼ cups of the filling mixture and set it aside. In a large bowl, combine the cake mix, melted butter, and the remaining filling mixture. Stir by hand until thoroughly moistened.

Preheat the oven to 350°F/180°C. Line the baking sheets with parchment paper.

Shape the dough into 1-inch balls. Place the balls 2 inches apart on the lined baking sheets. Make an indentation in the center of each ball with your thumb. Fill each indentation with a rounded ½ teaspoonful of the reserved filling.

Bake the cookies for 10 to 13 minutes, or until set. Cool 5 minutes; then remove from the baking sheets. Cool completely on wire racks.

Makes about 5 dozen cookies

White Chocolate Macaroon Cookies

Karen Binder, Ballinger, Texas

This is a cookie that we love making. And the best part is I can make the cookies in advance and freeze them. After I thaw them, I drizzle on the white chocolate and colored sugar. These are super easy and very good.

1 (1-pound 1.5-ounce) pouch sugar cookie mix
½ cup (1 stick) butter or margarine, melted
1 large egg
1 cup sweetened flaked coconut
1⅔ cups white vanilla baking chips
½ teaspoon coconut extract
1 teaspoon shortening
Red and green decorator's sugar

Preheat the oven to 375°F/190°C.

In a large bowl, stir together the cookie mix, butter, egg, coconut, 1 cup of the white vanilla baking chips, and the coconut extract until a soft dough forms. Drop the dough by rounded teaspoonfuls, 2 inches apart, onto ungreased baking sheets.

Bake the cookies 9 to 11 minutes, or until golden brown around the edges. Cool 1 minute before removing from the baking sheets. Cool completely on wire racks, about 20 minutes.

In a small microwave-safe bowl, heat the remaining ⅔ cup vanilla chips and the shortening on high 30 to 60 seconds, or until the mixture can be stirred smooth. Drizzle over the cookies and sprinkle with colored sugars as desired.

Makes about 3 dozen

No-Bake Mice Cookies

Jo-ann Morin, Frankfort, Maine

These cookies require no baking, but are a favorite at my cookie exchange because they're so cute. It's a great cookie project for kids!

1 bag Oreos (not Double Stuf) for the "snowy base" that the mice sit on
1 bag Hershey's Kisses (for the noses)
1 jar maraschino cherries (in juice) with stems (for the mice bodies/tails)
½ cup slivered almonds (for the ears)
1 container Dolci Frutta (see Resources, page 329), melted in the microwave
   (commonly used to chocolate-dip fruits, it hardens to a shell)
1 tube red decorative gel (for the mice eyes and nose)

Carefully twist all the Oreos apart, trying not to ruin the white snow parts. (Eat the leftover tops.)

Unwrap a bunch of the Hershey's Kisses and put in a bowl. (Eat a few for stamina!)

Melt the chocolate in the microwave (right in the container, but don't forget to take the plastic top off!). Stir halfway through and be ready to use it as soon as it's melted; it hardens up fast.

Dunk a cherry into the Dolci Frutta melted chocolate; attach the Hershey's Kiss to the top of the cherry so the kiss becomes the nose of the mouse and the cherry is the body/tail. Stick 2 almond slivers between the cherry and Hershey's Kiss so that they become the ears. (Try to keep them upright because if they slip to the side, then they look like elephants instead of mice!) Dab a little gel on the Hershey's Kiss for eyes and one dollop on the top of the Hershey's Kiss for the nose. Repeat the process!

Peanut Butter Cup Cookies

Barbara Johnston, Santa Barbara, California

This is really easy and whenever I make it, it's always a really big hit!

1 bag miniature peanut butter cups
1 tube pre-made peanut butter cookie dough
Mini muffin pan
Mini muffin paper liners (1¼-inch diameter)

Place the entire bag of miniature peanut butter cups in the freezer; the candy is easier to handle if it is very cold. Remove from the freezer, unwrap, and remove the paper liners from all the candies. Place the candies in a plastic freezer bag and return to the freezer until the cookies come out of the oven.

Keep the cookie dough in the refrigerator until ready to use, it's easier to slice if it is cold and firm. Line the mini muffin pan with paper liners. Slice the chilled dough into ¾-inch slices and cut the slices into quarters. Place one-quarter slice of dough into each lined muffin cup.

Bake the cookies according to the directions on the cookie dough tube. Immediately after removing the cookies from the oven, place a miniature peanut butter cup in the center of each cookie. Remove from the pan and let cool.

Variation: Use chocolate chip cookie dough and top with chocolate kisses.

Makes about 2 dozen cookies

Strawberry Angel Cookies

Brenda Lieswald, Rosemead, California

My nephews love these cookies and they are really easy.

1 (16-ounce) package angel food cake mix
1 cup Smuckers Strawberry Preserves
3 tablespoons mini semisweet chocolate chips

Preheat the oven to 325°F/165°C. Lightly grease the baking sheets, or line with parchment paper.

Beat together the cake mix and strawberry preserves (do not add water) until evenly moistened. Continue to beat for 1 minute. Stir in the chocolate chips. Drop by rounded tablespoonfuls onto the prepared baking sheets.

Bake the cookies 10 to 12 minutes, or until the tops are just lightly browned. Cool 1 minute on the baking sheets, then transfer to wire racks to cool completely. The cookies will be pink, soft, and chewy.

Makes 3 dozen cookies

Easy Reindeer Cookies

Bernadette Feibel, Atascadero, California

Dough
1 roll of premade peanut butter or sugar cookie dough
¼ cup all-purpose flour

Decorations
1 large bag mini pretzel twists
Red-hots
M&Ms
Miniature marshmallows
Pre-made tube icing

Open the roll of cookie dough, place in a bowl, and mix in about ¼ cup of flour to make the dough stiffer. After adding the extra flour, place half of the dough onto wax paper and roll into a log 2½ to 3 inches thick. Form the log into a triangle shape by pressing down to flatten one side, then rotate, press down, and repeat. Keep turning until you have a nice even shape. The triangular logs should be about 7 inches long. Place the dough logs in the freezer for 1 hour.

Preheat the oven to 350°F/180°C. Line the baking sheets with parchment paper.

Remove one log from the freezer and, using a large, sharp knife, make thin ⅛-inch slices (or thicker, if you prefer). Place the slices on the prepared sheets, 2 inches apart.

Bake the cookies for 9 to 11 minutes, or until golden brown around the edges. Remove from the oven and let cool a minute or so. While the cookies are still warm, place the pretzels as antlers on two sides of the triangle. When cool, use the icing as glue to make eyes and mouth out of red-hots and M&M's along with some mini marshmallows for the nose. If you are allowing children to help, make sure the baking sheets are slightly cool.

Makes about 2 dozen cookies

Nutty Ribbon Sticks

Robin Olson

I found this recipe among my mother's old cookbooks and have adapted it for the easy section. Instead of making homemade pie crust, purchase ready-made pie crust from the refrigerated section of the grocery store.

1 box high-quality, premade pie crust (2 rolls)
½ cup jam of your choice
¼ cup finely chopped nuts (pecans, walnuts, or almonds)
1 large egg white, beaten
Plain and colored sugars for sprinkling

Preheat the oven to 400°F/200°C. Line the baking sheets with parchment paper.

Take 1 roll of the pie crust out and leave the other in the refrigerator. Sprinkle a pastry rolling mat lightly with flour and place the roll of pie crust on the pastry mat; flour the top lightly. Using a rolling pin, roll the dough out thinly to a thickness of ¹⁄₁₆ of an inch. Try to keep it as rectanglar as possible. Spread half of the dough with jam, sprinkle the nuts over the jam, and fold the remaining half of the crust over the filling. Lightly go over dough with the rolling pin to compress.

With a sharp knife, cut the dough into ½-inch strips, 4 inches long for short ribbon sticks or 6 inches long for longer ones. Holding both ends, twist the strip like a ribbon and transfer to the prepared baking sheets. Using a pastry brush, lightly brush the ribbon sticks with beaten egg white, then liberally sprinkle sugar over each cookie. For holiday sparkle add some colored decorator's sugars to some plain sugar.

Bake 9 to 11 minutes, or until lightly golden brown. Transfer to wire racks to cool.

Variation: Use apple butter or fig jam and make a basic cinnamon-sugar mix for the topping.

Makes 5 dozen ribbon sticks

Chocolate Billionaires

Robin Olson

1 (14-ounce) package caramels
3 tablespoons water
1½ cups chopped pecans
1 cup coarsely crushed crisp rice cereal
2½ cups semisweet or milk chocolate chips
1 tablespoon shortening

Line two baking sheets with parchment paper; set aside.

In a large heavy saucepan, combine the caramels and water and stir over low heat until melted and smooth. Stir in the pecans and cereal until coated. Drop by teaspoonfuls onto the prepared sheets. Chill until firm.

Melt the chocolate chips and shortening in a double boiler or heavy-bottomed saucepan, and dip the candies until coated. Return to the baking sheets and chill until set. Store in airtight containers.

Makes about 4 dozen candies

Tiger Nut Sweets

Robin Olson

Tiger Nut Sweets—also known as Tiger Nut Balls—are possibly the oldest recipe known to mankind. This recipe was found written on ancient Egyptian clay pottery shards called ostraca *dating back to 4000 BC. This is a very sweet treat and kids will enjoy the story behind it as they help you roll the balls.*

1 cup almonds
1 cup fresh dates, pits removed (or substitute dried dates)
½ cup walnuts
¼ cup water
1 teaspoon ground cinnamon
1 cup honey
Water to thin honey, if needed
Confectioners' sugar for rolling (optional)

Grind the almonds and set aside in a small bowl. Chop the dates into small pieces. Chop the walnuts.

Put the dates in a medium bowl and stir in the water. Use a bit more water if you are using dried dates. Add the cinnamon and chopped walnuts, and combine all the ingredients together. (Or you could put all of the above ingredients, except the almonds, in a food processor.) Roll the mixture into balls. Dip each ball in a small bowl of honey and roll until fully covered. (If the honey is too thick for rolling the ball, thin with water as needed.)

Remove the nut ball with a spoon and roll the ball in a small bowl of ground almonds. Place the balls on baking sheets lined with wax or parchment paper until ready to serve. Chill, if not serving immediately. The nut balls may also be rolled in confectioners' sugar to make them easier to handle.

Makes about 24 balls

Cappuccino Bonbons

Collette Fahrig, Houston, Texas

This recipe came in fifth place in Cookie-Exchange.com's 1st Original Cookie Recipe Contest and scored high marks for easiness and taste from the judges.

1 package (family size) fudge brownie mix
2 large eggs
¼ cup water
⅓ cup oil
1½ tablespoons instant coffee granules
½ teaspoon ground cinnamon
Mini pancake pans and mini cupcake liners

Preheat the oven to 350°F/180°C.

Combine the brownie mix, eggs, water, oil, instant coffee granules, and cinnamon. Stir with a spoon until well blended.

Using a measuring spoon, fill mini cupcake liners with a tablespoon of the batter each.

Bake for 12 to 15 minutes, or until an inserted toothpick comes out clean. Cool completely. If you're not transporting these to a cookie party, serve with a garnish of whipped cream and a dash of cinnamon. Refrigerate until ready to serve.

Makes 48 bonbons

Macaroon Kisses

Iris Grundler, Gaithersburg, Maryland

1 (24-ounce) package sweetened flaked coconut
1 (14-ounce) can sweetened condensed milk
2 teaspoons vanilla extract
1½ teaspoons almond extract
36 chocolate kisses

Preheat the oven to 350°F/180°C. Line the baking sheets with parchment paper.

In a large bowl, mix together the coconut, condensed milk, and vanilla and almond extracts. Drop by rounded teaspoons onto the prepared baking sheets.

Bake 10 to 12 minutes, or until browned around the edges. Immediately press chocolate kisses in the center of each macaroon. Leave on the baking sheet for 3 minutes, then transfer to wire racks to cool completely.

Makes 3 dozen cookies

Creating Your Cookie Exchange Party

Common Hosting Concerns

The concept of a cookie exchange party is simple. Your friends come over, everyone swaps cookies, and you go home with an assortment of cookies. *What could possibly be complicated about that?* Many hostesses plan and look forward to hosting their parties all year long. We all put so much energy and effort into this party that when expectations are not met, it becomes a disappointment. Hopefully, you'll learn something from this list of the common problems that hostesses experience at one time or another. While the vast majority of letters I get are from happy hostesses who launched successful CE's from tips they got from my Web site or newsletters, I do get letters asking for help. The first thing I tell these people is "Don't worry, you're not alone"; just hearing that makes them feel better right away!

1. **Can't get the party started.** There are some potential hostesses that can't seem to get their parties off the ground. It often starts like this: They'll ask their friends what they think of the concept and the response is: "I don't bake" or "Sorry, I'm not interested." Everyone has a different opinion of what they think a cookie exchange is: from not knowing at all, to participating in good or bad cookie parties. The concept really appeals to some people, and to others not at all. Find new people who like the concept right away instead of trying to convince those who don't. If you can pull off one party with a few new people, that means you'll have made some new friends in the process. Your old friends will eventually find out that you've created an annual tradition, and they may end up changing their minds about attending.
2. **Others telling you how you should host your party.** For some, planning and creating their first cookie exchange party will become a lesson in assertiveness training. Friends and relatives may give opinions on how they think you should host your

party. Thank them for their advice and tell them that you'll take what they've said into consideration, then decide if you want to incorporate their ideas or not. You are allowed to hold the party the way that you want because, after all—*it's your party.* Customize it any way you wish.

3. **RSVP's and no-shows.** The average amount of attendees is about 50 percent of the complete invitation list. It's rare for all guests to show up, so if you want twelve guests, invite twenty-four. Realize that everyone is busy during the holidays. The guest list will change a little, year after year, but you'll probably notice a core group that you can count on to show up every year. *Répondez s'il vous plaît* is a French phrase that translates to "Respond, if you please." There are two issues with the RSVP. The first is people who don't respond at all. There's no nice way to say this. It's rude to not respond to an invitation; however, some people never host parties or have others to their home. They may not realize how disappointing it is to a hostess to have her invitation ignored. It's up to you to decide how many offers to extend to someone before you remove them from your list. My level of tolerance is two ignored invitations; they won't get a third. If you're invited to a party (of any kind) and you responded with "Yes, I will attend," please do your best to show up. Hostesses work very hard to create parties and take their head count seriously, especially with a cookie exchange. Last-minute cancellations and no-shows are the single most dreaded situation by anyone who hosts a party. Did I just hear an "amen"?

4. **Those who come empty-handed but want to take home cookies.** If you've got this problem, you've agreed to let people come to the party without bringing cookies. I've been asked if someone could come to my party but not swap cookies. I politely, but firmly say "No. There's a purpose to this party and that is to exchange cookies." I also tell them if they feel they just can't bake, they are welcome to go to a real bakery and buy six dozen high-quality cookies and participate. I like to say, "What you lack in time spent baking, you'll make up for in expense." Allowing non-baking, non-swapping guests can be a slippery slope, especially for someone like me who has many non-bakers bake and attend. It wouldn't take many years to degrade the whole party with a large number of non-baking guests. The party works best when everyone is participating in the same spirit.

5. **People who ignore your rules or themes.** As hostess, you never want to make guests feel badly. You never know if some just didn't read your rules carefully enough or even at all. Hostesses largely are gracious and overlook many things that fall below their expectations. If your invitation states "no no-bakes," and no-bakes show

up, if only one, brings them, or even two, it's okay. A few can get lost in the shuffle, and there won't be a dramatic loss in overall quality. If you stated a color theme and a friend dresses in something odd that sticks out like a sore thumb, stand her behind someone for the group picture, with only her face showing. Don't sweat the small stuff. Life isn't perfect, no matter how hard we all try. Manage expectations. When it's finally party time, the vast majority of parties go off without a hitch.

6. **People who take much more than their fair share.** This is a rare problem, but when it does happen, it can be upsetting to the hostess, especially if she's received complaints from others. A few days after the party, have a little chat with the person and explain why taking double the cookies that she brought is taking from others in an unfair manner. Give the person a second chance and invite her again. If she does it again, consider not inviting her in the future.

7. **Husbands who don't want to leave the house.** The majority of cookie exchange parties are still "girls only" and most husbands are happy to take the kids and leave for three hours. However, if this is an issue for you, your choices are to move your party to a friend's house, a restaurant, a rented hotel room, or a clubhouse. You can also make your cookie party one that includes husbands and/or children. One hostess shared a creative fix that she came up with. While she and her friends were swapping cookies in one room, her husband and his friends were swapping unique beers in another room. If there's a problem, there's usually a workable solution. You could also incorporate men into your party by making them cookie-tasting judges.

8. **Friends bringing other friends.** If someone asks you before the party if they can bring a friend, decide whether you want an extra person you may not know. This is your choice and you're not obligated to entertain your friend's friend. It's okay to limit your party and say no. Another situation with "other friends" is when they are a surprise guest at your front door on party day. There's no fix here; just smile and greet the new person as if you invited her yourself. The bright side is if it's your goal to create a large cookie exchange, you can take advantage of this opportunity to grow your party.

9. **Burnt cookies, poor-quality cookies, same old cookies year after year.** Burnt and poor-quality cookies: This is how the "bakery rule" was born. To guests: If you have burnt or ruined your cookies, please go to a real bakery and buy six dozen high-quality cookies. Do not bring burnt cookies to a cookie exchange. Poor-quality cookies: You should bring cookies as good and as high-quality as you'd like to take home. Do not bring store-bought cookies. No one who has spent several hours baking will

be excited to take home Oreos or Nutter Butter cookies topped with canned frosting and sprinkles. The same old cookies year after year: If this is a problem for you, then contemplate having a theme for your next party. The first cookie party you ever give can merely state, "Bring your favorite cookie." After that, some people get in a baking rut or are just not very creative and bake the same thing every year. When you implement a theme, you are guiding the group to seek out new recipes. Story time is more fun this way. Variety is the spice of life!

10. **No rules, no-bakes, no quality control.** Hostesses that don't use any rules or guidelines run the risk of burning their party out and losing attendees because of quality issues. The reason I created my rules is that I received complaints from my family and attendees about the poor quality of the cookies. Too many brought no-bakes, and some cookies featured odd main ingredients like potato chips and saltine crackers, launching the "must use flour" rule. You can use the word "guidelines" if you please, but I prefer the word "rules" because it's more attention-getting. *Rules were also made to be broken,* which happens, even at my parties. If from eighteen guests, I end up with sixteen to seventeen different types of cookies and one or two no-bakes, I can live with that. The good news is that my guests, who are friends, relatives, neighbors, and parents of my kids' friends, from those early 1990s cookie parties, still come to this day. So no guests were harmed or permanently insulted in the creation of "The Rules of the Cookie Exchange."

Creative Invitations

Most people are comfortable now using the modern conveniences of e-mail and the Internet, and hostesses are taking advantage of online services to send out party invitations. Whether virtually, or on paper, send out invitations using the theme of the party. Many hostesses are opting to do both, by sending a paper invitation and then following up with an online service to help keep track of RSVP's and the cookies. If there's no special party theme involved, it's always appropriate to use a Christmas theme since the vast majority (98 percent) of all cookie parties are held in December. (See Other Types of Parties and Swaps on pages 319–24.)

Sending a Save the Date is becoming popular with cookie exchange hostesses. It's a simple notification that you send out in September or October to inform your guests what day you'll be hosting your cookie party. Asking guests to set aside that date makes it less likely that they'll forget or schedule over your party, and they'll know to look for your invitation. Everyone's calendar fills up quickly in December. A Save the Date is not the full invitation, it should be brief. Example: *Save the Date! Robin's Cookie Exchange Party will be on December 12th at 2:00 P.M.* Save the Dates can be sent by e-mail, postcard, or a magnet for the fridge.

Invitations can range from simple to elaborate, costly to relatively inexpensive, and limited only by your own imagination. If money isn't your main concern, you could go to a print shop and have professionally imprinted invitations made. Some hostesses do this; however, the majority create their own. The scrapbooking and stamping communities are well known for their creative invitations. Take a cue from them and visit a local craft store for holiday and themed stamps, stickers, and card stocks in every color. You could send 8 × 10-inch or 5 × 7-inch postcards, note cards, tri-folds, and scrolls. *Do something different every year!*

The list below contains ideas for sending stand-out cookie party invitations.

Handmade Invitation I. Who doesn't enjoy receiving a lovingly handcrafted party invitation? Last year I held an Invitation Contest at cookie-exchange.com. The winner was Allison Ward of Fowlerville, Michigan, who created a gingerbread-themed invitation in the shape of an octagon. There are eight fat, cute, little gingerbread boy tabs, appearing to be in a circle when closed. When you pull on the tabs it opens up the invitation, and inside are the party details, plus a miniature wooden rolling pin glued into the center. It's adorable. See Allison's award-winning invitation online at cookie-exchange.com/contests/.

Handmade Invitation II. I must share one of my absolute favorite handmade invitations *ever,* submitted to the same contest, and winning second place. Diana Watkins of San Antonio, Texas, assisted by her equally talented daughter Kia Davis, created invitations using the theme "'Twas the Night Before Christmas." Kia found the perfect small storybooks. Diana and Kia then rewrote the story to make it their own personalized version and glued it over the pages in the book. They placed the book, with a ribbon tied around it, in a box along with a Santa and stamped the top of the box with a Christmas stamp. On the inside bottom of the box they placed the Cookie Exchange Rules, put the book on top of that, and mailed a box to each invitee. It's quite a keepsake. See photos at cookie-exchange.com/contests/2009/invitation/watkins/index.html.

'Twas the Day of Diana's Fourth Annual Cookie Exchange

'Twas the day of Diana's Cookie Exchange, when all through the house,
Not a cookie was burning, not even the one in the hand of her spouse.
The bar was fully stocked by the chimney with care,
In hopes that the Cookie Makers soon would be there.

The neighbors were nestled all snug in their beds,
While visions of slumber danced in their heads.
And Church in his robe, and I in my apron,
Had just settled down thinking "How great to be the cookie patron."

When out on the lawn there arose such a ruckus,
I put down my spatula and got up off my tukus.
And what to my wondering eyes should appear,
But all the Cookie Makers, "How early they are this year!"

The sun just appearing for waking eyes to inspire,
They seemed all comfy in their nighttime attire.
More rapid than eagles they flew to their trunks,
And opened their doors as their containers stacked with a clunk.

"Now Eva! Now, Linda! Now Hope and Debbie,
On, Cookie! On, Kia! On Marcus and Becky.
To the top of the porch! Come on hurry up ya'll,
Don't stumble! Don't falter, Be sure not to fall.

And then in a twinkling they were all at the door,
All excited and anxious to see what was in store.
And just as I had descended the stairs,
The front door flew open and they all stood there.

From the way they were dressed they must have rolled out of bed,
As their hair stood crazy on top of their heads.
They had wrinkles and creases, not one pant had been pressed,
WOW; they really took this PJ thing to heart when they dressed.

I greeted them all as a good cookie hostess should,
Giving them each a hug and a necklace in the place where they stood.
They all seemed hurried, and they all seemed wild,
Because they knew their cookies must be creatively styled.

Before I could say another word, they went straight to work,
With pilings and stylings by careful hands with no jerk.
They laid their cookies in the most extravagant way,
I was surprised at how some cookie formations did stay.

When the cookies were placed for all to see,
We wined and we dined all our hearts filled with glee.
After the cookies were packed and the party held in high esteem,
I heard them all shout: Oh, I shall bust my inseam!

—Diana Watkins and Kia Davis

You can see other great examples online at cookie-exchange.com/contests/.

Poetic Invitation Contest Winner, Cookie-Exchange.com, 2009

Dashing through the snow, in a four-door SUV,
Over the curb we go, gotta get some groceries!
Bells on ovens ring, making spirits bright,
What fun it is to cook and bake for the Cookie Party night!

Cookie swaps, cookie swaps, cookies all the way!
Oh what fun it is to bake six dozen for the day!
Cookie Swap, Cookie Swap, cookies all the way!
Oh what fun it is to make a side dish or entrée!

Off to mail the invites, I quickly checked the date.
December 12th at 4 o'clock, it's okay if you're late!
There will be drinks galore, and many games to play,
A prize for the best cookie, and one prize for display!

Cookie swaps, cookie swaps, cookies all the way!
Oh what fun it is to leave the children for the day!
Cookie swaps, cookie swaps, cookies all the way!
Oh what fun it is to go, so respond without delay!

—Tracey Weaver

See all nine submissions: cookie-exchange.com/contests/2009/invitation/2009_invitation
.html.

Handmade Invitation III. The front of the invitation: *You're invited to fill up your cookie jar at . . .* then in the middle is a cutout of a cookie jar with gingerbread cookies showing. Beneath that it says *Christine's 8ᵗʰ Cookie Exchange.* Inside the invitation, it says:

December 13ᵗʰ is the date this year
Upon which at my house you should appear
By 11 am plan to arrive for the trade
With your 6 dozen cookies already made.

Please bring an ornament gift for a game we will play
No need to wrap it, but if you want, you certainly may.
There will be munchies and beverages to eat and to drink.
We'll laugh and enjoy plenty of merriment, wink, wink.

It's a busy time of year, so we'll try to party fast,
But you're welcome to stay long and make the gala last.
A copy of your recipe to the party you must also bring,
Please RSVP by 12/6 with an email or a telephone ring.

—Christine Harpel, Fort Collins, Colorado

Christine has been sharing her party photos with us since she had her first CE in 2001. You can see this invitation and other great examples online at cookie-exchange.com/invitations/.

Memories Invitation. Gather group photos of past years of your cookie parties. Arrange like a collage, write the year underneath the photos. Add details of the upcoming cookie exchange party. Scan, add some clip art, and make color copies.

Message in a Bottle. A tropical-themed cookie party invitation could include the party details on "aged paper" that you could create by burning the edges, then rolling the paper as a scroll and stuffing it into a bottle with a couple of shells and confetti at the bottom.

Elegant Scroll. Speaking of scrolls, mail them in a tube or hand-deliver the invitation, written or printed on high-quality stationery or card stock, rolled and tied with a gold or silver ribbon. Quite elegant.

Recipe Card Invitations

From the kitchen of: (your name)
Recipe for: Cookie Exchange Party
Ingredients: 6 dozen homemade cookies
1 large platter to carry home your cookies
4 cups of smiles
5 quarts of laughter
1 extra-large happy heart

Mix together smiles, laughter and an extra-large happy heart for (your name) Annual Cookie Exchange Party. Set aside (date) from (time) for the holiday gathering. Add coffee, tea, or cider to this casual affair as you enjoy the friendship of others. Plan to bring 6 dozen home-made cookies for the exchange. RSVP.

Yield: An assortment of cookies and lots of holiday cheer!

Karen, cookie-exchange.com board member

And another . . .

Recipe for a Cookie Exchange

Ingredients:
30 fun, sassy women
30 × 6 dozen cookies

Mix on Sunday, December 10, at 6 Baker St.
Combine with festive cocktails and shake well
Stir in friends old and new
Add lots of cheer
Toss in holiday music and a dash of a cozy fire
Mix well with a handful of tasty treats
Blend well from 3~5 pm

Yield: 30 happy women with lots of cookies!

—Susan DeBay, East Granby, Connecticut

Wooden Spoons. Buy some inexpensive wooden spoons. In permanent marker, write the date on the front of the spoon. Write or print your invitation on a 4×5-inch card and punch a hole in the corner. Thread a red ribbon through the hole and tie a bow around the base of the spoon handle. Mail in a tube or hand-deliver.

Recipe Card, Returned. Add a cute holiday recipe card to your invitation with a request that the guest send it back with the recipe for the cookies they'll be bringing. (Add a self-addressed, stamped envelope.) Make recipe books to give out at the party. Send cards of various patterns to different people, so when you make copies and put them all together, there's interest and variety to the finished recipe book.

Customized Key Chains and Magnets. Go online and order customized key chains for your Save the Dates. This way no one can claim they forgot the date of your party! Make your own magnets from the craft store or order a bulk supply online.

T-shirt Invitation. Go online and order customized T-shirts with your basic party information or, if you're crafty, purchase plain T-shirts for your guests and use transfers or stamps with fabric paint and glitter glue and put your basic party information on the T-shirt. Advise everyone to bring their T-shirt to the party and have everyone autograph them with permanent markers. You could also ask guests to wear the shirts to the party. Have a signing party, but make sure to have a piece of cardboard to place under the T-shirt, so the permanent markers don't touch the skin.

Edible Invitations. Special delivery! Hand-deliver, or send by postal service, a big sugar cookie or gingerbread cookie with the party date written in icing on the cookie. Include a paper invitation with the details, rules, etc. If mailing, take great care in packaging to prevent breakage.

Please Come to a Christmas Cookie Exchange: A Poem Invitation for Neighbors

'Tis a month before Christmas when on our fair street,
There are still many neighbors whom I have yet to meet.

267

With our weekends very full, I'm hoping you're still available
To bring some festive cookies to set out on the table.

We'll get the day started with a little fun and some treats;
Then you can trade with some others and take plenty home to eat.

Just mix up some batter and a colored sprinkle or two;
Drop by in the morning for a visit and a warm brew.

Bring 5 dozen cookies on your favorite holiday platter.
(If you don't celebrate "Christmas," shoot, that doesn't matter!)

Since it's for just us gals, please don't wake kids or the spouse
Alas the party takes place at my little "mouse house."

If you simply can't make it and still want the sweets
Drop off your exchange cookies to later receive your platter of treats

You'll receive takeaway bags to pack up some tasty goods.
Do come festively dressed and we get to know the neighborhood!

A guest named Kay left this lovely poem on the cookie-exchange.com message board, for her neighborhood cookie swap.

Theme Objects in Invitations. If possible, stick an object or item from your theme inside the invitation. Your party is essentially starting in the mind of the guest from the moment they receive the invitation.

- The Red Feather theme party: Place a red feather in the envelope.
- Alice in Wonderland: Add a playing card as the entry ticket into the party.
- Gingerbread theme: Enclose a gingerbread-scented tea packet (Celestial Seasonings makes Gingerbread Spice Tea).
- The Afternoon Tea Party: Place a tea bag of Earl Grey in the envelope.
- A Medieval theme: Make the outside of the invitation look like a medieval family crest insignia.

- A Sexy Santa party: Glue a piece of small white marabou feather boa to the invitation, for example, line the top of bi-fold card stock.
- A Secret Spice Swap: Place a teaspoon of nutmeg, cinnamon, or other spice in a sealed baggie.
- Viva La Fiesta theme: A bit of colorful paper confetti glued or sprinkled loose in the envelope would be appropriate.

Magazine Cover. There are several companies that offer personalized magazine covers that can be used as a unique Christmas card, a birthday greeting, for graduations, a special anniversary, and most importantly—a thoroughly unique cookie party invitation! How excited would your friends be to see their faces on the cover of a magazine? Simply e-mail the company a good clear group shot from last year's CE party. There are dozens of magazines to choose from. (See Resources, page 331.)

Scented Paper. Invigorate the senses! Ginger-scented paper would be perfect to use for a Gingerbread theme party. You could try to find pre-made scented paper or make your own. Here are three simple ways to add scent to your invitations. Do these before you print.

- Dab a little essential oil directly onto the top or corner of the card, using a cotton ball or Q-tip, but realize it may discolor the paper. Test it first.
- Infuse a whole box of invitations indirectly. Take a 13-gallon kitchen trash bag and lay it on a table in an area not to be disturbed. Take cotton balls and put essential oil on them, then stretch them. Place the scented, stretched cotton balls to the back of the bag. Use a tall, sturdy glass vase to prop up the bag like a tent. Spread the envelopes, paper, or card stock in the bag around the tenting item; be careful not to allow the cotton balls to touch the paper as they may stain. Pull the strings of the bag together as tightly as possible to close, and leave for 48 to 72 hours.
- If you own a perfume atomizer, spray your paper with a fine mist, before printing, and allow to dry thoroughly. Dilute essential oils 75 percent with glycerin, which can be found at your local health store, along with the essential oils. Good holiday scents are ginger, clove, pine, cinnamon, vanilla, and peppermint.

Holiday Cookie Exchange Poem Invitation

It's time once again to let the baking begin,
we'll have a cookie party to get the season started.
Yule bake for a day but don't be dismayed,
your hard work and effort will surely be repaid.

So get out your butter, sugar, and vanilla,
mix them together, and make a sweet treasure.
You must know it's not just one or two dozen,
last year—remember? It was a dozen dozen!

Here are some rules they are not meant to be cruel
but without them you see, there won't be much glee.
No store-bought or no-bakes—no these just won't do.
The point is, it's Christmas so let's see what you can do.

So bring a family favorite or try something new,
call with your recipe so we won't have two.
The count must be perfect so no one is left out,
so please call with your answer so the word can get out.

Bring your dozens all packaged to go.
Place them in a tin or a bag and a bow.
Please attach the recipe, that would be sweet,
so when we get home your recipe we can repeat.

No husbands or children, please leave them at home;
if you brought them all I would need the Super dome.

This was left on the cookie-exchange.com message board by Lydia—it's a cute invitation for hostesses that require a dozen cookies per person.

Talking Invitations. Purchase audio greeting cards. Your own voice inviting guests to your party will surely get their attention and even become a keepsake. Talking invitations are available at stationery stores, drugstores, and online stores. Write out the party details, too. (See Resources, page 331.)

Invisible Invitations. This could be a unique Save the Date, especially for the Red and White Party, the Mardi Gras Party, or the Alice in Wonderland Party. Take a piece of white card stock or paper and write your basic invitation details on it in white crayon. Place a crayon of your chosen color in the envelope. In pen or pencil write COLOR ME in small letters at the top or bottom of card. Your cookie party invitation will magically appear to your invitee when they color over the paper.

Creative Themes for Your Parties

20 Easy Holiday Decorating Ideas

Decorating your home is very important in setting a mood and creating the right spirit when guests arrive at your party. Since most cookie exchange parties are held during the holiday season and winter months, below are some basic decorating ideas for a Christmas theme or Winter Wonderland party. Most could be altered to suit other special party themes. (See Party Themes, page 276, and Seasonal Parties, page 321.)

1. Set the mood and get the spirit going before people even walk into your house by adding luminarias along the walk and placing welcoming holiday or themed wreath on your front door. You'll save up to $25.00 by making your own wreath, if you have access to pine trees. Simply take two or three wire hangers and untwist them with pliers. Form into a circle, and intertwine the wires, then use pliers to twist the wires tight, so that none are poking out. Wear gardening gloves (to prevent sap from getting on your hands), and snip the pine boughs with clippers. Weave pine boughs in between the wires to hold. When the wreath is the size that you want, wrap boughs using florist wire to perfect shape. Make a little wire loop as a hanger for your door. Decorate your wreath with bows, bells, ornaments, and pinecones. *Voilà!* A homemade wreath can also be given as a prize.
2. Make homemade luminarias to line your sidewalk by saving and using old soup cans. Remove the labels, and clean and store the cans until ready. If you'd like to make large luminarias, use coffee cans, and spray-paint them silver or gold. Create

designs like snowflakes and stars by punching holes in the can with a large sturdy nail and a hammer. (Wear heavy-duty gloves for safety.) Place luminarias with lit candles on cement sidewalks. Use tea candles. These are safer than paper bag luminarias, can be reused, and will last forever.

3. Light up your outside walkways by using outdoor Christmas lights. It's useful and safety-minded to light up your sidewalk or footpath as well as festive for evening cookie parties.

4. Place a small check-in table near the front door. It should have the name tags (that you've pre-made, or have a pen handy) and a holiday display with a poinsettia, theme items, and a candle or two. If there's enough room, parting gifts can be displayed there, too.

5. Make cookie or candy container pots: Using a hot glue gun, glue candy canes, side by side and standing on end with their hooks at the top, to the outside of a terra-cotta pot. Fill with cookies or candy. Buy candy rods and surround a plain white candle. Use a glue gun to secure the canes to the candle and then tie a red ribbon around the center. This makes a great holiday decoration as well as a gift or prize.

6. Candles should be lit safely around the house and powder room an hour or less before the party.

7. One of my mood-setting favorites is a simmering pot on the stove of drinkable pot-pourri, which is hot apple cider with cinnamon sticks, a dash of nutmeg, and a few cloves floating in it. My guests rarely drink it; however, it makes the house smell like Christmas.

8. Don't forget to have Christmas music playing gently in the background. Make your song mix well in advance of the party.

9. Create an eye-catching dining table centerpiece by placing red, green, silver, or gold colored glass ball ornaments in a large crystal or glass bowl. Place the top clip point downward and not showing. Sprinkle the balls with glitter, or insert a few silver or gold twigs peeking out, or mount a candle in the middle.

10. I just love poinsettias, and the larger the better. Visit warehouse stores like Costco and Sam's Club for the large varieties at a good price. However, poinsettias are poisonous, so be careful if you have pets. I put the real plants on tables and counters and faux silk poinsettias on the floor.

11. To create a Winter Wonderland look, attach white Christmas lights around the doorways inside of your house. Stick removable utility hooks onto the ceiling and hang Christmas lights from them. Lightweight ornaments can be hung from the strung ceiling lights.

12. Create a cookie wreath centerpiece for your table by arranging Christmas cookies in

a wreath shape on a large platter. If you're daring, place the cookies directly on a fresh tablecloth.

13. Recycle! Save your large coffee cans all year long. Spray red paint on the outside of the cans. When dry, tape doilies against each can and lightly spray with white paint to create a snowflake design. There are many uses for the cans, and they can be used as cookie tins to give away. Instead of painting the can, you can glue wrapping paper around them. When I was a young, poor newlywed, I used decorated coffee cans as a base for homemade holiday centerpieces to give as gifts and to decorate my own house. Fill them with real or artificial flowers.

14. Wrap faux pine boughs and Christmas lights around a stair railing or banister inside your home. Use faux as opposed to real pine, due to sticky sap and pine needle droppings.

15. Use cut pine boughs for centerpiece bases and your fireplace mantel. To prevent sap from sticking to your table or mantel, discretely place wax paper or paper towels underneath pine boughs. (Use Goo Gone to remove sap.) Evergreens give a beautiful holiday look for free. Replace boughs when they start to dry out. (Caution: Pine is highly flammable when dry. Keep it away from fire.)

16. Create a beautiful holiday basket with pinecones and lights. Paint the cones with silver or gold spray paint or simply leave plain for a rustic look. Take white Christmas lights and wind them around the pinecones; tuck the wires as far into the cone as possible. Add a few small faux poinsettias; if you wish. (Situate near an outlet.) This is one of my favorite high-impact, low-cost holiday decorations! Store securely in an airtight container for the following year. Makes a great gift or prize.

17. Nothing makes a house feel warmer and cozier than a glowing fire in the fireplace. Make the fire at least an hour in advance of the party so that it calms down to a low, simmering fire.

18. For apartment dwellers who don't have a real fireplace, you could buy a faux fireplace and mantel. Some have realistic-looking flames and even come with heaters, for practicality. Another option is to purchase just the mantel and make a multi-candle display. If all else fails, pop in the yule log DVD.

19. Replace pictures on walls with Christmas and holiday framed art. Here's an idea I came up with many years ago. I went around to various antique stores and bought a lot of old December issue magazines from the 1920s and framed the Christmas ads. Back then all the art was hand drawn. They're beautiful to look at and quite the conversation pieces.

20. Invest in nice holiday linens and be sure to take advantage of after-Christmas sales!

25 Cookie Themes

Many hostesses like to ask their guests to bring cookies with a theme. Themes are, of course, optional. During the actual cookie-swapping portion of the party, we often like to take turns talking about the cookies we baked and why we chose them. Themes can add a dimension of challenge for the baker, and interest at story-telling time. For non-bakers, choosing a cookie to bring is a challenge, and giving a focus through a theme helps guide people by narrowing down the choices.

1. Your "Favorite" cookie: I recommend this only for a first cookie exchange—how many years in a row can you ask for a favorite cookie?
2. Heritage Cookies: Bring the cookie of your ancestral origin.
3. Cookies *must* have or *must not* have chocolate as an ingredient.
4. Classic Wintertime Treats.
5. Candy Land Characters: Mamma Ginger Tree, The Gingerbread People, Lord Licorice, Mr. Mint, Gramma Nut, Jolly, Plumpy, Princess Lolly, Queen Frostine, King Kandy, Gloppy the Molasses Monster. Decorating for a Candy Land–theme party would be fun!
6. Shaped Cookies: Cookies must have a shape besides plain old, boring round; cut out, molded, pressed, spritz.
7. Traditional Christmas Cookies.
8. Cookies with a cereal incorporated into the recipe.
9. How the Grinch Stole Christmas: Ask guests to use green decorations for cookies and to keep cookies small to represent the Grinch's stinginess.
10. Cookies with any candy incorporated into the recipe.
11. The Healthiest Cookie or Most Decadent Cookie.
12. Must be Sandwich Cookies.
13. Original Cookie: Make up your own recipe. (For advanced bakers.)
14. Hostess's Choice: Hostess sends the recipes to the guests to bake.
15. Cookies must contain fruit, or fruit and nuts, or whatever ingredient you choose.
16. Cookies must be frosted or iced.
17. Grandma's Favorite: May be different from heritage cookies.
18. Colors: Specify all cookies must be red, green, or your color choice. (This could

coincide with a dress or party theme, like Winter Wonderland: blues, whites, silvers.)

19. A Signature Cookie Recipe from your favorite famous chef (this would also be a good potluck theme).

20. Secret Spice: Hostess mails a secret spice or ingredient to each baker and has them incorporate it into a recipe. Alternatively, just e-mail the secret spice information to each baker.

21. Willy Wonka Cookies: Must incorporate a Wonka candy product into the cookie recipe.

22. Sugarless Cookies: No sugar—white, brown, or fake! This will take some creativity, but the cookies must be sweetened with anything but sugar, such as molasses, corn syrup, maple syrup, golden syrup, honey, jams, juices, dates, and any other natural sweeteners. Recommended for advanced bakers. (See Resources, page 330.)

23. For children, teens, 100 percent non-bakers, and those who simply love no-bakes, you could hold a "no-bake and sweet treat"-*only* exchange. Variation: Hold a bars-*only* exchange.

24. Exotic cookies from around the world: The hostess can choose the country or allow the guests to choose from any country they wish.

25. The cookie theme could be "Incorporate Tropical Ingredients," like pineapple, coconut, macadamia nuts, lemon, lime, orange, etc.

Party Themes

Themes can add a special touch in making your cookie exchange party more memorable, and a little goes a long way. You don't have to spend a fortune, or hire a party planner, to successfully pull off a theme. You could implement a party theme through the foods you serve, a centerpiece, specialty drinks, certain types of music, a party game, a costume (easy to hard based on your group's capabilities), posters, inexpensive props from a local party store or an online store. Don't overdo your themes. If you have a dress-up theme, then go easy on the cookie theme. You know what's best for your group. Themes help raise the energy and excitement of your guests. As the years go by, themes help distinguish one party from another. The themes that follow are assorted by ability: Beginners (8), Intermediate to Avid (6), Advanced (6).

Themes for Beginners

Ugly Christmas Sweater
- Have everyone wear their ugliest Christmas sweater and have a voting contest for prizes.
- Variation: Ugly Christmas Jewelry Contest

Hat Party
- Instruct group via invitation to create a fun hat at home for a contest at the party.
- Alternatively, create an activity by going to the craft store and buying items to create hats.
- You'll need: Poster board, scissors, glitter, colored tissue, feathers, buttons, pipe cleaners, colored markers, fake gems, elastic bands. Fun! *Don't forget to take pictures!*

Pajama Party
- Invite guests to show up in their Christmas jammies.
- Vote for the cutest or best, give a prize.
- The prize could also be . . . surprise! . . . another pair of Christmas jammies. Buy 4 sizes: S, M, L, XL. Return unused or re-gift at Christmas.
- Give nightcaps as a party favor. (See Resources, page 331.) What a cute photo you could have with everyone in their jammies and nightcaps!
- Breakfast or brunch foods would be appropriate for this party, no matter what time you hold it.

Ancestral Background Party
- Have everyone bring cookies from the country of their ancestral background.
- Variation: Invite them to wear their ancestral clothes.
- You could also make this party a potluck and have guests bring a dish from their country of origin.

The Red and White Party
- Advise everyone to dress in red or white. This is an easy theme for your guests to follow. Everyone owns a red or white blouse, shirt, sweater, or T-shirt.
- Variation: Red Feather. Place a red feather in the invitation envelope and instruct guests to incorporate the feather as part of their outfit any way they please. The least they can

do is pin the feather to their outfit like a brooch. The results look very nice at picture time.

- Specify that only their tops need to be red or white so that people don't have to shop for a full outfit just to attend your party.
- Variation: A red silk poinsettia. If you choose the poinsettia theme, don't send it by mail, it's too bulky. Just instruct in the invitation for everyone to incorporate a silk poinsettia into their outfit, as everyone has access to those.
- Variation: Christmas ribbons. Everyone uses ribbons as accessories in their hair, as necklaces, belts, etc.
- Have the group vote and award a prize for the best outfit.

'Twas the Night Before Christmas

- Send out storybook invitations. (See Creative Invitations, pages 261–71, for detailed instructions.)
- Advise everyone to wear their pajamas, as it goes with the theme.
- Give nightcaps or Santa hats as party favors. (See Resources, page 331.)
- Make a large chimney table centerpiece for the cookie table.
- To see the most spectacular rendition of this party visit cookie-exchange.com/exchanges/2008/watkins/index.html. *You will be inspired!*

Sexy Santa Party

- Have everyone come dressed as their own rendition of a sexy Santa and hold a contest.
- This theme relies on the ingenuity of your guests. Can you hear the laughter? (Especially when Grandma walks though the door!)
- Caveat: Think carefully about whether this idea is appropriate for your particular group.

Gingerbread

- Gingerbread decorations for a Christmas party are classic and always so appealing.
- Send ginger- or cinnamon-scented invitations. (See Creative Invitations, pages 261–71, for creative ideas.)
- Construct a life-size gingerbread man out of cardboard. Paint and decorate it to greet your guests at the front door.
- Make a gingerbread centerpiece, serve a ginger cake, have apple cider brewing on the stove.
- You could form and fashion cute gingerbread tiaras as a group craft activity or give everyone a matching gingerbread theme apron.

- Play a word scramble game out of the ingredients in a basic gingerbread recipe. (You can download two versions at cookie-exchange.com/party_games/.)
- Give homemade chocolate-ginger truffles or gingerbread cookies with guest names on them as parting gifts.

Themes for Intermediate to Avid

Christmas Movie Character
- Have everyone dress as their favorite Christmas movie character: Rudolph the Red-nosed Reindeer, Frosty the Snowman, The Grinch, The Abominable Snowman, Scrooge characters like Tiny Tim, The Ghost of Christmas Past and Present, *It's a Wonderful Life*'s Mary Bailey, *Elf*, Little Drummer Boy, Nutcracker, Disney characters. Vote for the best dressed.
- Hold a Best Costume Contest, prizes could be tickets to the latest hit movie.
- Check the Resources, page 331, for where to find costume rentals.

Viva la Fiesta
- Incorporate an Hispanic theme by using red, white, and green for your decorations.
- This is one of the few themes for which I'd recommend you purchase nearly all the party goods from a local party supply or online because the items are not expensive.
- Buy a piñata, which can be used as a centerpiece until it is time to play: i.e., bash it to pieces to get the hidden treasures. Add baking items such as cookie cutters, measuring spoons, recipe cards, and spices.
- Decorate your tree with hot chili pepper and cactus lights and all manner of "South of the Border" like maracas and crepe paper decorations.
- Fill piñatas with candies, containers of Mexican jumping beans, and maybe even some small gift cards. (See Resources, page 331, for piñatas.)
- Serve foods from the South-of-the-Border Menu, page 290.

A Victorian Christmas
- Serve an afternoon English tea. (See English Afternoon Tea Menu, page 294.)
- Enclose a sealed tea bag in the invitation envelope.
- Use nice damask table linens and place snacks and tea on large serving trays.
- Place small vases of red or white roses around your room.

- Decorate your Christmas tree in a Victorian fashion.
- Find a local costume store and see if you can rent extravagant period hats with large feathers. (See Resources, page 331.)
- If you own real silver and china, this party would be a great excuse to pull it out and use it.
- Go to a vintage or antique store to pick up gifts and prizes.
- If you don't own a china set, then go to secondhand or antique stores to pick up mismatched tea cups.
- You may find yourself pleasantly surprised at the affordable treasures you'll find at a secondhand store. Don't forget the teapots!
- Lastly, a vintage beaded purse would make a lovely prize.
- See the Resources, page 331, for tea etiquette and create a mini poster display for guests.

Christmas Luau Party
- Place red, white, or green leis on your guests as they arrive, and wish them a Merry Christmas in Hawaiian; say, *"Mele Kalikimaka!"*
- For games you could have a limbo contest; young guests will enjoy that although older folks may not participate, so be sure to have another game that all ages can enjoy.
- For decorations, make a centerpiece starting with a pineapple and finishing with traditional Christmas items.
- Decorate with fake palms trees using Christmas lights and ornaments.
- For musical ambience, play Don Ho Christmas music.
- Serve appetizers on skewers, sticking out of a pineapple. (See Hawaiian Pupus Menu, page 294.)

Winter Wonderland
- Invite everyone to dress in silver or white and/or light blue.
- Decorate your house with a lot of white or silver Christmas lights and candles.
- Drape silver garlands from the corners of the ceiling, going across the room. Hang shiny paper snowflakes from the garlands and ceiling using different lengths of ribbon.
- Create a faux Christmas tree of white and blue balloons in an unused but visible corner. Use large balloons for the base and graduate to smaller balloons for top. Keep balloons together using double-sided tape. Place a small light behind it, being careful not to touch the balloons. Sprinkle the balloon tree gently with silver shredded confetti or white glitter.

- Decorate your room using silver garlands, white candles of different heights, and Christmas ornaments in various shades of blue.
- Sugar cube ice castles or igloos would make an excellent centerpiece for a Winter Wonderland Theme. Create a base out of plywood or heavy-duty cardboard. Spray the base with white paint. Depending on the size centerpiece you want, purchase several boxes of sugar cubes. Build the castle or igloo by stacking the sugar cubes, bonded with white or clear glue. When finished, glue white, sparkly confetti or tinsel on the base.
- Consider serving the Swedish or German Menu, see page 295.

Elegant Party

- Instruct guests through the invitation to dress up in their most elegant and glittery attire. (Advise that they use something they already own, and not shop specifically for the party.)
- Serve foods from one of the following menus: the Gourmet Brunch, the Afternoon Tea, or the French Menu. (See pages 289, 294, and 298.)
- Be sure to serve drinks in martini glasses, no matter what the drink is, for that elegant touch! (Do a toast at picture time.) Plastic martini glasses will work, too.
- Use your finest linens, china, and silverware, if possible. And, there is plasticware that *looks* just like silver; it's amazing! (See Resources, page 331.)
- Midway through the party, everyone will be wishing they weren't wearing high heels. Play a fun game where they have to take their shoes off to play, called appropriately "The Shoe Game" (in the party games chapter, on page 309). This memory game would be great for a large group of twelve or more. After the game, inform everyone they are free to leave their shoes off. *Did I just hear a collective sigh of relief?* If money is no object, hire Fabio to carry everyone back to their cars.

Themes for Advanced Hostesses

Medieval/Renaissance Party

- Check your local party store or costume store for medieval specialty items. Look for crowns, jester hats, and royal scepters. If you can find any type of prop with a "knight in shining armor," *bonus points.* (See Resources, page 331, for costume rentals and Mardi Gras.) There are many party stores online that sell theme supplies and props at a reasonable cost.

- Create a Queen's robe out of a gold, red, dark blue, or burgundy furry sofa throw blanket and, using safety pins, pin a white feather boa along the edge. This is a good economic solution for a onetime-use item.
- Make a family crest for your front door, adorned with Christmas greenery.
- Create an elaborate centerpiece using a lot of sugar-dipped fruit and platters filled with food and large candles of different heights throughout. The idea you should have in your head is the elaborate feast given by the Ghost of Christmas Present in *Scrooge* (1970, Albert Finney, my favorite!). Not that extreme, of course, but it's the best vision of a medieval feast, *ever.*
- For Best Cookie contest or game play, be sure to "crown" the winner. Make a big deal out of the presentation. Toot a horn and exclaim: "Hear ye! Hear ye! I doth would lik-eth to present to ye, the most righteous Queen of the Cookie Exchange!" Then place the robe and crown onto the "Queen" and hand her the royal scepter. Then proclaim: "You may now bow to the Queen!" Have your camera ready and take pictures!
- For ambience, keep lighting low, think of the haunting and romantic castle look. Place flickering candles in large sturdy silver or pewter candlesticks and bowls of fruits and nuts around your party rooms.
- Use a lot of pine boughs and cones. The colors to use are forest green, royal blue, burgundy, or dark purple; think dark gemstone colors.
- The best music to fit this theme perfectly is to play Mannheim Steamroller Christmas albums.
- Look up your family crest online (or make one up). Print it and place it on poster board or frame.
- Make a menu on a small poster board using Old English. (See Medieval/Renaissance Menu, page 296.) Again if money is no object, hire Fabio in costume to greet your guests.

Alice in Wonderland Mad Hatter's Tea Party

- An Alice in Wonderland–style, topsy-turvy tea party would be rollicking good fun for a cookie party!
- Invitation: "Don't be late! Don't be late, for a very important date! The Queen of Hearts requests your presence for a Cookie Swap, Tea, and Mad Hat Party."
- Do the usual instructions for a cookie party. Then, on a playing card, using a permanent marker, write, "Please bring this prize ticket to get into Wonderland." Put the playing card into the invitation envelope, along with a bit of glittery confetti, for magic. Have a white rabbit stuffed animal with greeting sign, to greet your guests at the door.

Place an upside-down hat and a sign that says, "Drop tickets here!" In the middle of the party do a raffle with the entry tickets.

- Advise guests to make a crazy hat for the Mad Hatter's Contest, or make the hats a craft activity.
- Decorations and effects: Everything in Alice's world is topsy-turvy, large and small, and nothing matches. Go to a vintage, antique, or secondhand store and pick up non-matching tea cups and teapots—the crazier looking, the better.
- Use different colored plasticware and paper plates.
- Place stuffed animals around in odd places, like the corner of a table, floor, or hang them from ceiling—cats, frogs, fish. Bonus points, if you can find some plastic pink flamingos!
- Make posters on poster board of playing cards, mushrooms, large clocks, and the Cheshire cat.
- String colored Christmas lights in an X shape across the ceiling, and hang lightweight paper lanterns and tinsel.
- Use non-matching chairs for the tea party table.
- Make table place cards out of cookies, each with a guest's name. Place a sign near the gingerbread cookies that says OFF WITH THEIR HEADS!
- If you have extra tea cups and saucers from your vintage store forays, create a center-piece out of cups and saucers, putting the smallest on the bottom and stack upward. Use a hot glue gun and start on a wood base for support.
- Topsy-turvy presents are another prop that you can create inexpensively, with huge impact. Gather an assortment of cardboard boxes in various sizes and gift-wrap them. You'll need about twelve wooden dowel rods, scissors, and clear duct tape. Visualize a Christmas tree shape out of the boxes; the finished height should be five to six feet tall. The dowels should be at least ½ inch thick for sturdiness and about 12 inches long. Some will have to be sawed in half for different tilt angles. Stack boxes, largest on bottom, and as you stack, tilt them at unreasonable angles, using the dowel rods and clear duct tape for support. Punch holes in the boxes with scissors as necessary. Stick stuffed animals in crevices to keep the dowels from showing.
- Construct signs that say THIS WAY and THAT WAY and place them around the party area.
- Use the Afternoon Tea Menu, page 294, and make signs that say EAT ME or DRINK ME for the food table.
- Activities: Entry ticket raffle, Mad Hatter's Contest, play croquet in the den, award prizes!

Mardi Gras/Twelfth Night Party The Mardi Gras season begins on January 6, or the twelfth night after Christmas. This custom is descended from the Saturnalia celebrations of ancient Rome. Twelfth Night is the beginning of a celebration to mark the end of the holy holiday season. For the last two thousand years, forms of this traditional "letting loose" party have been celebrated annually all over the world. People dress in outrageous costumes, sing, dance, tell stories, and eat special foods, which vary by region.

- The colors used to decorate for your party should be the official colors of Mardi Gras. Purple represents *justice*; green represents *faith*, and gold, *power.*
- Start out by decorating for a Medieval/Renaissance theme and then keep going by adding masks and beads.
- You could purchase all the masks for your guests and give them out at the party or make a crafting event out of creating the masks. To make masks, you'll need supplies that can easily be found at a craft store. Start with inexpensive, plain masks, Elmer's glue, beads, glitter, trims, sequins, and many colorful feathers. Hold a contest for the best mask and let the group vote.
- Serve the traditional Mardi Gras King Cake, also known as Twelfth Night Cake or *galette du roi.* The King Cake is similar to a Danish pastry or cinnamon roll and decorated in Mardi Gras colors. (The French version contains frangipane cream, a pastry cream made with almonds.) Each King Cake typically has a small plastic baby (a symbol of the Holy Day) placed inside. The tradition is that each person takes a piece of cake hoping to find the plastic baby inside. The person who receives that special slice and finds the plastic baby is crowned Queen of the cookie party; have a special crown for her (or him if you allow men at your party).
- Serve food from the Louisiana Menu, page 291, or the Medieval/Renaissance Menu, page 296.
- For drinks serve Lamb's Wool, a traditional English and Irish Twelfth Night drink made of cider or ale, sugar, spices, and roasted apples, and Wassail, which is an ale drink with spices and honey. (See Resources, page 330, for the drinks listed above.)
- For games, play the Twelve Days of Christmas Icebreaker listed in the party games chapter, page 304.
- A theme-appropriate parting gift could be homemade Creole seasoning in little tins or baggies, and you can attach a recipe for Jambalaya.
- See Resources, page 331; look for Mardi Gras.

1950s Party The fabulous '50s! What a fun era to play in, and with so many possibilities. Decide whether you want do an adult style '50s party or a classic '50s teenager-style party. You could morph some ideas together from both styles. For teen-style party, the dress would be bobby sox, saddle shoes, poodle skirts, or a Pink Ladies jacket; guy wear would be cuffed blue jeans, white T-shirts. The movie *Grease* would segue perfectly into a '50s party.

- For a classic '50s teen-style party, send 45 records with paper invitations and enclose some holly stickers to get the Christmas theme going.
- For a more adult theme, look up classic '50s style invitations and use '50s retro fonts, which can easily be found on the Internet.
- For teen decorations, incorporate a Mr. Potato Head toy into your food centerpiece.
- Decorate your Christmas tree in 1950s or 1960s style. Use strands of large Christmas bulbs, in standard colors: red, white, blue, and green, a lot of silver tinsel, and round, shiny plain ornaments in red, silver, blue, and green. Aluminum-looking trees were also "in."
- Visit an antique store and see if you can find a calendar from the 1950s to display prominently. Look for 1950s magazines, and cut out and frame the ads.
- Place a life-size cut-out of Elvis, James Dean, or Danny Zuko with a real Santa hat on, to greet your guests at the door.
- Party favors: Cat eye glasses and chiffon scarves; hand out before picture time.
- Some fun '50s games and contests to play would be a hula-hoop contest, yo-yo contest, a bubble gum–blowing contest, a *Grease* trivia contest (shout out answers or write on paper), a dance contest with teams doing the Jitterbug, the Stroll, the Cha Cha, and the Lindy Hop.
- For prizes give silly 1950s items like fuzzy dice and wax lips. There are some really high-quality retro candy collections available online. Nostalgic candies will surely bring a smile to those who remember the candies of their childhood like Candy Necklaces, Dots, Candy Cigarettes, Bubble Gum Cigars, Wax Bottles, etc.
- The basic '50s teen foods are hamburgers, hot dogs, fries, milkshakes, and root beer floats.
- For an adult 1950s party, see the 1950s Theme Party Menu listed on page 299.
- For parting gifts, give Revlon lipsticks in '50s classic colors like In the Red, Cherries in the Snow, and Fire and Ice.
- Hold a contest for "Best '50s Hair!" Examples are The Flip, Beehive, Page Boy, Pin Curls, and Bettie Page bangs.

- There are many fun '50s props available on the Internet.
- Music: A lot of Bing, of course! For an adult '50s party, there's a wonderful 1950s three-album set called *Christmas Cocktails* (Complete Set, 72 songs). Search online for the best price.
- See Resources, page 331, for a '50s party.

1960s Party

- Up to 1965, life was very much like the mid to late 1950s. For an early 1960s theme party, encourage guests do their best "Jackie O" by wearing pearls, pillbox hats, and white gloves. Award a prize for best costume.
- Making pillbox hats could be a craft activity.
- Go to an antique store, buy some 1960s magazines, cut out the automobile and kitchen ads, and then frame and display around your party rooms and in your powder room.
- For the early '60s Christmas look, it was quite common to see simple paper cutouts as decorations, usually purchased at a drugstore (or 5&10 cent store) and taped up to the windows and sliding glass doors.
- Purchase 3-D cutouts made of honeycomb tissue in the middle, to use as a centerpiece, from your local Hallmark store, drugstore, or look online for vintage paper decor.
- Decorate your Christmas tree 1950s or 1960s style. Use strands of large Christmas bulbs in standard colors: red, white, blue, and green, a lot of silver tinsel, and round, shiny, plain ornaments in red, silver, blue, and green. Aluminum-looking trees were also "in."
- Go to a secondhand store or eBay and try to procure a rotary phone. Oh, the memories, it took so long to make prank phone calls back in those days! *Did I say that?* (Party lines were a blast, it was like an audio-only version of the Internet.)
- Serve foods from the 1960s Elegant Dinner Party Menu, page 300.
- From 1965 on, the staid conservatism of the 1950s era disappeared, seemingly overnight. Next stop, the Swingin' '60s! Purchase an Austin Powers life-size, cardboard cut-out to welcome guests. Put a real Santa hat on his head.
- For music, play *The Beatles Christmas Album* and do a search for 1960s Christmas music.
- Guests could wear mini skirts with long boots, or white go-go boots, and midi and maxi skirts.
- For the late '60s, a hippie-style party is in order. Ask guests to wear flowery peasant-style dresses and put flowers in their hair.

- Follow decorating instructions (below) and menu for the 1970s themed party (page 300).
- See the Resources, page 331, for a '60s party.

1970s Party
- The '70s started in hippie and ended in disco. For a hippie party, invite guests to dress in bell bottoms, tie-dye T-shirts, fringed vests, love beads, headbands, peace signs, and ankh necklaces. If you don't want to go crazy hippie, you could be middle-of-the-road '70s. Along with jeans, there were corduroy pants with polyester patterned blouses, and shoes were Dr. Scholl's, desert boots, clogs, and platforms.
- Invitation ideas: The '70s was the homemade era, so make your own invitations. Use flower power in Christmas colors.
- Common colors were earth tones, like dark brown, rust, avocado, lime, or army green, mustard, and orange.
- The Christmas trees were often fake, with tinsel garlands and homemade ornaments like macramé and strung popcorn. Big-bulbed Christmas lights were still used in the early '70s and the miniature lights came into vogue in the late '70s.
- If you own a lava lamp, now would be a good time to pull it out and build your table centerpiece around it.
- Disco balls are easy to find and *scream* '70s. There are many '70s party kits available online.
- Contests and games: '70s Trivia Contests, Mad Libs, Musical Chairs, Charades, Best '70s Outfit; have a Disco dance-off and award the best and worst dancers. Have the group perform "Y.M.C.A." Game prizes could be cherry or bubblegum lip gloss, Rubik's Cubes, and mood rings.
- For crafts, buy some lanyard (aka gimp) in Christmas colors and have guests make a bracelet or key chain. Do you remember the butterfly, zipper stitch, and box stitch? (See Resources, page 331.) Another craft from back in the day was to make leather friendship bracelets with beads added.
- For Christmas music play the Carpenters, and be sure to visit iTunes for a good mix, as a lot of '70s bands put out at least one Christmas song. Don't forget to download the dogs barking "Jingle Bells," a '70s radio staple.
- Serve from the '70s Party Menu, page 300, or the Fondue Party Menu, page 299.
- Give your guests a homemade Pet Rock as a parting gift. *Have a nice day!*
- See the Resources, page 331, for a '70s party.

25 Party Menus

I'm quite sure that there are some sit-down dinners at cookie exchanges, but at most cookie exchange parties, the foods are served buffet style. This way guests can roam around, chat, and mingle while they eat. The menus below can be used for either sit-down dinners or buffet-style dinners. The food menu theme does not have to be the same as the overall party theme, although it can be. In addition, there can be a cookie theme, which is different from the party theme.

To allow space for the buffet and the exchange, use different rooms. At my parties the dining room features the cookies, and the den and kitchen have the party food.

If you're running dry on ideas, a creative food menu theme can help inspire you to come up with your party theme. Think different, unusual, and exciting! Doesn't everyone eat enough ham and turkey in December? These sample menus are merely a starting point, if you care to have a food theme. The goal was to come up with different and interesting menu combinations in which the majority of the foods could be made in advance and served hot in chafing dishes, soup or stew pots or slow cookers, and casseroles. Feel free to mix and match where applicable and, of course, add your own special touch!

You do not have to feel compelled to serve alcohol at your party. I simply added drinks that went with the theme or era for your convenience in case you wanted to offer an appropriately themed alcoholic drink.

The food is ready—so let the party begin!

The American Brunch

Egg, Bacon, and Cheese Casserole
Creamed Chipped Beef on Biscuits
Chocolate Chip Silver Dollar Pancakes
Quiche: Bacon and Cheese, Spinach and Feta, Ham and Cheese, Mushroom
Hash Brown Casserole
Corned Beef Hash
Sausages
Texas French Toast
Cinnamon Bread French Toast
Platter of Breads, Rolls, and Muffins

Yogurt, Granola, and Fruit Parfaits
Baked Apples

Orange Juice, Wine Spritzers, Coffee

Gourmet Brunch

Eggs Benedict
Gravlax on Toast Points, topped with Finely Diced Red Onions,
Chopped Hard-Boiled Eggs, and Capers
Fresh Fruit Compote
Strawberry or Banana Crepes with Crème Fraîche
Russian Blinis with Caviar or Smoked Salmon,
Dollop of Sour Cream

Pastry Tray with Petits Fours, Chocolate Eclairs, Mini Fruit Tarts

Mimosas, Blood Marys, Coffee

Deli Brunch

Platter with Nova Lox, Cream Cheese, Sliced Red Onions, Lettuce,
Tomato, Muenster Cheese, and Capers
Variety of Toasted Bagels
White Fish Salad
Matzoh Brei (Scrambled Eggs, Onions, and Matzoh)
Blueberry Blintzes
Fruit Platter
Noodle Kugel
Bowl of Cottage Cheese, with Side Bowls of
Granola and Fruit Toppings

Mandel Bread
Rugelach
Halvah

Dr. Brown's Black Cherry Soda, Cream Soda, and Ginger Ale
Manischewitz Wine, Coffee

South-of-the-Border Menu

Taco Bar: Chicken or Beef, Tomatoes, Guacamole, Sour Cream, Green Onions,
Shredded Lettuce, Diced Tomatoes, Gourmet Hot Sauces
Carne Asada for Fajitas (or Beef, Chicken, Pork, or Shrimp)
Seven-Layer Taco Dip
Tamales and Taquitos
Bacon-wrapped Shrimp Stuffed with Cheese and Jalapeños
Tortilla Chips served with Salsa Verde
Queso Fundido (Mexican Fondue)
Pork Carnitas
Fresh Fruit Skewers

Flan served with Mini Churros
Spicy Mexican Chocolate Cookies served with Vanilla Bean Ice Cream
Watermelon Granita

Sodas, Margaritas, Mojitos

Under the Sea Menu

Shrimp Cocktail
Ceviche
Seafood Canapés: Smoked Oysters on Crackers, Dill Shrimp Dip on Toast Rounds,
Crab Cheese Ball with Crackers
Tuna or Salmon Salad served with Cocktail Breads

Lobster Bisque
Bacon-wrapped Shrimp with Dipping Sauce
Crab-stuffed Mushroom Caps
Vegetable Crudités
Crab Louis Salad
Fried Calamari with Lemon Dipping Sauce
Flounder Stuffed with Crab Imperial
Sautéed Scallops in a Parmesan-Lemon Butter Sauce over Pasta
Maryland-style Crab Cakes

Fruit Tart
Lemon Sorbet

Sodas, White Wine, Spritzers

Louisiana Menu

Louisiana Sunburst Salad
Gumbo
Jambalaya
Baked Shrimp Creole
Mini Muffalettas
Coleslaw
Red Beans and Rice
Salad

Bananas Foster
Bread Pudding with Hot Rum Sauce
Pecan Pie

Café au Lait, Iced Tea
Cocktails: Hurricane, Sazerac, Ramos Gin Fizz

Southern/Soul Food Menu
Fried Chicken
Barbecued Ribs
Macaroni and Cheese
Coleslaw
Collard Greens (or Spinach)
Black-eyed Peas
Orange Fluff
Candied Sweet Potatoes
Cornbread

Hummingbird Cake
Chess Pie
Peach Cobbler

Southern Sweet Tea, Spiked Fruit Punch, Pink Lemonade

Japanese Menu
Ginger Salad
Miso Soup
Edamame
Sushi and Sashimi
Shrimp and Vegetable Tempura
Gyoza Dumplings
Tonkatsu (Fried Pork Cutlet) with Pungent Dipping Sauce
Yaki Soba

Green Tea Ice Cream

Tea, Sake, Soda

Thai Menu

Tom Yum Goong Soup
Spring Rolls with Dipping Sauce
Pork Satay served with Peanut Sauce
Pad Thai
Gaeng Panang Gai (Coconut Chicken Curry)
Khao Ob Sapparod (Baked Pineapple Rice with Chicken and Cashews)

Banana-Coconut Cream Custard
Coconut Sorbet
Bananas and Lychees in Sweet Coconut Milk

Lemon Soda (Num Ma Now), Hibiscus Tea (Cha Ka Jeape)
Cocktails: Bangkok Cooler, Siamese Sour, White Lotus Flower

Chinese Menu

Crab Rangoon
Pot Stickers
Spring Rolls and Egg Rolls served with Sweet Sour Sauce
Lettuce Wraps
Shrimp Toast
Moo Shu Pork
Sweet-and-Sour Chicken
Barbecued Spareribs

Mango Pudding

Chinese Cocktails, Jasmine Tea, Tsingtao Beer

Hawaiian Pupus Hors d'Oeuvres Menu

Lomi Lomi Salmon

Rumaki

Teriyaki Beef Skewers

Crab Rangoon

Char Siu (Spareribs)

Coconut Shrimp

Ahi Poke

Bacon-wrapped Pineapple

Hawaiian Kalua Pig (Slow Cooker)

Huli Huli Chicken

Teriyaki Mahimahi

Banana Bread

Fresh Tropical Fruits Platter

Sweet Potatoes

Coconut Cake

Fruit Punch, Sodas

Cocktails: Blue Hawaii, Mai Tai, Piña Colada, Lava Flow

English Afternoon Tea

Muffins, Scones, and Crumpets served with Clotted Cream, Lemon Curd,
Jams, and Preserves

Delicate Finger Sandwiches: Cucumber and Herb (Mint or Dill), Smoked Salmon,
Egg Salad, Tuna Salad, Watercress

English Trifle

Dainty Pastries

Variety of Teas: Black Teas, Oolongs, Green Teas, Herbal
Flavored Waters

Swedish Smorgasbord

Platter of Soft and Crisp Breads served with Compound Butters
Cold Sliced Meats and Cheeses served with Various Mustards
Hot Meats: Swedish Meatballs, Ham, and Sausages
Cold Seafood: Shrimp, Crab, Caviar, Pickled Herring, Gravlax, Anchovies
Baked Salmon or White Fish
Flying Jacob (Casserole of Chicken, Bananas, Bacon, and Peanuts)
Cold Raw and Pickled Vegetables: Radishes, Variety of Olives, Sliced Cucumbers
Cold Salads: Potato Salad, Egg Salad, or Coleslaw
Raggmunk (Potato Pancakes)

Morotskaka (Swedish Carrot Cake)
Swedish Tea Ring
Daim Torte

Sodas, Juices, Coffee, Glögg (Mulled Wine)

German Menu

Canapés: Egg and Anchovy Spread on Crackers,
Ham on Buttered Dark Bread
Cucumber Salad
Pickles, Olives, Celery
Potato Salad
Sausages served with Dusseldorf Mustard
Mini Reuben Sandwiches
Spaetzle (Little Dumplings)
Zwiebelkuchen (Onion Pie)
Sauerbraten (Sweet-and-Sour Pot Roast)
Schlachtplatte (Sausages, Sauerkraut, and Potatoes)

Schwarzwalder—Black Forest Cake
Linzertorte

German Beer, Wines

Medieval/Renaissance Menu

Cheese Platter with Dark Breads like Pumpernickel and Rye
Cranberry-Orange Scones and Butter
Mushroom Tarts
Canel Cucumber (Cucumbers with Cinnamon Sugar)
Sausages in a Savory Sauce
Cheese, Egg, and Onion Pie
A Sop of Onions
Roasted Beef
Chawettys (Fifteenth-century Meat Pie)
Roasted Chicken

Crustade Lombarde (Fruited Custard Pie)
Chardwardon (Spiced Pears) topped with Swithin Cream
Gyngerbrede
Fruyte Fritours (Fruit Fritters)

Hippocras (Spicy Mulled Wine), Missionary Punch, Mead (Honey Wine)

See Resources, page 331, for links to many of these recipes.

Italian Menu

Bruschetta
Antipasto Platter
Caponata
Ensalata Caprese
Gourmet Pizzas (Chicken, Goat Cheese, Pineapple, Spinach)

Portobello Mushrooms Balsamico
Chicken Marsala
Fettuccine Alfredo

Tiramisu
Apple Crostata
Tartufo, Lemon Granita, Chocolate Gelato
Cannolis

Sodas, Cappuccino
Cocktails: Campari and Soda, Bellini, Rossini, Caruso, Limoncello

Greek Menu

Greek Salad
Tiropita (Greek Cheese Pie)
Raw Veggie Platter with Garlic Hummus Spread
Feta and Olives
Roasted Eggplant Spread with Toasted Pita Bread
Fried Zucchini with Tzatziki Dipping Sauce
Spanakopita (Spinach Pie)
Lamb Souvlaki
Moussaka (Beef and Eggplant Casserole)

Loukoumades (Honey Puffs)
Baklava (try my Baklava Cookies on page 158)
Anomala (Chocolate-covered Roasted Almonds)

Sodas, Juices, Vyssinatha (Non-alcoholic Sour Cherry Cordial)
Cocktails: Acropolis, Blue Aegean Angel, Greek Doctor

Indian Menu
Roti (Bread)
Raita (Yogurt Dip)
Dalchini Palau (Cinnamon Fried Rice)
Dal Makhani (Lentils, Beans, and Onions with Tomatoes and Cream)
Dahi Ki Dal (Split Pea and Yogurt Soup)
Palak Paneer (Spinach Curry with Cheese)
Baigan Ka Bharta (Mashed Eggplant)
Pork Kebabs
Shrimp Curry
Tandoori Chicken

Badam Phirni (Almond Pudding)
Kheer (Rice Pudding)

Ginger Ale, Spiced Tea, Mango Lassi (non-alcoholic, can be spiked)
Beer: Taj Mahal, Kingfisher

French Menu
Olive Tapenade with Crackers
Vegetable Crudités
Frisée (Salad) with Goat Cheese, Pears, and Caramelized Walnuts
Smoked Salmon Terrine served with Toast Points
Mini Quiches
Savory Onion Tart
Foie Gras and Pâtés served with Crusty Breads
Baked Brie en Croûte topped with Toasted Almonds
Salad Niçoise
Chicken Marengo or Coq au Vin
Ratatouille
French Gourmet Cheese Platter

Fruit Tart
Pâtisserie: See Resources, page 330, for link

French Wine

Fondue Party

Gruyère or Emmental Cheese Fondue served with French Bread and Raw and Blanched Vegetables
Steak Fondue in Hot Peanut Oil or Beef Broth, served with Various Dipping Sauces

Chocolate Fondue served with Pound Cake, Strawberries, Pineapples, Berries

Sodas, Wine

1950s Theme Party

Bowls of Chex Mix, Peanuts, Potato Chips
Sour Cream and Onion Dip served in a Hollowed-out Cabbage
Canapés: Deviled Ham, Hot Cheese Puffs, Salami on Ritz topped with Gherkin, Pimiento Spread
Melon Ball Cocktail served in a Cut-out Melon
Dried Beef Log
Guacamole Dip on Crackers
Cheesy Stuffed Celery (Cheddar or Blue Cheese combined with Cream Cheese, Piped)
Deviled Eggs
Three-Bean Salad
Molded Jell-O Salad
Pigs in a Blanket
Lobster Newburg served in Croustades (Mini Puff Pastry Bowls)
Tuna Noodle Casserole
Beef Stroganoff

Chocolate Soufflé
Peppermint Pie
Baked Alaska

Sodas, Coffee
Cocktails: Whiskey Sour, Singapore Sling, Manhattan

The 1960s Elegant Dinner Party

Tomato Aspic
Bay Shrimp in Cocktail Sauce
Pineapple Cheese Ball served with Ritz Crackers
Waldorf Salad
Wilted Spinach Salad
Gelatin Salad in a Fancy Mold
Chicken Divan
Beef Wellington
Turkey Tetrazzini
Potatoes au Gratin
Asparagus in Lemon-Butter Sauce

Lemon Meringue Pie
Baba au Rhum

Soda, Coffee, Tea
Cocktails: Old-fashioned, Tom Collins, Dry Martini

1970s Theme Party

Dips: Lipton Sour Cream 'n' Onion Dip, Guacamole, Clam Dip
Chips: Pringles, Nacho Cheese Doritos, Ruffles, Fritos
Bowls of Trail Mix

Canapés: Deviled Ham on Triscuits Topped with Gherkin, Tuna Salad on Cocktail Rye,
Spam (and leave the can out for laughs), Salami and Cheese on Ritz Crackers

Salad Bar: Iceberg and Romaine Lettuce,
Tomatoes, Sliced Red Onions,
Olives, Mushrooms, Shredded Carrots, Alfalfa Sprouts, Sunflower Seeds,
Avocado, and Homemade Croutons served with Thousand Island, Creamy Italian,
French, or Ranch Dressing

English Muffin Pizzas

Crepes with Fruit like Strawberries or Blueberries
and Whipped Cream or Savory Crepes such as Sautéed Onions
and Mushrooms with a Béchamel Sauce

Mini Quiches

Pita Pocket Sandwiches

Ambrosia or Watergate Salad

Pigs in a Blanket

Broccoli and Cheese Vegetarian Casserole

Meatballs in Jelly Sauce

Teriyaki Shish Kebabs

Carrot Cake

Sara Lee Cheesecake with Cherries

Bowl of Pop Rocks and Pixy Stix

Coke, Pepsi, Dr. Pepper, Fresca

Fruit Punch with Ginger Ale and Sherbet

Celestial Seasonings Herbal Teas

Cocktails: Tequila Sunrise, 7 & 7, White Russian, Harvey Wallbanger

Lighter Fare Menu

Fresh Veggie Platter with Low-Calorie Dips

Fresh Fruit Kebabs with Sweet Neufchâtel Dip

Vegetable Crudités

Hard Cheeses and Crackers Tray

Salads
Turkey and Veggie Wraps
Poached Fruit Compote

Sorbet, Granita

White Wine, Wine Spritzers, Iced Tea, Juices

The American Casual Menu

3 to 6–Foot Submarine Sandwiches (pre-sliced)
Mushroom Caps filled with Sausage Stuffing or
Gorgonzola Cheese or Crabmeat
Slow Cooker Pulled Beef in BBQ Sauce served with Split Rolls
Cold Spinach Dip served in a Bread Bowl
Hot Chipped Beef Dip with Sliced French Bread
Hot Artichoke Dip, Crackers, and Veggies
Veggie and Fruit Platter

Sodas, Wine, Beer, Hot or Cold Cider, Coffee, Tea, Punches

Breaking the Ice

The purpose of party activities and games is to get people circulating, make new acquaintances, and break the ice! We often invite people from different parts of our lives who don't know each other. A group activity that involves laughter quickly bonds, and strangers become friends. Games get people moving around and raise the energy in the room.

Activities and Party Games

Who Am I?

Decorate a nice holiday basket and fill with pencils and small sheets of paper. Have everyone submit one entry with the name of a famous person, then fold the paper and place it in the basket. The hostess will then tape a piece of paper with a famous name to each guest's back. Have an assistant hand you a random submission. Guests walk around while they're socializing and ask random people questions to figure out who they are. You are only allowed to ask one person one question as to "who you are." Am I male or female? Am I in politics or entertainment? Am I famous or infamous? This is a fun game all by itself and doesn't require a prize. You can also create a Christmas version, and ask for famous Christmas movie characters.

Poem Contest

Notify guests through the invitation to write a short and cute six-line (or more) poem about the cookie exchange. Have each participant bring their poem to the party and tell them not to share it with anyone. The hostess puts all the poems into a basket and then goes around the room and has everyone draw out one. Everyone takes turns reading a poem aloud. When all are finished reading (and laughing hysterically!) the hostess gives each guest a piece of paper to vote for their favorite poem (not their own). She then collects the results and announces a winner.

Can't Say Cookie

Using candy canes, make necklaces with red or green ribbons. When the guests arrive, give each guest a necklace to wear. Guests aren't allowed to say the word "cookie." If the person says "cookie," they lose their candy cane necklace to the person who caught them saying the word. At the end of the cookie exchange, the person with the most candy cane necklaces gets a prize.

The Purse Scavenger Hunt

The person who pulls the most items out of their purse from the hostess's master list wins a prize! You can make up your own list or use this one to start: $10 bill, 2005 penny, grocery receipt, safety pin, business card (specify for a doctor or beauty parlor), lotion, pen, comb, shopping list, mirror, roll of LifeSavers, mints or gum, lipstick (lip gloss or lip balm), nail file, earring, ticket stub, eyeglass case, scrunchie (pony tail tie), coupon, postage stamp, Starbucks card, dental floss or pick, speeding ticket, hand sanitizer, an iPod, tissue, perfume.

Twelve Days of Christmas Icebreaker

Print out several copies of the song "The Twelve Days of Christmas." Mark them consecutively with the numbers 1 through 12 (the first one is marked #1, the second #2 . . . when you get to the thirteenth one, you start again with #1, etc.). At your party, pass out one to each person. Everyone with a #1 must stand and sing the first line of the song, now and each time it comes up again. (For example: "On the first day of Christmas my true love gave to me, a partridge in a pear tree.") When they are finished singing they should sit down. Then, everyone with papers marked #2 has to stand and sing the second line now and each time it comes up. (For example: "On the second day of Christmas my true love gave to me, two turtle doves . . ."). When they are finished they sit down and those with #1 must stand and sing their line again ("and a partridge in a pear tree"). Then they sit down and those with #3 stand up and sing, etc. There's a lot of getting up and down and some very funny singing and a great way to get everyone laughing! (You can find the lyrics online at cookie-exchange.com/party_games/.)

The Present Game

To play this game you will need:

- A prize in a box, gift-wrapped in a dozen layers; use lots of tape!
- One pair of bulky gloves or knitted mittens; this makes it more challenging.
- An Elf hat or Santa hat plus a scarf.
- One die in a pie pan, for passing.

The gloves, hat, scarf, and wrapped box are placed in the center of the room. Choose a person to begin the game by rolling the dice. The first person to roll a six runs to the middle of the room and puts on the hat, scarf, and gloves. They attempt to unwrap the present as fast as they can. The bulky or slippery gloves should make this difficult. They have to work quickly because the next person to roll a six takes the hat off the person in the center. The person in the center stops immediately and takes off the scarf and gloves and gives them to that person, and returns to the group. The game continues like this until the package is completely unwrapped, and the person who finally unwraps the prize is the winner and gets to keep it!

Pass the Stocking

Fill a stocking with a lot of Christmas-related items. For example: a candy cane, Santa figurine, coal, nutcracker, garland, bells, ornaments, cinnamon stick, cookie cutter . . . Gather your party group in a circle and pass the filled stocking from person to person. Let each person feel the items in the stocking (no peeking) and when everyone has had a chance to feel all the items in the stocking, have the participants write down all the items and objects they felt. When everyone is done and has submitted their paper to the hostess, she will pull everything from the stocking to reveal the actual items. The person who correctly guesses the most items wins a prize!

Tools: Paper, pencils, and magazines or clipboards to write on.

Dirty Santa (Gift Exchange)

Advise your group through the invitation to bring a wrapped gift for a gift exchange. Decide in advance how much you want the items to cost. Example: "Bring a $10.00 wrapped gift, for a gift exchange game we'll be playing."

When guests arrive at the party, have them place their wrapped gifts under the Christmas tree or on a gift table.

Let's say that you have fifteen guests participating. Create fifteen small pieces of paper and number each piece, 1 through 15. Place the numbers in a basket. Have everyone draw a number from the basket to determine their order.

The person who drew the number 1 unwraps any gift they choose from the pile and then shows it to the group. Each successive participant, in the order of their number, has the option of opening a new gift *or* stealing an already opened gift. If a person decides to steal a gift (and become a dirty Santa!), the person whose gift is stolen gets to repeat his/her turn and either steals another person's gift (he/she can't immediately steal back the gift that was just stolen from him/her) or unwrap a new gift.

This cycle of stealing continues until a new gift is chosen, at which point the turn is passed to the participant with the next number from the drawing.

Since items can be stolen up to three times, the gifts in your possession are not yours to keep until the game is declared over. The game is over once all numbers have been drawn from the basket.

The Memory Game

Place about twenty items on a large Christmas platter or baking sheet. Make the items random objects that you have around your house. Don't use a theme because that makes remembering easier. Provide each participant with pencil and paper. Present the tray and allow the participants to view it for 2 or so minutes. Remove the tray and have everyone write down as many objects as they can remember. The person who correctly guesses the most items wins a prize.

Tools: Paper, pencils, and magazines or clipboards to write on.

Variation: Display only kitchen gadgets.

Blind Auction I

Through the invitation, ask everyone to fill a brown paper lunch bag with items from home. Nothing new, just random items they think others would find cute, funny, or useful. Hold a blind auction with the assorted bags. You can use Monopoly money or make your own. Decide how much money to give out and when someone has run out of money, they're out of the auction. Let people team up and split their winnings if they want.

Blind Auction II

After two decades of cookie parties, I discovered that I had lots of random prizes and overstock collected from years of after-Christmas sales expeditions. Therefore, at my 2008 cookie exchange I didn't need to ask anyone to bring anything, and I provided all the blind auction items. Now for the fun part, which my girls really loved. In 2008, the stock market crashed not too long before my party. Real money was nearly worthless, and everyone (in the whole wide world) was depressed and worried. I decided to lighten the mood for my party and auction, so I printed my own "funny money." I printed out $100,000.00 bills and digitally "glued" ten different famous male celebrity faces where George Washington's face should be. I gave everyone ten bills of $100,000 each, totaling a million dollars. To hear twenty-three women trying to out-shout each other was hilarious. "I bid $300,000 dollars!" I bid $500,000 . . . I bid a MILLION DOLLARS!!!" I auctioned twenty-three prizes, so everyone won something. When the action was over, the girls were fighting over who got to keep George Clooney and who got to keep Brad Pitt! This was definitely a hoot. If you don't want to spend money on the prizes, you could ask each guest to bring a $5.00 wrapped gift, ornament, or white elephant. The celebrity funny money is a special download for subscribers of my free newsletter.

Reindeer Antlers Game

The object of the game is to see who can build the biggest, baddest Reindeer Antlers the quickest! Divide your group evenly into teams, for example, five teams of three people each or three teams of five each; it's your choice on how to split your groups. Have each team choose a leader. That person will be the Reindeer for their team. Give the leader of each team a pair of pantyhose. Place a bowl with assorted balloons near each group so all players can easily access them. Set a time limit, such as ten minutes, for team members to blow up the balloons and then hand them to the lead Reindeer, who will crazily attempt to stuff the balloons into the pantyhose. When the timer goes off, the Reindeer leaders have to all put on their "antlers" immediately, and whoever has the best "rack" wins! Give little gifts to the winning team members.

Tools: A few large bags of assorted sizes of balloons, cheap panty hose (from the dollar store), a timer, and your camera, because you won't want to miss taking a picture of this game!

The Right/Left Christmas Gift (Ornament) Exchange

This is a popular game to play at cookie exchanges. In the invitation, specify that everyone bring a small wrapped gift or ornament in the $5.00 to $10.00 range. The hostess reads a letter aloud while everyone follows the directives of the letter by passing their ornaments right and left.

(See cookie-exchange.com/party_games/ for twelve different Left/Right stories to print.)

Christmas Bingo

This family favorite game with a Christmas theme can be purchased online; the cost is between $5.00 and $10.00. Alternatively, you could make your own customized version with your word processor or graphics program.

New Year's Resolutions

Take 8 × 11-inch sheets of paper and cut them into nine pieces. Make enough for the number of guests participating. Hand each guest a slip of paper and a pencil. Have each of your guests write down five New Year's resolutions and sign their name. The hostess will be the reader and not participate. Only the hostess knows who wrote what. Now hand each guest another piece of paper that will be the answer sheet, and have them number the paper according to the number of guests present. The hostess pulls a paper slip randomly and that will be #1. The hostess reads it aloud, and keeps track of who wrote what by placing the paper with the resolutions face down, in order, when done reading. The guests have to guess who wrote the resolutions by writing on the answer sheet. At the end of the readings, state the persons' names in order who wrote the resolution and then see who guessed the most correctly. That person wins a prize.

Who Did That? (Icebreaker Game)

Take 8 × 11-inch sheets of paper and cut them into nine pieces. Make enough for the number of guests participating. Hand a paper square and a pen or pencil to each guest. Have each person write something down that nobody would ever guess that person has ever done, such as "I have bungee jumped" or "I've swum with sharks" or "I've gone skydiving." Put all the responses in a basket. The hostess will pull out one at a time and read them aloud. Everyone then tries to figure out who did what. This is always a great icebreaker, everyone learns something unusual about each other, and there's lots of laughter.

Make a Christmas Tree

Give each guest a piece of green, yellow, and red construction paper. Each guest has to then hold the piece of paper behind their heads and rip a Christmas tree from the green sheet, a star from the yellow sheet, and a stocking from the red sheet. The guests then tape their tree together. Have the group vote for the best artistic rendition and then award a prize to the winner. Variation: Have them rip angels and make the prize an angel ornament or angel tree topper.

The Shoe Game

Gather your group in a standing circle, but don't tell them why. Make sure they are all paying attention. Start the countdown. "Ready? Five, four, three, two, one!" and then yell "Kick off your shoes and toss them in the middle!" Everyone will look around frantically, trying to recall who was wearing what shoes, and then toss their shoes into the pile.

Taking turns, clockwise, the person whose turn it is has to pick up a shoe and attempt to correctly match it to the rightful owner. If they are correct, they stay in the game, but they just knocked out the person whom they correctly guessed. The person who got knocked out collects their shoes and leaves the circle. If the person they guessed was the wrong person, they are out of the game and have to remove their own shoes from the circle.

The person who correctly matches the shoes now has a choice: Keep going to knock out more people *or* say "Next" and then the next person takes a turn. (They have to tell the truth if it's their shoes.) It's going to get down to two people who obviously know their own shoes.

The hostess has a choice on how to end the game and declare a winner:

- The last two are winners, give 2 prizes.
- Have the last two play rock, paper, scissors.
- Have a die in a pan and have them roll a six to win.

Possible prize? Give a gift certificate to a shoe store!

Ornament Games
Pass the Ornament. Supplies: A drinking straw for each person, and lightweight ornaments. Pass the ornaments down the line, person to person, by inhaling and exhaling on the straw to hang on to or release the ornament. No hands! Each person who drops the ornament exits the game until one person who remains is declared the winner!

Musical Ornament. This game is similar to musical chairs. Get everyone in a circle. Hand a guest a non-breakable Christmas ornament to pass around, from one person to the next. Play cheerful Christmas music. Randomly stop the music. When the music stops, the person holding the ornament is out of the game. The last person holding the Christmas ornament wins a prize.

Guess the Baby
Collect baby pictures in advance, by e-mail, of all guests. Print out and tape them on a large poster board with a number next to them. Give the guests a sheet of paper on which you've already printed the names of the guests in no particular order. Have the participants try to match up the names with the baby faces! *Can you hear the ooohs and aaaahs?* The guest with the most correct guesses wins a prize.

Holiday Fashion Show
Supplies: Scissors, a stapler, tape, crepe paper in different colors, newspaper. Break the group up evenly into teams. Tell everyone they are going to put on a fashion show and they must choose one person as their model. Set a timer and give them ten minutes to come up with the best outfit. Have the groups vote. Give the winning team members a small gift.

Gingerbread House (Activity and Prize)

Make a gingerbread house—just the house itself, no decorations. Have each guest do one part of decorating it, i.e. the doors, windows, walkway. (You supply the decorations.) They then put their name into a hat, and at the end of the party, one name is chosen to take the house home for their Christmas centerpiece.

Christmas Trivia

You'll need supplies like pens and pencils, a hard surface to write on (a magazine or clipboard works), and copies of the games for each guest. Many games are available online, some are free and some are to purchase. You could come up with the questions yourself. Check out cookie-exchange.com, where I offer free games to download and have some special party game resources for my newsletter subscribers.

The Card Toss

Set out a laundry basket and have ready three Christmas cards. Set up a line, real or imaginary, that each person will stand behind to play the game. One at a time, each person comes up to the line and has three chances to toss a card into the basket. This is harder than it sounds! A variety of card sizes and weights makes it more challenging, also. If you have a lot of people playing, you can use two baskets and six cards, to allow two to play at the same time. If you want, you can have play-offs with those who did the best and tied, until you have only one winner and award a prize.

Unscramble the Cookie Names

Make a list of two dozen cookie names. Then on another piece of paper rearrange the letters. Make copies for your guests. Hand out pencils and provide something to write on such as a magazine or clipboard. Give a prize to the first person who completes the list. (Also preprinted on my Web site, cookie-exchange.com, and available as download through my newsletter.)

Pin the Nose on Rudolph

Alternatively, "Pin the Beard on Santa," a spin-off on "Pin the Tail on the Donkey." Check your local party stores.

The Scarf Game

Take a winter scarf and wrap it around your neck. Tell the others something the scarf can be used for. For example: "A scarf can be used for swiping out dust bunnies from under the bed." Continue passing the scarf until everyone has participated. After awhile you begin to get some really unique and funny responses (along with demonstrations with the scarf!).

Decipher the Canticles

Guess the Songs of Christmas. This is a word twist game where you have to figure out the meaning. Here are the first three:

1. Exclamation, Member of the Round Table with missing areas.
   Answer: "Oh, Holy Night."
2. Boulder of the Tinkling Metal Spheres.
   Answer: "Jingle Bells."
3. Vehicular Homicide was Committed on Dad's Mom by a Precipitous Darling.
   Answer: "Grandma Got Run Over by a Reindeer."

There are twenty-five canticles. Go to cookie-exchange.com/party_games/, and print out the question and answer sheets. Make this a timed game and award a prize.

The Raffle Game

The purpose of this game is to reward those who follow your cookie exchange party rules. Hostesses report back that doing the raffle helps with attendance and compliance of rules.
   Example:

You'll receive one raffle ticket *if you arrive to the party on time.*
two *tickets if you wear holiday earrings.*

three tickets *if you make holiday cookies* (or the theme asked for).
four tickets *if you wear holiday attire.*
five tickets *if the cookies are on a holiday platter.*

The person with the most tickets gets a prize. Give out prizes for first, second, and third place. Make up your own raffle rules and put them in the invitation.

25 Ideas for Prizes, Party Favors, and Parting Gifts

Historically, hostesses have always given party favors and parting gifts at cookie exchange parties. You needn't feel pressured to do so, it's your party, therefore you can make up your own rules and you don't *have* to do anything more than host the party. However, if you'd like to give contest prizes, favors, and parting gifts, here are some crafty and creative ideas to get you started.

1. **Cookie Recipes.** Give cookie recipe books—like this one!
2. **Homemade Cookie Recipe Books.** Use the recipes for the cookies that will be featured at the upcoming CE party, or an accumulation of recipes from past cookie exchanges. Have guests e-mail their upcoming recipes in advance of the party. Print, then staple together, or use a hole punch, and tie together with a festive ribbon. Purchase festive holiday stationery for the book cover, and add your name and the year:

   Robin Olson's 20th Annual Cookie Exchange
   2009 Cookie Recipes

   If you want to add a personal touch, don't bind the book, but have it all ready to go in a room that won't be used for the party, like a home office. During the party, take a digital group party picture. Discreetly scamper off into your office, download the photo, and print copies of the picture for the main page. Enlist a close friend or relative to assist you in quickly binding the booklets. The process of downloading, printing, and binding should take under ten minutes, if everything works right and your printer doesn't jam. Or ask the guests to bind their own, providing festive ribbons for the hole punches.

For further personalization, turn this into a group activity. Have the group sit in a circle. Pass out pens and something hard to write on, like a clipboard or magazine. Pass out the newly created cookie recipe books, so that everyone has one. This next part would be akin to signing school yearbooks.

Have each person write their own name on the front cover, so everyone will know whose recipe book it is. Then each guest will pass the book to the person to their left, clockwise, and each person will write their signature on their own recipe page. Keep passing until everyone has signed all the books.

The only thing they have to do is write their signature, but advise the group to feel free to add more if they desire, by writing a little personal note to the owner of each book, if they know a person well. Advise the group to also put next to their name how many CE parties of yours they've attended: "Leslie Kelly, fourth timer!" or "Judy Willis has attended five times!" *Voilà*. A low-cost and highly personalized keepsake!

3. **Snowman Soup Mix.** Here's an easy recipe for Snowman Soup. Place directly into a Christmas mug or a zippered baggie: 1 packet of pre-made hot chocolate mix, 2 to 3 chocolate kisses, a dozen mini marshmallows, a small candy cane. Attach the poem to the mug or baggie. If using a mug, decorate with cellophane wrap or tulle. Attach the following poem:

Snowman Soup

A little cup of cocoa,
I'm sending your way,
For you to sip and enjoy,
On some cold lonely day.

As you sip this cocoa,
Its warmth will warm your heart.
Just like our friendship warmed mine,
Right from the very start.

4. **Homemade Potpourri.** Give out dried herbs from the garden like lavender, lemon balm, etc., wrapped in tulle and tied with a pretty ribbon.

5. **Ceramic or Glass Holiday Platters.** Hand these to guests right before the cookie swap and have them use it for their take-home cookies. This gift can be rather expensive, so it works best when you have a small cookie exchange, which would be five to ten people. Nice holiday baskets would work well, too. *Keep an eye out year-round for sales!*

6. **Kitchen Utensils.** Give utensils that have to do with baking as gifts or prizes—rolling pins, whisks, spoons, parchment paper, or assortment of cookie sprinkles, decoratively wrapped and tied with ribbon.

7. **Christmas Coffee Mugs.** Fill festive mugs with mixed nuts, Hershey's Kisses, Reese's Peanut Butter Cups, or peppermints.

8. **Commemorative Christmas Ornaments.** Imprinted with the year on them.

9. **Cookie Cutters.** Cookie cutters make great prizes or parting gifts. Tie a ribbon around each one. Hang them like ornaments on a miniature lighted Christmas tree by your front door. Very festive! Tell everybody to take one as they're leaving.

10. **Homemade Breads, Treats, and Candies.** Give homemade baked items such as mini banana bread loaves, Amish friendship bread (see recipe on www.robinsweb .com/food/breads.html), old-fashioned popcorn balls, peanut brittle, peppermint bark, homemade toffee, gingerbread fudge, or chocolate truffles, decoratively wrapped. (See Tiger Nut Sweets, page 252. Attach history.)

11. **Homemade Extra-Large Gingerbread Man Cookie,** personalized with the recipient's name.

12. **Plants.** Give small plants such as African violets in 4-inch pots, tied with a festive ribbon. If you know how to propagate plants, this is a really thrifty and low-cost way to give nice gifts. Plants that are especially easy to propagate are pathos, spider plants, Coleus, and creeping Charlie. Asparagus ferns clumps can be divided. Miniature mistletoe or holly plants would be festive, too.

13. **Holiday-scented Candles.** If you're inclined to be crafty and thrifty, gather straight twigs, and stand up vertically against a pillar candle, surround with a rubberband to keep the twigs in place. Hot-glue the twigs, then remove the rubberband and tie a wide red or gold ribbon around it and make a bow—rustic, handmade, and useful.

14. **Personalized Christmas Stockings or Santa Hats.** The Santa hats are very cute if everyone wears theirs at picture time.

15. **Themed Aprons, Tea Towels, Oven Mitts, Trivets.** Possible themes could be the 1950s, Victorian, or Santa.

16. **Customized Gifts.** Use an online service like CafePress (www.cafepress.com) to create your own custom mouse pads, mugs, clocks, T-shirts, etc. Some items if ordered in bulk, fifteen or more, are approximately a one-third discount of their base prices.

17. **Small Prizes for Group Game Winners.** Ideas for cute and cost-efficient prizes include ornaments and holiday notepads from a dollar store; small (1 to 3-ounce) bottles of hand lotion or perfumes. Recycling is always a good idea: Make gift tags from old Christmas cards—cut out cards, punch a hole in corner, stick a ribbon through, and tie a knot. Wrap the gift tags in cellophane in groups of 8 to 10 cards. Also, give small tins or baggies of dried herbs from your garden or purchased in bulk from warehouse-type stores.

18. **Homemade Luminarias.** See page 272 for instructions on how to make them.

19. **Christmas CDs.** Give the gift of your favorite music.

20. **What's Your Favorite Store?** The best gifts are something you would buy for yourself. I often give gifts from my favorite stores like Bath & Body Works. My ladies have received full-sized bottles of my favorite scented shampoos and lotions that I picked up at the semiannual sales, usually January and July. Always a big hit!

21. **Homemade Cheese Spreader.** Go to a thrift store and raid their silverware bin for stainless steel spoons. (Real silver is very hard to hammer.) Look for spoons with a nice design on the handle. They don't have to be matching. You will then need a hammer, a hard, flat surface, and a towel. Put the spoon on the hard surface, like a cutting board, and cover with the towel. Gently beat the round part of the spoon and flatten it. You've just created a really nice butter or cheese spreader! Tie a ribbon around the neck of the spreader. Give it as is with a little note attached, or make some homemade compound butter or cheese spread to go with it. This is a nice, useful, but completely inexpensive gift that will last forever! (My Dad taught this it to me when I was a teenager.)

22. **Easy Winter Bird Feeder.** Gather large pinecones, stick florist wire around the top of each, and make a loop for hanging on a tree. Spread peanut butter on the cone, then roll in birdseed. Wrap them in cellophane and tie with pretty ribbon.

23. **Christmas Jewelry.** Holiday jewelry such as necklaces, earrings, and bracelets is always a welcome gift. These are nice items worth buying at after-Christmas sales for the following year's parting gifts or prizes.

24. **Quick Sweet Breads, Brownies, or Cookie Mixes in a Jar.** Take your favorite cookie recipe and use only the dry ingredients. Place the ingredients in a clean glass

jar. Create a tag with instructions on what to add and how to make the breads or cookies. Wrap the jar with a pretty bow. This makes a great parting gift or prize.

25. **Homemade Cinnamon Tree Ornaments.** Combine 2 cups of ground cinnamon with 2 cups of applesauce, then roll out with rolling pin and cut out with cookie cutters. Punch out a hole at the top and thread with a ribbon for hanging. Smells like heaven! Optional: Sprinkle with glitter. Keep on racks until completely dry, then store. These ornaments retain their smell for up to five years.

Buy the large bottles of cinnamon at Costco or Sam's Club.

Other Types of Parties and Swaps

Hosting a Children's Cookie Party

Hosting a children's cookie party can really be fun! The party suggestions are broken down by ages; two to seven years old, eight to twelve, and thirteen years and up. Customize your party for your group's age and ability level.

Two to Seven Years Old

Boys and girls between the ages of two and seven are too young to bake and bring cookies or even appreciate the concept of swapping and trading, so make this a cookie decorating party. You'll need other moms to help if there's more than a few kids. Simply provide sugar or gingerbread cookies and give each child a little baggie of royal icing (snip the corner off), other squirtable colored frostings, and bowls of candies. Supplies you'll need: a large plastic tablecloth, moistened paper towels, cookies, candies, icing, and your camera.

Eight to Twelve Years Old

This is the age group where kids may start to show an interest in helping you bake, and depending on their ability level, let them do as much as they're capable of. Boys may still be interested in helping you bake a little, but may become less interested as they get older. You could have a cookie exchange party with this age group as long as all the mothers are on board to help. The kids understand the concept of trading, but they still need baking supervision. I'd recommend keeping this group small, no more than eight. Plan to play some party games, in particular from this book: Can't Say Cookie, The Present Game, Pass the Stocking, Reindeer Antlers, and Christmas Bingo. Recipes from this book for the this age group would be *any* in the Bar, Tartlets, and Turtles chapter and the Easy Treats chapter as well as any cookie listed as Easy elsewhere in the book. I would like to highlight that Thumbprints, Shortbreads, Russian Tea Cakes, and Mexican Wedding Cookies are particularly easy for kids to help with. They would love rolling cookie dough into balls and then into either ground nuts or confectioners' sugar, or sticking their thumbs into the dough to make thumbprint cookies. The cookies and treats that I think would appeal to children the most are: Peanut Butter Cup Cookies, Bird's Nests, Cathedral Windows, Rolo Turtles, No-Bake Mice Cookies, and Easy Reindeer Cookies. If you want fun, kid-friendly cookies, but prefer them be real baked cookies (as opposed to no-bakes, which feature candy as the main component, the base or incorporated), choose the Candy Cane Twists, Peanut Butter Christmas Mice, Chocolate Reindeer Cookies, Santa's Whiskers, or Butter Thins. These are cookies with *a little bit* of candy for decoration but are listed as Intermediate or For Advanced Bakers, which of course means you, Mom, are going to do most of the work, but you can have the kids help decorate the cookies. With this age group you could also have the group bake a batch of cookies together.

Thirteen Years and Older

Okay, now it's just a girls' party. Teenage boys like to eat cookies, but honestly, if you ask your fourteen-year-old son if he wants to host a cookie exchange party, he'll look at you like you have two heads. This age group of girls has two choices for a party. The first choice is a cookie exchange party where they bake the cookies at home, because starting around thirteen years old, they are capable of baking by themselves without supervision. However, teenagers enjoy activities, are highly social, and work well in teams, therefore I'd recommend a baking party. How many teens to invite depends on the size of your kitchen. If you have a small kitchen, invite no more than four girls, a medium-size kitchen, five to six, and if you have a large kitchen, no more than eight girls to keep chaos to a minimum (speaking from experience). By invitation, have everyone bring certain ingredients to make the cookies. You could help your daughter (if she needs it) choose two or three cookie recipes, and then help her break down the ingredients and make a homemade invitation. Since this is the age group of sleepovers nearly every weekend, you could also incorporate the baking party into a pajama party and let them play games and contests from this book, which they are old enough to read and pick out for themselves.

Seasonal Parties

By popular choice, cookie exchange parties are held primarily during the Christmas holiday season, anywhere from the day after Thanksgiving up to Christmas Eve. However, there's nothing stopping you from hosting a cookie party during another season, if you are motivated to do so. Also, who said exchanging has to only be *cookies?* Let's throw some ideas around and instead of starting off with "why," let's begin with *"why not?"*

Other Holidays That Could Feature a Cookie Swap

Hanukah. There are very few types of purely Jewish cookies, mainly just Rugelach, Macaroons, Mandel Bread, and Hamantashen, so create variety by starting with the two Mandel Bread recipes from this book and adding Macaroon Kisses, Apricot Jewels, Baklava Cookies, Oatmeal Crispies, Sesame Thumbprints, and the Best Ever Sugar Cookies using cookie cutters in the shapes of dreidels, the Star of David, and menorahs. Decorate the cookies with blue and white icing. *L'chaim!*

Valentine's Day. Any cookie can be made with red or pink coloring to fit the theme. Try heart-shaped Sugar Cookies, Sweeties, Pinwheels made with strawberry or raspberry jam, Strawberry-filled Tea Cookies, Cream Wafers, Cherry Bonbons, Hidden Kisses, Cherry Cookies, Macaroon Kisses.

Mardi Gras. Serve, or have everyone trade, mini King Cakes with fun prizes baked inside. Use the Mardi Gras Twelfth Night theme listed under Party Themes (page 284). This would be a colorful, fun, and tasty party, and I would probably include men.

St. Patrick's Day. I would include men in this one, too, since beer is always featured at any St. Patrick's Day party! Another recommendation would be to have everyone bring an Irish dish. You make the corned beef and cabbage and have others bring everything else. Recommended cookies from this book are: Best Ever Sugar Cookies cut out in shamrocks, rainbows, leprechauns, etc., Sweeties (but use green food coloring instead of red), Espresso Shortbread, Colorful Cream Cheese Pinwheels in white and green, Irish Chocolate Mint Squares, Irish Lace Cookies, and Thumbprints but substitute mint jelly or add a drop of green to apple jelly. Basically, any cookie that could be made green with food coloring and decorator's sugar could be used to fit this theme.

April Fools' Day. Have everyone make April Fools' cookies. What is that, you ask? April Fools' cookies are cookies that look like one thing but taste like another! This could be accomplished by implementing a variety of different spices, extracts, colorings, icings, or ground nuts. Examples: Looks like a classic gingerbread, but tastes like chocolate or looks like a classic shortbread, but tastes like peppermint. Looks like a Lemon Melting Moment, but tastes like cherry, or looks like a peanut butter cookie, but is cinnamon flavored. Here's an eye-popper, Deviled Eggs, which are little meringues created in the shape of an egg, but cut in half, and where the yolk would be in a real egg, place a spoonful of lemon curd. I think you get the idea now. If you have a creative and advanced baking group, an April Fools' Cookies Exchange would work very well and story time would be a blast!

Easter. The theme party for Alice in Wonderland would work well for an Easter party. Cut out Best Ever Sugar Cookies in shapes like eggs, bunnies, and tulips, then ice or frost using pastel food colorings. Cookie recipes from this book that would be good for Easter could be Colorful Cream Cheese Pinwheels, Lemon Melting Moments, Apricot-Cream Cheese Thumbprints, Spritz Cookies, Cherry Bonbons, and Cathedral Windows, using white chocolate. Party favors or placards could be made out of the Bird's Nest (no-bake) recipe. Use white chocolate instead of butterscotch and instead of topping with cherries, stick 3 colored jelly beans or Jordan almonds on top to look like eggs. *Be sure the White Rabbit greets your guests at the door.* Since Easter always features candy, how about a homemade Candy Exchange? Any no-bake would do.

Cinco de Mayo (The Fifth of May). Serve a Taco Bar with all the trimmings and ice-cold Margaritas. Cookies could be sugar cookies in traditional Hispanic shapes, Spicy Mexican Chocolate Cookies, Peruvian Alfajores, Churros, Mexican Wedding Cookies, and serve Tres Leches cake for dessert. See Party Themes—use Viva la Fiesta (page 279)!

Mother's Day. A perfect time for a tea party. The cookie recipes should concentrate on family hand-me-downs. Make this a special mother-daughter party. Have everyone take turns stating how much their mother means to them and to share one specific life lesson that they learned from their mother. (Have tissue boxes handy and take pictures before this part.) Hostesses: A great party favor to give at the beginning of the party would be to create homemade corsages for all of the mothers in the group. Use a different color and type ribbon for each mom. Then make a simple bracelet out of the matching ribbons for the daughter(s), for matching sets.

Christmas in July. For party decorations, go with a patriotic theme, or literally "Christmas in July." A third option would be to mix the summer season and Christmas elements together and feature Santa wearing a bathing suit, and carrying a surf board. (Search online for "Surfing Santa.") This would be the time to feature a Cookie and Treat or Candy Party so that you could feature no-bakes and keep everyone away from their ovens, *if they choose.* Serve or swap the Nanaimo Bars as they're a cold, refrigerated bar cookie, Chocolate Billionaires, a candy treat, or the Chocolate Oatmeal Cookies, which are boiled and then cooled for a summer party. Another possibility is to hold a contest to see who can come up with the best-tasting, but lowest-calorie cookie, which would appeal to summer sensibilities. What about a "bars only" theme to limit time spent in front of an oven? How about Lemon Bars and Cherry Coconut bars? Other fruity, therefore summer-appropriate, baked cookies from this book could be: Pineapple-filled Cookies, Banana Bread Cookies, Orange-Nut Pinwheels, Sesame Thumbprint Cookies, Lemonade Cookies, and Dreamsicle Cookies with Glaze.

Halloween. Hold a costume contest and give prizes for best decorated theme cookie, spookiest cookie, or best platter presentation. Cookies from this book could include: Best Ever Sugar Cookies and Gingerbread cut-outs with basic Halloween shapes like witches, half-moons, cats, candy corns, and pumpkins. For decorations use red, orange, green, and black food colors, icings, sprinkles, and Halloween candy. For witches' broomsticks, make Bird's Nests aka Haystacks (from page 235) and stick them on clean 3-inch twigs for the broom handles. Sprinkle the cookies with black decorator's sugar. Other cookie suggestions are: Basic Butter Cookies, Spritz Cookies, Cream Wafers, Pinwheels (using black and orange food color and sprinkles), Orange-Cream Cheese Chocolate Chip, Pecan Lace Sandwich Cookies with Orange Buttercream (add black food dye to the cookie base), No-bake Mice Cookies, Iced Gingersnaps, Caramel Apple Cookies, Apple Butter Brickle Tarts, and, lastly, convert the Nutty Ribbon Sticks into Witches' Fingers by adding black decorator's sugar. "Polish" the fingertips with Wilton red sparkle gel icing. Make eyeball cookies out of Australian Chocolate Wheaties: Dip in melted chocolate around the sides for eyelids, and top with M&M for pupil. (Note: Black food coloring is available at most craft stores and online. You can also make your own by combining equal parts of red, blue, and yellow food coloring in a small, clean empty glass bottle.)

Other Swapping Ideas

When the economy is down, sharing, trading, and exchanging items and/or services within your group of friends makes good sense. Here's a list of items *other than cookies* that could be the focal point of swap or exchange parties.

- Wine, gourmet cheese, tea, main-course dishes, appetizers, soup swaps, raw cookie dough, cakes, cupcakes, pies, breads, etc. If it can be eaten, it can be swapped. If presenting perishables, have everyone bring a Styrofoam cooler. The recipes can be shared, too.
- Crafts: Everyone brings their specialty. A great way to gather gifts for the holidays.
- Books you've already read.
- Electronics: DVDs, CDs, video games.
- Plants, herbs, and vegetables from your garden.
- Baby clothes in good condition. The hostess would keep track of ages to make sure there are good matches. Also, swapping outgrown baby equipment such as strollers, changing tables, and car seats, as well as kids' toys could be valuable.
- Gather a party for the purpose of discussing talents, and agree to swap services. Everyone needs a babysitter, a hairdresser, a plumber, an electrician, etc.
- Home decorations: knickknacks, pictures, lamps, and collectibles.
- Kitchen gadgets or small appliances. Trade your extra coffee bean grinder for a Slap Chop, or that Blooming Onion cutter that you had to have for something that is useful, like a Microplane grater.
- Host a Glamour Swap. Trade new or barely used clothes, jewelry, handbags, shoes, and accessories. Inform everyone to bring 5 new or like-new items. Display in groups; everyone takes home 5 new items.

As you can see from the list above, the sky's the limit. So go have fun, make a party out of trading, and benefit from some new items and services.

Now go forth and exchange! Because the only things in life worth keeping are intangible.

Acknowledgments

To my Cookie Exchange: Most of you consider yourselves to be "non-bakers." Thank you all so much for stretching yourselves, and spending your valuable time doing something that you wouldn't normally do, which is bake. I appreciate the thoughtfulness and the time spent to bring good-quality cookies to share with the group. You're an inspiration to all potential cookie exchange hostesses who think they can't give this party because their friends don't bake. I often get kudos from all over the world for the photos of the pretty, appealing cookies that appear at my parties. I appreciate each and every one of you and all of your efforts over the years! In no particular order: Leslie Kelly, Becky Campbell, Debbie Rogers, Joyce Buttrey, Louise Guard, Judy Willis, Maria Moreno, Rosa Polen, Nancy Wert, Iris Grundler, Charlene Dillingham, Angela Sammarco, Patrice Datovech, Emily Korber, Peggy Ols, Zina Merritt, Donna Dorsch, Jackie Wray, Suzie Troia, Toni Ebert, Donna Dlubac, Lisa Cullen, Ruth Dike, Cheryl Berger, Debby Griffith, Janet Albright, Anne Goldman, Diane Lewis, Charlene Clark, Ann Hallock, Sandy Pingatore, Tracy Thomas, Krista FitzGerald, Penny Roberts, Mary Jean McCarthy, Terri McHugh, Chris Carr, Julie Jones, Judy Broseker, Sue Callaway.

A huge thank-you to all who shared their family or favorite cookie recipes, which helped turn this book into a worldwide cookie exchange party.

To my daughter, Stephanie Olson. Thank you for everything you've done to assist with my cookie parties, from baking to decorating, from food preparation to taking photos of the party. *You are the best* and I am so proud of you and your accomplishments. The world is your oyster.

My dear friend and hostess with the mostest, Holly Murphy, with whom I co-hosted my first cookie exchange two decades ago. Also, a "shout-out" to all who attend Holly's fabulous cookie parties. When Holly waves her magic wand, magic happens. Everyone in Santa Barbara knows that!

My kindred CE sisters: To all the wonderful women around the world who've generously shared their cookie exchange party experiences with us all, through stories, photos, details, and recipes. For me, this group has helped create a global community, and has imparted the vision for all the possibilities of what an annual cookie exchange party can be.

Special thanks and acknowledgments: To Rosy Levy Beranbaum, for permission to reprint your classic gingerbread recipe. I also appreciate the time you've spent sharing valuable baking advice with me, so that I could, in turn, share it with others.

Susan Sias, thank you for your cookie decorating tips section and the cover photo of the cookie shield. Also, thanks to David Sias for your photography of the cover cookie in icing.

To Aparna Balasubramanian of Panaji, Goa, India, for your beautifully written instructions on how to make ghee and Ghorayebah (Arabic Cardamom Shortbread Cookies).

Parts of the Medieval Menu are credited to The Richard III Society of Canada.

Thanks to Joelen Tan of Chicago for telling me about the "reverse cookie swap."

To Allison Ward, Diana Watkins, Tracey Weaver, and Christine Harpel (and so many others) for sharing their creative and original cookie exchange party invitations, which so many find so useful.

Cate Dimisa, thank you for your excellent baking skills and delicious cookies (Mommy Magic Cakes, www.mommymagiccakes.com).

Special thanks to those who baked for or attended the photo shoot party: Donna Soule, Iris Grundler, Leslie Kelly, Nancy Wert, Rosa Polen, Peggy Ols, Patrice Datovech, Mary Jean McCarthy, Terri McHugh, Donna Dlubac, Debby Griffith, Cate Dimisa.

To my lifelong taste-testers, husband Kim Olson and sons David and Sean Olson. If I say test the cookies and you eat them all within five minutes, I know they must have been good.

Step-aunt Carol Bierwagen, thank you for sharing your mother's, Rose Friedrich's, cookie recipe collection with me. I know that my mother always looked forward to eating them.

Much appreciation and thanks to my wonderfully patient editor at St. Martin's Press, Elizabeth Beier, assistant editor Michelle Richter, and everyone else at St. Martin's who worked on this book.

Heartfelt gratitude to my literary agent, Peter Steinberg, for your guidance, professionalism, and patience.

This book wouldn't exist without the inspiration, guidance, and knowledge freely shared by so many people over the years. *Thank you all.*

Conversion Charts

U.S. Measurement Equivalents—Volume to Fluid Ounces and Grams

16 tablespoons	= 1 cup	= 8 ounces	= 226.8 grams
12 tablespoons	= ¾ cup	= 6 ounces	= 170.1 grams
10 tablespoons +2 teaspoons	= ⅔ cup	= 5.33 ounces	= 151.1 grams
8 tablespoons	= ½ cup	= 4 ounces	= 113.4 grams
6 tablespoons	= ⅜ cup	= 3 ounces	= 85.05 grams
5 tablespoons + 1 teaspoon	= ⅓ cup	= 2.667 ounces	= 75.61 grams
4 tablespoons	= ¼ cup	= 2 ounces	= 56.70 grams
2 tablespoons	= ⅛ cup	= 1 ounce	= 28.35 grams
1 tablespoon	= 1/16 cup	= ½ ounce	= 14.7 grams
3 teaspoons	= 1 tablespoon		
1 teaspoon		= ⅙ ounce	= 4.734 grams

International Liquid Measurements

	Standard Cup	Tablespoon	Teaspoon
USA	236.6ml	15ml	5ml
UK	250ml	15ml	5ml
Canada	250ml	15ml	5ml
Australia	250ml	20ml	5ml
New Zealand	250ml	15ml	5ml
Japan	200ml	15ml	5ml
India	200ml	10ml	2.5ml

Temperature Conversions

This temperature table is useful for those who have old recipe books that only instruct: "Bake in a moderate oven."

Fahrenheit	Centigrade	Description
225°F	105°C	Very Slow or Very Cool
250°F	120°C	Very Slow or Very Cool
275°F	130°C	Cool
300°F	150°C	Slow
325°F	165°C	Very Moderate or Moderately Slow
350°F	180°C	Moderate
375°F	190°C	Moderately Hot
400°F	200°C	Hot
425°F	220°C	Hot
450°F	230°C	Very Hot
475°F	240°C	Very Hot
500°F	250°C	Extremely Hot

Resources

Special Ingredients

Unusual, hard-to-find ingredients: Kalustyan's online store has a great variety of world-wide ingredients, including many called for in this book, such as ghee, rice and organic flours, desiccated coconut, crystallized fruits, extracts, flavorings, jams, high quality chocolates. www.kalustyans.com.

Castor sugar: The English Tea Store, www.englishteastore.com.

Chocolate-filled peppermint candy canes or peppermint candy canes: specialty candy shops or online at www.hammondscandies.com.

Cocoa powder: Ghirardelli, www.ghirardelli.com, ScharffenBerger, scharffenberger.com, or Valrhona, www.valrhona-chocolate.com.

Copha or Kremelta (solid vegetable shortening made of coconut oil): www.simplyoz.com/products/aussie_food/groceries/cooking_supplies/copha.

Desiccated coconut: This is drier, nonsweetened, and similar in size to coarse bread crumbs. Find this product at your local Latin, Asian, African, or international markets or online at www.americanspice.com, or do a regular "shopping" search for best price.

Dolci Frutta: Look in the fresh fruit and vegetable section of your local grocery. If your store doesn't carry it, e-mail the company to find out the closest location. Or go to www.dolcifrutta.com.

Dulce de leche: Can often be found in your local grocery in either the Latin section or baking supplies, near the evaporated and condensed milk. I recommend Nestlé, for flavor, above all others.

Flours: White whole wheat-flour: King Arthur Flour, www.kingarthurflour.com. Rice flour: Bob's Red Mill White Rice Flour, www.bobsredmill.com, or Arrowhead Mills Rice Flour, www.arrowheadmills.com. Oat flour: www.arrowheadmills.com. (All the flour companies listed have USDA Certified Organic products.)

Lard: Good-quality lard to bake with is harder to find than cheaper, hydrogenated lard, which is readily available. Go to a health-minded grocery store and read the labels—look for nonhydrogenated lard.

Lyle's Golden Syrup: My local grocery recently started carrying this product. If yours doesn't, there are numerous links to buy it online.

Sugar substitutes: Search articles at www.allrecipes.com with the exact phrase.

Nonfood Baking Supplies

For the French Menu, a great link for recipes, if you wish to bake your own pâtisserie: www.frenchpastrychef.com.

Mardi Gras drinks: "Lamb's Wool," a traditional English and Irish Twelfth Night drinks. www.barnonedrinks.com/drinks/l/lambs-wool-2977.html, www.ehow.com/how_2061921_make-lambs-wool-epiphany.html, or visit www.cookie-exchange.com/cookbook/resources.html.

Some recipes from the Medieval Menu can be found at The King Richard III Society of Canada, www.home.cogeco.ca/~richardiii/recipes.html.

Cookie cutters: www.cookiecutter.com, www.thecookiecuttershop.com. For **Hispanic-themed cookie cutters:** Visit www.cookiecutter.com, look under "Western" for chili peppers; www.sweetartfactory.com and the H.O.Foose Tinsmithing Company, www.foosecookiecutters.com, under "Southwest."

Cookie scoops: Pampered Chef, ice cream/cookie scoops—www.pamperedchef.com.

Parchment baking paper: Reynolds brand at www.reynoldsparchment.com, and for the eco-minded, unbleached parchment paper can be found at www.greenfeet.com.

Refrigerator and freezer deodorizer: Prevent odors in fridge and freezer. Search online for the specific brand "Fridge Aid Deodorizer" and for the best price.

Weight scales: Recommended is the KD-7000 Digital Stainless-Steel Food Scale. Search online for best price. Digital scales at your local Wal-Mart, Target, K-Mart, etc., will range in price from $15.00 to $35.00.

Wilton cookie press, and other cookie decorating and baking supplies: www.wilton
.com. Search your local craft store before an online purchase—they may carry Wilton
products.

Miscellaneous Party Resources

Costume and party stores: www.partycity.com. I get a lot of my party supplies (for cookie
parties and other occasions) from my local Party City store. Party America also has
stores all over the country, see www.partyamerica.com. Online only: Anderson's Giant
Party Store, giantpartystore.com.

Costume rentals: Search online for a local costume rental store nearest you. Try www
.costumelocator.com.

Disposable silver plasticware: At Costco and online at www.webstaurantstore.com.

For '50s, '60s, and '70s parties: See my online Resources page, www.cookie-exchange.com/
cookbook/resources.html. There are too many resources to list here.

Gimp (lanyard): refresher course, www.boondoggleman.com.

Mardi Gras: www.mardigrasoutlet.com.

Nightcaps: www.mooncostumes.com, www.frankbeecostume.com, www.costumes4less
.com.

Party invitations online: www.mypunchbowl.com, www.evite.com, www.sendomatic
.com.

Personalized magazine covers: www.fakemagazines.com, www.covermefamous.com,
www.yourcover.com.

Piñatas: Available at Target, Toys "R" Us, and Kmart, as well as online.

Talking invitations: www.soundexpressiongreetings.com, www.vocalgreetings.com.

Tea etiquette: www.tealaden.com/teaweb/etiquette.htm.

Please note that the Web sites listed in this book are not guaranteed to exist in the future.

Index